THE
WINNING
TICKET

*Copublished with the Eagleton Institute of Politics,
Rutgers University*

THE
WINNING
TICKET

Daley, the Chicago Machine, and Illinois Politics

MELVIN A. KAHN AND FRANCES J. MAJORS

American Political Parties
and Elections

general editor:
Gerald M. Pomper

PRAEGER SPECIAL STUDIES • PRAEGER SCIENTIFIC

New York • Philadelphia • Eastbourne, UK
Toronto • Hong Kong • Tokyo • Sydney

Library of Congress Cataloging in Publication Data

Kahn, Melvin, 1930–
  The winning ticket.

  (American political parties and elections)
  "Copublished with the Eagleton Institute of Politics,
Rutgers University."
  Includes index.
  1. Chicago (Ill.)—Politics and government—1951—
2. Nominations for office—Illinois—Chicago. 3. Daley,
Richard J., 1902–1976. I. Majors, Frances J. II. Title.
III. Series.
JS708.K27 1984 320.8′09773′11   83-24727
ISBN 0-03-069298-9 (alk. paper)

Published in 1984 by Praeger Publishers
CBS Educational and Professional Publishing
a Division of CBS Inc.
521 Fifth Avenue, New York, NY 10175 USA

456789 052 987654321
Printed in the United States of America
on acid-free paper

To Hannah Kahn and Earl S. Johnson,
two genuine humanists

Acknowledgments

I owe a great debt to the many people who made this book possible. Joyce Purcell's contributions to several chapters, particularly those dealing with Chicago politics, were invaluable. As an unabashed machine foe, she also challenged constantly my analysis of the late Mayor Daley and the machine.

Ray Chancey and the Jackson County Illinois Democratic Organization admitted me to their inner councils, tutored me in the art of practical politics, made me a gubernatorial co-campaign manager, and, along with Clyde Choate, enthusiastically sponsored me for state office. I will always value the trust and friendship of Ray and Mary J. Chancey and my friends in the Jackson County organization.

Former alderman Leon Despres, Justice (ex-senator) Thomas A. (Art) McGloon, and County Commissioner John Stroger shared their expertise over a period spanning fifteen years. They represent three vital segments of Chicago politics respectively—a machine critic, a former top Daley lieutenant, and a black leader. This book has profited immeasurably from their perceptive insights. I am also grateful to the politicians who appear in the book; they provided most of the raw material. In accordance with traditional machine policy, many prefer to remain anonymous.

Wendy Bousfield and Steve Hathaway, of Wichita State University, critiqued the manuscript with sharp stilettos and upgraded both the style and content. Sandy Schuster helped proof and caught several errors. Dick Simpson performed as a virtuoso; he provided both an incisive interview as an antimachine leader and a superior manuscript critique from his perspective as a political scientist. Coral Tait Smith performed an excellent job of typing several drafts and the final manuscript and contributed helpful suggestions on the fine points of diction.

Many colleagues provided needed encouragement at various stages: the late Orville Alexander, John Jackson III, Jack Van Der Slik, and the late Karen Zink of Southern Illinois University encouraged my early efforts; and Ken Ciboski, Jim Kuklinski, Jim Sheffield, and John Stanga of Wichita State University prodded me to complete the project.

Wichita State University generously provided a sabbatical and support services, and I am particularly indebted to Fred Sudermann, director of Research and Sponsored Programs, Dean Lloyd Benningfield of the Graduate School, Deans Paul Magelli and Martin Reif of the Liberal Arts College, and James McKenney, political science department chair.

Adrienne (Kahn) Halevi-Blume was supportive of my political involvement and Sharonah, David, and Miriam Kahn as well as Sandy Schuster have given strong support over the long years of the project. To each and every one of the persons mentioned above, I express my deep and enduring gratitude.

To maintain their friendship and good will, I absolve them of responsibility for any and all errors.

M.A.K.

My loving thanks to my family—Sarah, Mary, Austin, and Troy—for their encouragement and their patience.

F.J.M.

The authors wish to give special thanks to the department of Special Collections, The Joseph Regenstein Library, The University of Chicago for their permission to quote at length from an editorial in the *Dziennik Chicagoski.*

Authors' Note

A note concerning the authorship: Melvin A. Kahn's participant-observer data and interviews have been supplemented by collaborative research on Mayor Daley, Paul Powell, and the ethnic history of Chicago to provide background for a fuller understanding of the political actors who appear in these pages. The coordination of this diverse material and the final conceptualizations and writing of the book reflect the joint efforts of the authors.

Contents

Prologue:
The Frame of Reference

In 1969, I sought the Democratic nomination for Illinois superintendent of public instruction, and the case study that follows thus represents the viewpoint of a former participant-observer in both Illinois and Cook County politics.

Competing with fourteen others for the party's endorsement was in itself an absorbing experience, but, beyond that, it led me to an intensified interest in the internal workings of the political organization that dominated the candidate choice—the Cook County Democratic central committee (hereafter referred to as "the machine" or "the organization"[1]). It seemed to me that by focusing on the nomination process—on how the most tightly organized, best-disciplined American political organization of the 1960s went about the task of slating candidates for office—I might gain some new insights into its structure and functioning. The presentation of my findings represents one purpose of this book.

A second purpose, which stems from the first, is to generate some questions about the future of Chicago politics. The changes that Cook County politics have undergone in the last twelve years have seemed all the more startling and confusing because of the contrast afforded by the two decades of relative stability that preceded them. As of this writing, the organization is atomized and has experienced difficulty in nominating as well as in governing. Mayor Washington's initial struggles with alderman Ed Vrdolyak and the city council lead one to ask whether a reformer can govern Chicago effectively. By analyzing the Daley machine's informal network for achieving ethnic consensus, I hope to provide a bench mark for comparison between then and now.

As I began to examine my own political experience of the 1960s, and added interviews with Illinois politicians and research, I developed a perspective on both the Cook County organization and on Mayor Richard J. Daley that differs somewhat from other interpretations. My interpretation of the machine is that it was not a strict hierarchy but, rather, a stratarchy, or reciprocal deference structure, wherein the leader often tempered policies he favored to preserve a coalitional balance. This coalitional balance undergirded the slating of candidates that satisfied the party's multi-ethnic leadership and the voting base that maintained the machine. Thus, if self-perpetuation were the prize, the slatemaking session was the arena. E. E. Schattschneider has stated that in the nominating process "one may hope to discover the locus of power within the party. . . . "[2] My data suggest that "loci," rather than "locus," might better describe the origin of party power with respect to the nominating process in Illinois during the Daley era. In slating candidates for state or national office, diverse party elements located at various layers of the political structure initiated power and deferred reciprocally in more than one direction.

But before proceeding to the particulars of the case study at hand, I would like to establish a context for it by examining briefly the history of nominations in the American political system.

John Adams's description of the "smoke-filled room" caucuses of his day has been quoted too frequently to cite it again. Since Adams recorded his observations, the methods of candidate selection have changed, though not necessarily improved. The importance of nominations as a political institution nevertheless remains undiminished, because they are the *sine qua non* of a democratic society. And although Americans usually perceive the general election as the key contest, it represents only the final choice among the few contenders who remain. It is the nomination process that winnows the potential candidates, refines the ultimate choices, and provides voters with identifiable alternatives in the general election. As Hugh Heclo states it:

> In both Britain and the United States the key locus of choice is in the preelection selection process. Though more dramatic and publicized the election itself is far less important—in the sense of the number of alternatives eliminated—than the selection, when one from a large number of potential candidates is designated. As a systems analyst once said, "If I can set the options, I don't care who makes the choice."[3]

Although the major purpose of the nominating process is to select candidates from whom the voters may choose in the general election, nominations also serve other important political requirements. One of these is "structuring the vote," which Leon Epstein has described as "the imposition of an order or pattern enabling voters to choose candidates according to their labels (whether or not the labels appear on the ballots)."[4] The party label serves as a meaningful frame of reference for the voter.

Nominations also serve to unify the party behind legitimatized and agreed-upon candidates. Schattschneider points out that "in an election the *united front* of the party is expressed in terms of a nomination" and indicates that "if a party cannot make nominations it ceases to be a party."[5] Of course, the party's continuing vitality depends upon viable nominations. The "wrong" choice may engender apathy, or even hostility, in party supporters; but a candidate whom party loyalists perceive as acceptable can assure the party continued allegiance from its financial backers and rank-and-file workers. Generally speaking, an acceptable candidate is one committed to traditional party values, amenable to the idea of patronage,[6] and attuned to the policy needs of major interests aligned with the party.

Frank Sorauf points up the party's high stakes in the nomination process when he says that "the consequences of the nomination process bulk large. The images of the candidates of a party are to some extent its images; the candidates' reputations and stands on public issues become the party's. Furthermore, the candidate with whom the party goes into the election campaign determines to a great extent its ultimate chances for victory. The nomination of candidates, moreover, offers the party a major opportunity for uniting its wings and factions behind acceptable candidates. In short, it is crucial to a political party who its candidates are, both for the winning of elections and for the building of internal unity and cohesion."[7]

The consequences of the nomination process are no less significant for society than for the parties. The candidates' personal and political skills and priorities contribute, for better or worse, to the ideal of representation and to the people'e sense of political efficacy. As a matter of fact, the evolution through which the nomination process has passed since John Adams's day illustrates a continuous trend of more public involvement at the nomination stage.

Initially, the American parties nominated their candidates in the caucuses, private meetings confined to political leaders. President Andrew Jackson and his Democrats excoriated the elitism of "King Caucus," however, and shifted the emphasis to conventions wherein party activists chose delegates who, in turn, selected the candidates. During the Progressive Era, many dissidents demanded the direct primary, with its vision of "rule by the people" instead of "boss domination." In our own day, scholars have empirically challenged the rationality of the average American's voting decisions;[8] but the direct primary has taken root and has developed into the most frequent mechanism of nominating candidates for state offices.

The direct primary has not been a benign development for the parties, even if one can point to particular national or state officeholders who would not have survived the nominating process had it remained in the hands of the parties. But the direct primary has not affected all the states to the same extent; and within states in which both parties are competitive, party leaders still exert considerable control over the nomination process.

They manage this most often by means of the preprimary endorsement, and though the manner in which party leaders control nominations through the preprimary endorsement varies, the leadership commonly designates the individuals the state convention will later ratify. Sometimes, party leaders simply pick the men and women whom the organization is then asked to support in the primary election. The important variable, however, is not the manner of choosing but the party's commitment to that choice.

Scholars of American politics are in wide agreement concerning the critical role that nominations play in the American political process and are compelled to examine it again and again in relation to the parties, the people, and democratic government. This book examines one type of leader-controlled nomination by focusing on the state of Illinois at a time when party leaders chose a slate of candidates that, without subsequent ratification by a state convention, the party supported in the primary election.

In this case study, I will employ two social science concepts as heuristic tools or frames of analysis for examining the power relationships that existed within the Cook County Democratic party organization and between the machine and the state party. The first of these concepts is Ferdinand Tönnies's *Gemeinschaft-Gesellschaft* interpretation of modern society;[9] the second, Samuel Eldersveld's "stratarchy" concept of power distribution.[10]

Gemeinschaft-Gesellschaft offers a useful framework from which to view humanity's struggle to survive, politically as well as otherwise, in the modern world. On the one hand, citizens must perform in the *Gesellschaft* milieu, which best translates as urbanized, industrialized society—a world characterized by impersonality, preoccupation with economic struggle, change, and social relationships based upon law.

In short, it is a cold, uncaring world dominated by depersonalized relationships and formal contracts. But modern man also seeks out the intimacy, pscyhological comfort, and economic simplicity of *Gemeinschaft*, or the small, folk community, characterized by emphases on the personalized relationships of family, kin, and neighbors, subordination of economic competition to group cooperation, and social relationships based upon custom. It is a warm "in-group," a social environment identified by a feeling of unity among its members, in which informal status, rather than formal contract, prevails.

One theme of this work is that the machine, both in its everyday operations and in the important nomination function, carefully balanced the worlds of *Gemeinschaft* and *Gesellschaft*: It paid heed to its members' desire for financial status and for professional prestige (and likewise acknowledged the needs of organized labor, business and industry, and the institutions of formal government), while at the same time it also paid careful attention to the *Gemeinschaft*-oriented identifications of the many Chicagoans who lived in and identified with their respective ethnic communities. I maintain that an important part of the political genius of Mayor Richard Daley was his ability to bridge successfully these two worlds.

The machine's necessary acknowledgment of Chicago's conglomerate interests together with *Gemeinschaft*-rooted party supporters in both Cook County and downstate made unavoidable its recognition of its decentralized power structure. Relevant to this political fact of life is Samuel Eldersveld's utilization of Lasswell's and Kaplan's "stratarchy," or "reciprocal deference structure":[11]

> By *stratarchy* is meant an organization with layers, or strata, of control rather than one of centralized leadership from the top down. At each stratum, or echelon, of the organization there are specialized organs to perform functions at that level. Each stratum or organization is relatively autonomous in its own sphere, although it does maintain links above and below. There is, thus, the proliferation of power and decision making and a recognition that lower levels are not subordinate to the commands or sanctions of higher strata. The party develops this pattern of relationships— stratarchical rather than hierarchical—because of the necessities of collaborating with and recognizing local echelons for votes, money, personnel. Further, the party must cope with widely varying local conditions. A special component of stratarchy is reciprocal deference. Between layers there is a tolerance of

autonomy, of each layer's status and its right to initiative, as well as a tolerance of inertia. This deference stems from the absence of effective sanctions and the fact that the echelons need each other in the drive for votes and its other functions. Mutual need, mutual support, mutual respect, and much interechelon accommodation are the marks of the American party stratarchy.[12]

Eldersveld's stratarchy model describes a structure in which decision-making authority is dispersed to several strata and which functions by means of mutual accommodation or reciprocal deference between (or among) the variously located decision makers. However, Eldersveld's "command model" (which includes the "classic machine") is characterized by a chain of command in which power emanates at the top of the structure and decisions flow downward to the lower levels. In this model, Eldersveld says, "deference is strictly upward!"[13] Citing Milton Rakove's description of the structure of the Daley machine, Eldersveld concludes, "This then is the image of the classic machine."[14] My findings indicate that the machine contained elements of both the command and the stratarchy models, and, while certain elements of Eldersveld's definition of stratarchy were not present in the Cook County organization, reciprocal deference was much in evidence. Present also were "[m]utual need, mutual support, mutual respect, and much interechelon accommodation."[15] Centralization of leadership was not, in the Daley machine, incompatible with autonomy of decision making at several levels, nor tight discipline incompatible with flexibility.

The real outlines of the Daley machine's hybrid form confound the portraits of the organization drawn by some writers, most notably that of journalist Mike Royko.[16] The machine's movement in its day-to-day operations was accompanied by prolific, ongoing dialogue and discussion. And its leader's most characteristic mode of functioning was extensive bargaining, which sometimes resulted in reversal by the ward committeemen of policies he favored, particularly in the vital area of slatemaking. The ward committeemen were elected in the party's primaries, and it was they who selected the party's county chairman and they who could (and did) hold him accountable. Although Daley and the machine's top leaders often endorsed ward committeemen as candidates, independent challengers sometimes won. The relationship between the Cook County machine and the state party was also reciprocally deferential in nature and typically followed a pattern of mutual accommodation and bargaining. I therefore will examine the presence of stratarchy in two settings: the internal functioning of the Chicago machine and the interaction between the machine and the non-Cook County leaders of the state party.

Much of my data developed through the course of political activity and conversation while I served in four political roles: (1) regional gubernatorial campaign co-manager for Governor Sam Shapiro; (2) active participant in the Jackson County, Illinois, Democratic organization; (3) aspirant for nomination to state office; and (4) a student political activist in Chicago. I gathered other findings through formal interviews. To acquire the latter information, I usually had to assure the respondents I would not identify them. To honor this pledge I have used either composite characters, no names, or pseudonyms. After the slatemakers had chosen their nominees for the 1970 election, some allowed me to use a tape recorder when I interviewed them. In most cases, however, I simply took minimal notes to facilitate interviewee response and then went immediately to my hotel room and dictated. While it is not possible to give a precise and exact rendering of all specific words spoken during those interviews not tape-recorded, the minimal time lapse between interview and dictation allowed an accurate transcription of most of the words spoken and a faithful reporting of their meanings and emphases. The statements attributed to certain persons by the interviewees and the scenarios and characterizations they conveyed to the interviewer might not reflect verbatim, unbiased accounts of said characters and incidents. Wherever possible, I sought confirmation from a second, and sometimes a third, source; and any information of a dubious nature that could not be confirmed was excluded.

This work represents a snapshot-in-time analysis of nominations during the Daley era. Mayor Richard J. Daley died in 1976; Paul Powell, the downstate leader, died in 1970. Most of the data for the chapters on these men were compiled while they were alive; and, while findings from this period do have present-day applicability, their deaths and the inevitable changes that institutions undergo over time have altered the relationships between political leaders and their parties. My purpose is not merely to portray the main personalities involved in the story that follows but, more importantly, to describe and explain the parts they played in the slatemaking process.

With respect to my role as participant-observer, it provided both an unmatched opportunity for access to information and a danger of bias. I am certain that had I approached the machine members as an outsider/scholar there is no way I could have acquired most of my data. But as "one of them"—by following their norms and playing the game—I achieved a natural vantage point. Altogether, I informally conversed with or interviewed more than 180 people from several groups. These included active Democrats at all levels of the Cook County machine, ranging from precinct captains to Mayor Daley himself. With the exception of only two people, I met personally with every major downstate leader, every official of the Illinois state Democratic central committee, all leaders of the Democratic state legislative team, every Democratic state officeholder, and numerous downstate activists. Others included Democratic mavericks, Republican leaders, interest-group leaders, and journalists.

As an active participant in a political race, I was so determined to succeed that, later, when work on this book began I sometimes continued to think as a political aspirant rather than as a political scientist. Whether I have avoided the Scylla of participant bias or the Charybdis of overcompensation for my political prejudices is a question each reader must answer.

1
Political Baptism

The chair was vacant except for the symbolic swatch of purple and black crepe signifying Mayor Daley's absence. For twenty-two years Daley had reigned supreme over his city council. Although he had been a meticulous and systematic man, he had not planned events beyond his death; specifically, he had not designated a successor. It would be up to the council members now gathered to attempt an agreement on who would take Daley's chair in the council room. After two abortive efforts, they finally agreed that Michael Bilandic should serve until a special mayoral election could be held.[1]

The following day I watched the Cook County machine meet to select the man who would inherit Daley's other toga—that of the party chairman. The eulogies all sounded the same themes: Daley's greatest asset was his love for his family . . . he was a devout man . . . he was the greatest of leaders. . . . Then Congressman Dan Rostenkowski spoke:

> Mayor Daley was a man who could put you down in a second, and he could also make you soar to heights you never believed you could attain. He was a compassionate man. On Christmas Day he'd call me up and say, "Dan, just want you to know I'm thinking of you."
>
> Mayor Daley sometimes scolded. But when you were feeling low, he would really come through. You remember, I had an election in the United States Congress with a very disappointing result. The phone rang, I got on the line, and his voice said,

"Danny, what did they do to you? What can I do for you, Dan?"
That was the kind of man he was.

Following Rostenkowski, suburban maverick Lynn Williams
rose slowly. There were tears in his eyes, and his voice quavered. "I
often battled with Mayor Daley," he conceded. "The mayor and I
frequently agreed about ends, but seldom about means; and he often
treated me with humor—too much humor. [Subdued laughter.] But he
was always fair—scrupulously fair."

One after another, men stood to offer their recollections of Mayor
Daley. And as the eulogies flowed, my thoughts strayed to two
personal political experiences in which the mayor had figured
prominently.

My first major encounter with Mayor Daley took place in his
office on the fifth floor of city hall. The Democratic party's state
chairman had arranged the meeting because I was seeking the
nomination for state superintendent of public instruction, and my
county chairman and I had traveled 365 miles from Carbondale² to
visit with the mayor. Fifteen men aspired to the state superintendent's
office, but Daley met with only two of us individually. My next
meeting with the mayor, and with other party leaders, involved my
final efforts to gain their endorsement. It took place at the Illinois
Democratic state central committee slatemaking session. This event
capped a fascinating journey through Illinois during which I sought
supporters to transmit favorable signals to the mayor and his cohorts.
But in the Illinois Democratic party, one must follow protocol and
start with his or her political base. This is now it all began:

I first met Jackson County chairman C. Ray Chancey in 1968 at
a Carbondale whistle-stop rally for U.S. Senate candidate William
Clark. Because the campaigners were behind schedule, Chancey and I
had an opportunity to chat. He was a soft-spoken man of few words.
Soon after we began talking, he took a three-by-five card out of his
pocket and jotted my name, address, and phone number. Later, I
found out that Chancey always carried a supply of these cards so that
he could make a quick note of any information he thought worth
retaining and then file it away for future reference as soon as he
returned home. As I got to know him, I realized that this efficient
political leader, Chancey, wielded great influence as head of the
Democratic party in Jackson County, the locus of the largest number

of Democratic voters in all twenty-two counties of the Twenty-first Congressional District.³

Chancey was fifty-four years old in 1968 and had prematurely white hair. He had entered the real estate and insurance business after graduating from Southern Illinois University (SIU) and had prospered over the years. His financial independence enabled him to avoid a position in the patronage system and, thus, obligation to downstate Democrat Paul Powell, who, next to Mayor Daley, controlled more patronage jobs than any other single individual in the state.⁴ In addition to his financial autonomy, Chancey also differed from many party regulars in that he directly cultivated university people. Realizing that as SIU grew it would attract more Democrats and the party would profit, he succeeded in changing a strong Republican county into one with Democratic leanings. His encouragement of the SIU community took several forms: First, he appointed university precinct committeemen to key positions in the party. Second, he firmly backed State's Attorney Richard Richmond, who had gained heavy support among the SIU members of the Jackson County Democratic organization but whose overly intellectual and abrasive ways had alienated many nonuniversity rank-and-file party workers. Chancey respected Richmond's intellect and stood by him.

Another of Chancey's attitudes especially endeared him to SIU activists. During the 1968 Illinois presidential preferential primary, he upheld the right of university people to work for their hero, Senator Eugene McCarthy, even though Chancey and most of the other party members backed Vice-President Hubert Humphrey. He emphasized that whereas these factions might divide over Democratic presidential choices they would unify against Republicans, whether the conflict involved national, state, or county contests or the success of the party organization itself. He refused to pressure the McCarthy workers in the primary; and most of them supported Humphrey as well as the rest of the ticket in the general election. In 1972, Chancey at first opposed George McGovern for president; but when the South Dakotan captured the nomination, the chairman mobilized the entire organization behind McGovern's candidacy. The result paid off handsomely. Jackson County emerged as the only county in Illinois favoring McGovern in the general election. Not even Richard Daley's vaunted Cook County organization could match Chancey's feat.

Prior to every major election, Chancey held a clinic for election judges and precinct workers to review the nuts and bolts of effective precinct watching. He recommended sitting on a high stool, the better to look over the shoulders of those counting votes, and wearing a green visor for glare protection. Chancey also reminded them of the inadequacy of merely watching the ballot counting—they must also check the actual recording of votes. Everything considered, Chancey proved a masterful political leader.

Soon after we met, Chancey invited me to attend the next meeting of the Jackson County Democratic organization; and when I showed up that night he asked me to speak. I was apparently the type of non-ideologue he felt comfortable with.

Chancey and I met frequently during the next few months, and I attended meetings of the county organization on a regular basis. Because I saw many of the SIU people in the course of my daily life, I purposely sat with the nonacademic committeemen, who liked the idea that I preferred their company to that of the university crowd. After the meetings, Chancey and a few of the executive committee members drank beer at the Pump Room in Murphysboro, and, from my very first attendance, Chancey always invited me to join him and "the boys." I was grateful for the opportunity, especially since my social life in the college town of Carbondale had been limited to get-togethers with my university colleagues. It turned out that "the boys" and I had a lot in common.

This group consisted of men who were far more folksy than my SIU acquaintances. Harry Kilby, a stellar precinct committeeman, operated a barbeque stand and held assorted patronage jobs when the Democrats were in power. He was also a fixture at political gatherings, where he entertained those in attendance with his vast stock of earthy stories and served delectable food that he cooked on grills propped up on safety signs discarded by the state highway department.

Leonard Smith, a silver-haired, quiet, well-mannered man, operated two businesses, a tavern and a bookkeeping service. One of his DeSoto neighbors, John Batteau, who was also a student of mine, described Smith in the following way: "Don't let Leonard's gentlemanly appearance fool you—he doesn't like to fight, but sometimes he has to keep order in his tavern. He's the strongest man I've ever seen and can beat any three asses at one time." Aside from his reputed physical powess, Smith was a dedicated reader. As I got better acquainted with him, I learned that he constantly read books on politics, history, and biography. Idealistic and well-informed on the major issues of the day, he enjoyed having a political science professor to talk with.

Leonard was a political purist. He thought it immoral to wheel and deal for personal gain and thus had little use for Paul Powell, the downstate master of pork barrel politics. At heart a political maverick, he often supported idealistic candidates; but because of his precinct effectiveness (he kept meticulous records on his constituents and continuously rendered services for the party), Chancey and the pragmatic Democratic regulars accepted him.

Many others became my good political friends. John Travelstead, Chancey's trusted right arm until Travelstead went to work as a rural mail carrier, effectively handled all nuts-and-bolts matters during campaigns. He and I shared a fondness for extended political conversation. And then there was a state driving inspector, whom I first had met when he drove with me for renewal of my driver's license. After I had hit two curbs, he generously blamed it on the snow, passed me on my test, but begged me to improve my driving—if not for myself, then for the safety of my family.

I genuinely admired these new-found friends. In return, they valued the fact that a college professor liked them as individuals and respected their vote-getting abilities. Good friendships developed between us, and, in the process, I unknowingly constructed a political base for my future.

In early fall, 1968, Governor Sam Shapiro's campaign manager contacted Chancey and asked him to set up a "citizen's" headquarters, because the Shapiro forces wanted to establish an organization not publicly identifiable with the party leadership. Chancey chose Bob Brooks, a university member of his organization, and me to serve as cochairmen. One incident helped create good will with the organization workers. One afternoon, we faced the problem of erecting a ten-by fifteen-foot sign over Shapiro headquarters, and no support structure was available. A few SIU colleagues and I carried the sign, but the precinct workers solved the complex problem of how to set it into place. I joked, "Although the Ph.D. is great training for carrying a sign, it takes the brainwork of people not ruined by college to put it up." Everyone except my university colleagues enjoyed the observation.

Bob Brooks ran the headquarters, and my basic job consisted of organizing caravans throughout the Twenty-first Congressional

District. Campaigners distributed handbills and carried political signs praising Governor Shapiro, while I gave media interviews. I cut four radio tapes for the Jackson County organization and served as the featured speaker at several political rallies throughout both the Twenty-first and Twenty-second Congressional Districts. We would finish up with a mini-rally featuring either a combo or recorded music, and I would make a brief partisan speech from the rear of a flatbed truck. On one occasion, ethnic fervor, albeit misplaced, prompted a well-intentioned Democrat to shout, as he took a handbill from my son, "Shapiro for governor—good! It's about time they ran an Italian!"

Republicans won most of the state offices in 1968, and, generally, it was not a good year for Democrats. Our carrying Jackson County for Governor Shapiro by more than 500 votes, however, represented a significant accomplishment inasmuch as he lost throughout most of Illinois. After the campaign ended, I continued to attend Democratic organization meetings and enjoyed frequent contacts of both a social and political nature with Ray and Mary J. Chancey.

In the long, hot summers of southern Illinois in the sixties, the combination political rally/picnic—with good food, cold drinks, sunshine (or shade, as per one's fancy), and the familiar entertainment of political oratory (lofty or low)—constituted an agreeable way of passing a lazy weekend afternoon and evening. My wife and kids and I joined other families at these social affairs whenever possible. And I made a special effort to attend those at which Congressman Kenny Gray was to be the featured speaker. Gray, a former auctioneer, was the second-best stump speaker in the state (downstate Democratic leader Paul Powell took highest honors).

One night, performing at his stem-winding best, he blasted Republicans from an outdoor platform before a crowd of enthusiastic Democrats in Marion. It was mid-June 1969, with no political race in sight for another year and a half, but to southern Illinois Democratic party loyalists, listening to partisan rhetoric was much more fun than watching television and was also good for the health. It set the blood to pumping. Congressman Gray had gotten well under way, and now he spoke emphatically:

> There is a very real difference between us Democrats and those Republicans: We're for the working people, and they're for the

rich. We pass laws for the people—social security, agriculture, public education—and the Republicans oppose them. But what do the Republicans give us? I'll tell you what they give us: They just got through giving us the state income tax—that's what they give the plant workers, and that's what they give the farmer!

He held up a copy of the *Southern Illinoisan* newspaper and pointed to a story:

This shows that in our own state of Illinois the Republican legislature passed the income tax, and the Republican legislature did it under the leadership of their very own Republican governor. The Republicans did it over the objections of us Democrats. If somebody tells you that politics isn't very important, you can tell them that Republican politicians pick their pockets every single time. Yes, politics is real important. Republicans favor the fat cats, and Democrats favor the working people.

Congressman Gray issued a final salvo, and then the more than 200 party activists adjourned for liquid refreshments and resumed backslapping and handshaking.

Because chairman Ray Chancey and I frequently saw each other in Jackson County, we purposely spent our time that evening talking with others from the district. But when the crowd began to disperse, I approached Chancey: "Ray, could I talk with you?"

"Sure!" he replied, motioning me aside.

"Let me try out an idea on you. The *Sun-Times* has been blasting Ray Page [the Repubican Illinois superintendent of public instruction] for three days in a row. I think I can beat him. What do you think of my taking him on?"

"Sounds pretty good, Mel," Chancey responded, "but I can also see a lot of problems in your getting the nomination.[5] Let me talk it over with the boys on the executive committee, and then you give me a call about Wednesday."

When I telephoned Chancey at his office, he suggested lunch the next day; and though in the past he had always picked up the tab, he now announced, "You're coming up here to ask for a favor, so we're going to have a good lunch, but this time it's on you."

I met him at the Eagles Club, and we started out talking general politics. Then, introducing the idea of my running for state superintendent, the usually taciturn chairman made what was, for him, a speech:

"Mel, I've checked with the boys, and we're all behind you. You can count on Jackson County as a strong base. We'll help you in every way possible. We think you have excellent qualifications— you've got the Ph.D., and you proved in the Shapiro race that you know how to run a strong campaign.

"But it's going to be real tough, because Jackson County is just one of one hundred and two counties in Illinois. While I like to think that we're stronger than a lot of Chicago people give us credit for, we couldn't get Hubert Humphrey to campaign here, and it took all the arm-twisting we could do even to get Sam Shapiro down here. So this isn't the strongest base for launching a candidacy.

"However, we've never had a candidate from Jackson County, and we're certainly overdue. You demonstrated an ability to work effectively with the county organization, and we're behind you. Now, the first thing we've got to do is to go see Clyde."

"Clyde," in this case, happened to be Clyde Choate, who was a state representative from Anna, the state central committeeman for our congressional district, minority whip of the Illinois house, and the protégé of Paul Powell, the man who was known politically as "Mr. Southern Illinois." Choate also served as legislative leader of the downstate Democrats in the Illinois house. Chancey told me to call him back in a week, and in the meantime he would arrange a meeting with Choate. This schedule suited me fine, because I would be busy during part of that time attending the American Political Science Association convention in New York.

At the convention, Martin Dubin—Democratic party chairman of De Kalb County and a political scientist at Northern Illinois University—approached me about a "tremendous guy named Mike Bakalis," who was seeking the nomination for state superintendent. Dubin wanted to know if I would line up a speaking appearance for Bakalis. I was momentarily caught off-guard. I definitely did not want to help an opponent; but neither did I want to let anyone outside of Jackson County know I was in the running, for fear state committee-man Choate would hear about it from someone other than Chancey and me. I could not tell Dubin about my plans nor did I want to lie. I finally responded, "I work closely with Clyde Choate, and if he doesn't back anyone else and gives the green light for Bakalis, then I'll be glad to help out." It bothered me that I could not be more candid with Dubin, but I saw no other way to handle this situation.

Upon returning from the convention, I called Chancey, who reported that we had an appointment with Choate on the following Tuesday morning.

"Fine," I said. "Did you tell him what we want?"

"No," he replied. "When I'm asking a political favor, I never tip off people in advance, because, if I do, it can give them time to think of reasons to say 'no.' Let's just go down there and sort of surprise him."

Clyde Choate's formal education had ended with high school, but in shrewdness, general political savvy, and leadership ability, few could equal him. When he first ran for the state legislature, his main assets were his reputation as a Congressional Medal of Honor winner and his charismatic personality, for he lacked funds and had to run his campaign on an extremely bare budget. His advertising consisted of crayoned messages scribbled on grocer-donated brown bags, which he placed on the windshields of cars. He made a deal with a gas station owner for credit on the condition that if he lost the election he would not have to pay.

Choate and I had first met in 1968 at the Democratic National Convention outside the Sherman House Hotel. Later, he and his aide, Doug Kane, helped me when I co-managed Governor Shapiro's campaign in southern Illinois. During the campaign, both Choate and I spoke at a meeting of the Twenty-first Congressional District Democratic Women's Club. Choate told me afterwards that he liked my speaking style and invited me to speak at his 1968 Jefferson Day rally in Anna.

In addition to his legislative leadership role, Choate served as Union County Democratic party chairman and staged a gala affair every election year. This year, more than 700 enthusiastic party supporters and their guests crowded into the American Legion Hall, where benefactor Choate supplied the multi-course dinner and the drinks.

Choate served as master of ceremonies, and when it came my turn to speak, I found him energetically supportive. As I made each point, he would holler, "Yow-sah" into the microphone, setting off applause from the audience, or he would pound on the podium as a signal for yells and cheers. I found it easy to give a highly partisan, hard-hitting speech before this crowd that Choate manipulated at will.

When the Shapiro campaign ended, Bob Brooks and I held a dinner for the campaign workers and invited Choate to be a guest of honor and featured speaker. Exuding warmth and charm, he delivered a rousing speech and also answered questions freely, giving the audience an excellent analysis of both legislative politics and the inner workings of the Democratic party. Choate and his wife, Donna, bantered with us long after the dinner was over and thanked me several times for inviting them to be with the students. Both gave me warm embraces as they left.

I thus had every reason to believe that this powerful Democrat would be in my corner. After all, we had worked harmoniously and effectively in the governor's campaign, and Choate had used me as a featured speaker at his political rally. So I felt confident and eager when I learned that Ray and I were to meet with Choate at his farm. But in politics there are few paths devoid of obstacles, and I would soon discover that Clyde Choate would not provide me easy access to political office.

Chancey picked me up at nine in the morning, and we enjoyed a rustic drive on the winding road to Anna. Choate greeted us heartily, and when I complimented him on his farm and his beautiful horses, he became quite animated, expressing his enthusiasm for riding and his admiration for accomplished riders. At that point, I engaged in my first overt act of political hyprocrisy—I boasted about my wife's riding ability. In reality, she was then at home recovering from a broken arm sustained in a riding accident, and the year before had broken her leg in a fall from a horse. Though her riding was a big bone of contention between us, I did not convey my antipathy to Choate as he gave us a tour of his property and pointed out his elegant, prize-winning horses. An hour later, he took us inside, where Donna welcomed us warmly and offered us hot coffee and sweet rolls.

Chancey and I had discussed strategy on the trip down and had agreed that he should be the one to broach the subject of my political aspirations. So now he told Choate, "The Jackson County organization would like Mel to be the next state superintendent of public instruction. Mel did the right thing by coming to me first. Now we're doing the right thing by asking your support."

Choate looked suprised. "Well, I should have thought of that myself," he said. "Mel has good qualifications for the job. But I was hoping you were coming down here for something else. There's another position open where we need a strong candidate, and I was hoping you were going to ask Mel to run for state senator."

"Clyde, that's an interesting deal," I said, "but, frankly, I can't hack two houses and support my family on twelve thousand bucks a year."

"Well, I can see that it would be a problem. But a lot of the fellows in the legislature boost their income by selling insurance or something like that."

"I'm sorry to have to admit I'm not really suited for business," I responded. "Besides, a Jew can't hope to win in a basically Southern Baptist and Methodist . . . "

"No, no—you're wrong," Choate shot back. "Being a Jew won't hurt you. Some people still have bad prejudices against the Catholics, but there's very little, if any, against Jews."

Then Choate went on to explain why he thought running for state superintendent was not feasible. Many politicians in the state resented the political overrepresentation of southern Illinois, he said. Paul Powell occupied the position of Illinois secretary of state. Alan Dixon of nearby Belleville served as the number-two leader in the state senate. And still another neighboring politician, Lieutenant Governor Paul Simon of Troy, stood directly in line for the governorship should anything happen to Governor Ogilvie. Furthermore, Choate himself would become speaker of the Illinois house should the Democrats win in 1970. Thus, because of southern Illinois's disproportionate power, Choate did not think the state party would consent to yet another officeholder from our region—particularly the office of state superintendent, which, second only to the secretary of state, would control the largest number (more than a thousand) of Democratic patronage jobs in Illinois. Choate also warned me that other contenders had already begun their campaigns, one as early as two years before. At best, my candidacy would represent a long shot.

After Choate finished ticking off all of my candidacy's adverse implications for the party, he then let us in on his personal objection to my running for the state superintendent's office. Cook County leaders had approached him about running on the state ticket in 1968, but he had declined. Should Powell not run again for secretary of state in 1972, Choate would become the leading prospect for that patronage-rich office. If, however, a southern Illinoisan were state superintendent, the problem of geographical imbalance could very likely block Choate from the secretary of state nomination. Choate emphasized his party service of twenty-three years and indicated that, since I was a Johnny-come-lately of less than two years' heavy political activity, he did not intend to step aside. His argument was persuasive. I understood his position and would not insist on running, I told him.

At that point, Chancey stepped in. He reminded me of our agreement that he would do the talking, and, for the first time, I realized that I no longer functioned as a political free agent. I had requested support from Chancey and the Jackson County organization, and they had given it to me. Under our "contract," they now were pledged to seek my nomination, and I was committed to support their efforts. Furthermore, the organization now felt a substantial patronage stake in my future, and any decision to withdraw belonged to them, not to me.

Choate's logically justified reservations about the viability of my candidacy plainly were lost on Chancey. He reiterated my qualifications to run for the office: "Mel would make a very good candidate," he told Choate. "He was manager of the Shapiro campaign [Chancey exaggerated, for I had been only co-manager], and we won in Jackson County. He's a strong campaigner, and you yourself used him twice as a featured speaker. Besides, Mel's Jewish background will add great strength to the ticket in Cook County."

Then Chancey turned to a more convincing argument: "Clyde, over the years I've given you lots of strong political support and also raised a lot of money. And do you know where that money comes from? It comes from our organization and people like members of Mel's own synagogue."

Chancey paused to let his last statement sink in, and Choate looked thoughtful. Chancey spoke again: "Plenty of people in Jackson County want Mel to have the nomination. The boys in the organization want him to have it, and I want him to have it. If Mel is turned down, a lot of us will be very disappointed, and people will want to know why he was vetoed."

Choate was persuaded—persuaded against his will, clearly, but ready to lend his support nevertheless. Still, he could not resist repeating to me, "Even though you're well-qualified, it will be awfully hard for you to get the nomination. But if the Jackson County organization is determined, I'll give you strong backing."

I then volunteered, "Clyde, the patronage privileges of the county chairmen will depend on their loyalty to me; and if you go after any state office, I'll insist that all county chairmen receiving my patronage line up behind you."

This apparently took the sting out of Chancey's strong admonishment, for Choate now assumed the role of major advisor and outlined my basic strategy. He explained that, officially, the slatemakers consisted of twenty-four central committeemen, each of whom represented one congressional district and possessed voting power equal to the number of votes he received in the party primary. Consequently, the twelve from Cook County were "more equal" than the twelve from downstate, since the former represented almost two-thirds of the Democratic primary voters.

In essence, then, the Cook County machine provided major input on state slatemaking. The endorsements were consensual decisions, however, and the superintendent position traditionally went to a downstater. Thus, a prospective candidate's major task was to find backers who would send positive support signals to the slatemakers. Choate offered to take me to see Powell and Daley but repeated that my main job was to meet as many people as possible who could tell the "Chicago boys" what a good candidate I would make. He mentioned once more my late start and the heavy odds against me, but he cited, on the other hand, Paul Powell's bitter opposition to Adlai Stevenson III's receiving the nomination for U.S. senator. Powell supported downstater Alan Dixon of Belleville, but Choate felt pessimistic about Dixon's chances. "Powell will raise such a commotion against Stevenson that Daley and the boys may have to throw us a bone. The bone they throw might very well be slating Mel Kahn for state superintendent," he concluded.

Then he gave me some parting instructions: "Touch a few bases in downstate, and work real hard in Chicago. Use your labor connections and contacts with other Chicago people you know. The whole idea is to send strong signals to the slatemakers and let them know you're an effective campaigner. You've lived in Chicago, and you've lived in downstate—use all your knowledge to recruit every bit of backing you can get. At the right time, I'll help you, but you've got to gather support and run a good preliminary campaign."

As Chancey and I drove the thirty-five miles back to Carbondale, I reflected on the time we had spent with Choate and, particularly, on how the soft-spoken Chancey had reversed him. My students and I had recently discussed Samuel Eldersveld's concept of stratarchy, the dispersement of decision-making powers to several strata, or layers, within a political structure. I now mused that stratarchy evidently was at work in downstate Illinois politics: Ray Chancey could not commit himself to me without first clearing it with his executive committee. But, having done so, Chancey, a mid-level party official, then had managed to counter the initial stance taken by Clyde Choate, his political superior in the organization, who was also the legislative leader of all downstate Democrats. Nor was this the first time Chancey had blocked him. Now Chancey had turned Choate around, even though Choate had offered plausible reasons for not backing me. The concept of nonhierarchical decision making, or stratarchy, seemed strongly confirmed in the relationship between these two political leaders.

Moreover, Clyde Choate had bested someone several notches above him in the state Democratic hierarchy, Daley himself, by helping defeat the income-tax formula Daley and Republican Governor Richard Ogilvie had worked out. Finally, Paul Powell had defeated Mayor Daley's choice for speaker of the Illinois house in 1959 with the help of downstate Democrats, Republicans, and the Republican governor. All this had occurred at a time when many considered Mayor Daley the top state political leader in the United States.

But stratarchy is a two-sided coin. Although those occupying a lesser position on the scale—a Chancey, a Choate, or a Powell— might exert influence over Mayor Daley, nevertheless, to acquire a state nomination one must perceive power perspectives accurately. Chairman Chancey could not achieve the slating of prospective nominees for state office unless he had the backing of Clyde Choate, his state central committeeman, the approval of downstate leader Paul Powell, and the support of the most powerful Illinois Democrat of them all, Richard J. Daley. These reciprocal relationships, wherein leaders located at separate levels of a scale levied varying amounts of influence over one another depending upon time, place, and situation, lent weight to the concept of stratarchy. But stratarchy means "limited hierarchy"; and though differently positioned politicians needed each other and could exert mutual influence, as was evident in the domain of state nominations, Mayor Daley and the machine could tip the scales.

I was now able, from the stuff of my own experience, to start fleshing out and putting names to the theoretical outlines of the textbooks and the classrooms. To be sure, I had helped manage a governor's campaign in my area of the state. But to be starting on the road to my own nomination for public office, well, this gave me a different perspective on that reality we call political life. My road was to be a long one in every sense except the chronological, and in the short months ahead I would have to knock on all the doors of political influence to which I could find my way. Though it was the door on the fifth floor of Chicago's city hall behind which lay the highest seat of political power in the state, a direct approach to Mayor Daley was not open to me. But by making pilgramages to the sinecures of lesser luminaries, paying my respects, and pleading my case, I could approach the mayor obliquely, discreetly, and properly credentialed. My quest for endorsement would take place in two political arenas whose quality of life, history, and ethnic make-up contrasted as vividly as did the characters and style of the two men whose presence dominated them. These arenas were Richard J. Daley's Cook County and Paul Powell's downstate Illinois.

2
A City of Nations

I became aware of Chicago's diverse ethnic make-up fifteen years prior to my 1969 political race for the office of superintendent. As a graduate student at the University of Chicago, I frequently traveled by public transportation to the various ethnic enclaves of the city. When I worked at Goldblatt's Department Store on Christiana and Twenty-sixth Street, I attended celebrations and enjoyed Polish polka music at nearby Pilsen Park. Sometimes, after a Friday afternoon class in the social science building on Fifty-ninth Street, I would walk to the Sixty-third Street elevated train in the heart of Woodlawn's black ghetto and ride to Comiskey Park to watch the captivating "Minnie" Minoso and his "go-go" Chicago White Sox. I also worked part-time for the National Opinion Research Center doing in-depth interviews on Chicago's near-west side, where the spicy aromas and fast chatter at the neighborhood softball games suggested that Taylor Street was an Italian microcosm. And, in the summers, my friends and I would occasionally go to Sieben's open-air beer garden on the northwest side of the city to drink the good, dark German beer and sing drinking songs.

To anyone living in Chicago during the Daley era, this metropolis proclaimed itself a "city of nations." And the Democratic machine reflected the city: it relied heavily on its ethnic foundation for votes, finances, and leadership. In return, the machine proffered both *Gesellschaft* and *Gemeinschaft* types of rewards: jobs, access to key policy makers, and the public recognition and acknowledgment designed to maintain group pride. Because these relationships paid off handsomely for the machine, early in my campaign I set myself a central goal: to demonstrate to the slatemakers that I understood and had political support from the major groups comprising the machine's ethnic coalition.

While many people perceived Chicago as a single civic entity, the reality it assumed for its citizens was that of a mosaic of *Gemeinschaft* neighborhoods and communities. Natives thought of themselves not only as Chicagoans but also as residents of distinctly definable neighborhoods such as Chatham, Hyde Park, Logan Square, Albany Park, Canaryville, or the section so colorfully known as Back of the Yards. These neighborhoods contained ethnic enclaves, many of whose inhabitants belonged to "cousin clubs" that gathered for picnics and other social events, religious festivities, and national holidays, thereby reinforcing their kinship identifications within the ethnic group.

Richard Daley, of all Chicago's mayors, was the ultimate ethnic booster. He would purchase a tree in Israel, pay homage to the great Polish patriot Kosciusko, and honor the Italian-American community on Columbus Day. Of course, the machine did not limit its honors to these groups only, as Germans, Greeks, Slavs, Croatians, Lithuanians, and a multitude of others celebrated their most important holidays by marching down State Street resplendent in their native costumes. Daley usually led these processions. Nor did he forget his own Irish—on St. Patrick's Day, the Chicago River took on an emerald hue as the mayor led the annual parade.

In addition to community organizations and churches, the communication media bolstered this feeling of ethnic awareness in that many ethnic groups published their own weekly newspapers, several of them written in the language of national origin. Some radio stations supplemented their English programming with offerings in Polish or Spanish; others broadcast exclusively in one of these two languages. Within the black community, stations specialized in music and dialogue indigenous to black culture. To truly understand Chicago, and to comprehend the nature and operation of the machine, one must focus on these collections of individual neighborhoods, which often functioned as self-contained subcommunities.

As millions of Americans of ethnic origin have emerged from impoverished backgrounds to join the middle class (and, in some instances, the upper class), a great many of them have retained their ethnic awareness. Ethnic involvement created important political ramifications in Chicago. Instead of joining the higher-income Republican party identifiers, ethnics achieving financial success more often exerted influence and leadership within the Democratic party. Milton Gordon has delineated ethnicity's impact this way:

> From the cradle in the sectarian hospital to the child's play group, the social clique in high school, the fraternity and religious center in college, the dating group within which he searches for a spouse, the marriage partner, the neighborhood of his residence, the church affiliation and the church clubs, the men's and the women's social and service organizations, the adult clique of marrieds, the vacation resort, and then, as the age cycle nears completion, the rest homes for the elderly, and, finally the sectarian cemetery—in all these activities and relationships which are close to the core of personality and selfhood—the member of the ethnic group may if he wishes follow a path which never takes him across the boundaries of his ethnic structural network.[1]

It is true that not every ethnic group received equal treatment from the machine, but each generally felt it fared sufficiently well to continue the machine relationship. In fact, when most ethnic leaders compared the machine's material payoffs to the deprivation of their grandparents, they concluded easily that the machine functioned as a friend of the ethnic. Edward Chambers, assistant director of the Industrial Areas Foundation Training Center, emphasized the machine's ethnic appeal when he identified the Democratic party of Cook County as the "best ethnic organization in the nation, based entirely on jobs and self-interest. . . . Everybody gets something, including the Catholic Church and the Protestant black ministers who are put on the payroll."[2] During the early days of the Washington administration, the Chicago *Defender* printed a story on sixteen black ministers who were on the city payroll (ten of whom dated back to the Daley administration) at salaries ranging from $6.21 per hour to $27,060 per year.[3]

Jobs and self-interest of course provided most of the energy that made the machine run, but it is overstating the case to claim that the machine's success issued "entirely" from these. Although economic payoffs had to occur, the machine did not distribute material compensation equally, and it often substituted group recognition (a *Gemeinschaft* characteristic) for economic rewards. Emphasizing group recognition enabled the machine to minimize its expenditure of political capital (jobs, contracts, and so forth). Edgar Litt underscores this dimension of ethnic politics:

> Under this system, ethnic leaders are eventually taken care of in the allocation of material, divisible party benefits, while group members are psychologically recognized. Of course, that recognition implies the obligation to perform services and secure political favors, but among the consequences of recognition is that the potential for granting favors will in most cases not have to be realized. A political organization that always had to convert recognition into material benefits would soon be bankrupt.[4]

We later will note some of the material benefits machine members (and, occasionally, supporters) could count on. Nevertheless, the steady recognition accorded Chicago's ethnics diminished significantly the machine's need to provide expensive payoffs.

Recognition politics, moreover, served as a substitute for class politics, which might have posed a divisive threat to the machine's coalition. By pleasing supportive groups through recognition politics, the machine could side-step controversial issues that would produce clarion calls for effective action. Raymond Wolfinger says, "By structuring politics so that expectations are for recognition rather than substantive policies, ethnic strategies divert working-class energies away from substantive policy demands."[5] Now, the machine could not always avoid issues, but because it dominated Cook County's governmental units, it often could structure them so that they did not enter the public arena. E. E. Schattschneider's thesis prevailed: To the extent that the machine privatized inter-group conflict to the participants themselves, the dominant faction usually won. Conversely, to have permitted socialization of the conflict to the public arena would have diluted the strength of the individual groups involved, for outside parties likely would have decided the issues differently than would those initially concerned.

Particularly on the question of "neighborhood population stability" did white ethnic groups seek to prevent the conflict from entering the domain of public decision making. Those neighborhoods and subcommunities defined by ethnic lines wanted to maintain their identities as established over the years; they opposed the influx of new and "different" (black and Hispanic) people. In Chicago, the most segregated of northern cities, the code words "keeping the neighbor-hood the way it's been" meant "keeping the blacks out." This goal accounted significantly for the machine's successful operation in the many wards whose denizens were determined to preserve the status quo. The Daley machine's singular ability throughout the 1960s to keep favoring the white ethnics over the blacks in the two areas—jobs and housing—that affected the blacks with at least equal intensity, while simultaneously relying upon blacks for the electoral edge that kept the organization in power, struck me as ironic. To achieve this, however, the organization had to walk a tightrope, continually readjusting its relative payoffs to the loosely cohering elements of its ethnic coalition to prevent any violent shifts that might dislodge those on top. I would have to try to perform a minature version of this delicate balancing act, I assumed, were I to gain the broad-based ethnic support I would need for the nomination. It might not be easy to win the backing of Polish leaders, for example, and that of black politicians as well.

Even though I had lived in Chicago previously, in the summer of 1969 I did not possess as much general knowledge of the history and political development of Chicago's ethnic groups as I later came to acquire. But I was sharply conscious of the ethnic identifications of the individual politicians whose support I sought. Some of these men functioned overtly as spokesmen for their respective ethnic groups; others, while not serving directly as ethnic representatives, yet were alert to how their people fared in local politics. I, too, became increasingly sensitive to ethnicity's impact upon the Democratic machine when I began contacting Cook County political leaders. The following general sketch may further illustrate ethnicity's role in developing the political styles, attitudes, and goals of these men whose backing I needed.

People of eastern European extraction predominated among Chicago's Caucasian ethnics, and, of these, the Poles were by far the most numerous. It was the Poles more than any other group who supported native-language newspapers and radio stations. Within the Democratic voting bloc, the Poles were numerically second only to the blacks.

I had already met Roman Pucinski, the intelligent and garrulous congressman and ward committeeman, and I had hopes that I might win the support of this prominent leader among Chicago's Polish-Americans. My visit to Pucinski's Milwaukee Avenue ward head-quarters on Chicago's northwest side revealed a sign-plastered exterior and a spacious office inside. A secretary, a general office worker, and an administrative assistant comprised the staff. The office motif was patriotic, vintage 1930, and miniature American flags and two large lamps adorned with eagles took up much of the space on the clerk's desk. On the main wall hung a plaster American eagle with a four-and-a-half-foot wingspread. An outsized red, white, and blue vase ornamented with stars stood sentinel on the floor nearby.

In the waiting room beyond the reception area, a number of publications pertaining to the city of Chicago lay scattered about on tables. One pamphlet contained an index, allowing people to turn instantly to sections on legal help, jobs, and other services. Like the Chicago Democratic organization itself, Pucinski's headquarters emphasized personal assistance.

After I was seated in Pucinski's private office, we talked generally for a while, and then he commented upon his job and his feelings about it: "I work seven days a week. I enjoy the work, but I really question whether those people not in public life work as hard as those of us in politics. Being a professional public leader is a very demanding job, and it often means having to run around the clock. It means accepting all kinds of jobs and trying to do things for people. I find that it is an interesting job. But another fact that many don't realize is that you have to do a lot of studying and reading and keeping up with the issues."

Pucinski was concerned that ethnic politics uncontrolled and left unchecked would create disorder. In his opinion, only a Democratic party strong enough to work out agreements between ethnic groups could prevent chaos among what he called "this mosaic of minorities." He defended, too, the operation of the political machine, particularly that of his own ward organization.

When it came to the relationship between the Poles and the machine, Pucinski took the role of historian and talked about the roots of Polish politics in Chicago. He also freely suggested reading material and Xeroxed for me a copy of a newspaper article by Professor Martin Krug that described the great Polish migration waves of the late-nineteenth and early-twentieth centuries. These immigrants, according to Professor Krug,

> spoke a rudimentary, peasant's Polish, were mostly illiterate in their own language and, of course, the English language was totally alien to them.
> No work was too hard, too menial, too coarse or too

dangerous. They had no choice, and they could not be choosy about jobs, if their families were to survive in the new environment. This hard and demanding work was the single contribution of these millions of brawny and healthy immigrants, who without much complaining or rebelling, helped to make America the industrial giant it is today.[6]

In 1969, as I was beginning my campaign, the significance of this heavy Polish vote was not lost on me. Naturally, I wanted nomination support from this major population segment.

Historically, Chicago's Poles identified from the beginning with the Democratic party. In 1894, a *Dziennik Chicagoski* editorial made a strong case for Polish allegiance to the Democrats:

> For whom should the Poles vote?
> For the Democrats.
> And whom else should they vote for?
> For Polish candidates, regardless of political party.
> Why should we vote for the Democratic party?
> Because in reality it is the people's party and it stands for freedom.
> Who opposes all restrictions?
> The Democratic party.
> Who are the true friends of the working people?
> The Democrats.
> Who condemn Pullman so severely?*
> The Democrats . . . .
> . . . Who are restraining millionaires and exploiters?
> The Democrats.
> Who give every person in America the right to pray and speak in his own language at school?
> The Democrats.
> Who condemn the wicked A.P.A. [American Protective Association]?
> The Democrats. . . .
> . . . Which party did the most good for the Poles?
> The Democratic party.

---

*George Pullman manufactured sleeping cars for the railroads, required his workers to live in his company town of Pullman, Illinois, and influenced President Cleveland to send federal troops to break a strike that would become historically significant in the labor movement.

What are the proofs?

The Democratic administration employs hundreds of Poles, and more than a score of them are officials.

And the Republicans?

They always turned their back on us, or tried to buy us as if we were cattle.

Did they succeed?

No, they did not succeed and never will.

Are there any Polish candidates on the Republican ticket?

No, there are none.

Why?

Because, when a Pole tried to run for county commissioner, the Republicans placed a Negro on their ballot. Therefore, let the Negroes vote for them.

And who else?

The Pullmans . . . . [7]

Poles appreciated the policies of Democratic Governor John Peter Altgeld, a fierce opponent of the Pullman interests, and they regarded the Republican party as antiworking class. The *Dziennik Chicagoski* editoralized, "The Democratic Party, the true people's party, the party with a high regard for religion, ought to be our party. There is no room for us in the Republican Party."[8] The Poles perceived the Republicans as "the party of big business, puritanical prohibitionists, fanatical anti-Catholics, and narrow-minded educators trying to stamp out the Polish language," whereas they viewed the Democrats as "the party of working men's democracy and broad-minded toleration."[9] Thus began the tradition of the Chicago Polish community's attachment to the Democratic party.

Despite their large numbers, Poles achieved recognition very slowly in America, one reason being that many still regarded themselves as only temporarily absent from the mother country and planned nostalgically to return "home." In fact, prior to World War I, many Poles did not bother to become naturalized. After the war, however, they ascribed greater value to U.S. citizenship, and Polish-American leaders expressed dismay at the neglect accorded Chicago's Polish community. This concern took the form of two principal complaints, both directed against the Irish: first, the Poles were noticeably weak within the Irish-controlled Catholic Church hierarchy; and, second, the Irish-dominated Democratic party withheld the recognition Poles felt they deserved. Edward Kantowicz sums up the Poles' political goals:

[T]he recognition drive attempted to provide two types of satisfaction for Polonia's citizens. One was psychological, a sense of pride and prestige, a feeling of belonging, of being an insider, of having influence; the other was economic—politics meant jobs. Prestige came, for the most part, from gaining elective office or significant appointive position (high-level patronage); whereas the vast number of clerical and laboring jobs in government bureaus (low-level patronage) provided the bulk of economic rewards. Above all, the final goal of politics was the gaining of power; so the ultimate aim of the recognition drive was to wield political influence in Polonia's interest.[10]

In the mid–1920s, their struggle began to pay off, to the discomfort, however, of the Democratic party. Democratic Mayor William Dever greatly antagonized the Poles when he vowed to enforce the unpopular prohibition mandate of the Volsted Act; and, in the enforcement that ensued, overzealous police sometimes broke into private homes in search of bootleg liquor. The Poles denounced Dever's raids with the rationale that a man's home was his castle and therefore inviolate from government harassment. Kantowicz describes how the colorful Republican candidate, "Big Bill" Thompson, capitalized on this anti-Dever feeling among the Poles and other ethnic groups: Thompson "roared around the city proclaiming that he was 'as wet as the Atlantic Ocean' and that he would 'fire every policeman who enter[ed] a home in search of liquor.' Outraged at Dever's police, Polish-Americans at Thompson rallies responded with cries of 'hurray for beer and Big Bill!' "[11] The Polish community's switch to the Republicans was the deciding factor in Thompson's election.

But in the 1931 mayoral election, Republican Thompson wiped out his previous gains in the Polish wards when he referred to Czech Anthony Cermak as "pushcart Tony," and he particularly incensed Poles "by declaring the Democratic 'double-play combination' to be 'Szymczak to Zintak to Cermak.' "[12] Although the Poles now flocked back to the Democratic fold, they had served notice of their willingness to jump the political fence when the issues—or ethnic insults—warranted such action. Thenceforth, Chicago's Democratic leaders would take this possibility into consideration in their dealings with the Polish electorate.

The Poles, though numerically superior, often functioned ineffectively in the machine because of their tendency toward internal strife. When the organization decided not to reslate highly respected Polish Judge Edmund K. Jarecki on the grounds of party disloyalty in patronage matters, Polish ward leaders sided with the machine. (Jarecki did, however, defeat them in the primary.) In addition, the Poles frequently refused to engage in coalition building with other machine ethnic groups, with the result that their large numbers failed to achieve for them the highest leadership posts of party chairman and mayor, despite the presence of many outstanding Polish leaders.

Though largely apolitical with respect to other policy matters, the Poles rallied on issues pertaining to home ownership and taxation; and as blacks began to move into Polish areas this intra-city migration created severe tension between the two groups. The machine, while occasionally endorsing symbolic problack measures such as hard-to-enforce antidiscrimination laws, steadfastly opposed effectual open-housing ordinances. By keeping the question of segregated housing out of the public arena, the machine-dominated city government narrowed the scope of this vital conflict between neighborhood-segregationist ethnic groups (predominantly Polish) and blacks. Delimitation of the conflict thus resulted, for the most part, in the maintenance of the status quo—a highly desirable policy from the viewpoint of the white ethnics.

But the lines had been drawn, and many Poles rebelled against what they regarded as blatant black favoritism among liberals and the media. Michael Novak cites the resentful protest of one Polish-American interviewed by reporter Lois Wille:

> The liberals have always despised us. We have got these mostly little jobs, and we drink beer and, my God, we bowl and watch television and we don't read. It is god-damn vicious snobbery. We're sick of all these phony integrated TV commercials with these upper-class Negroes. We know they're phony.
>
> The only time a Pole is mentioned it's to make fun of him. He is Ignatz Dumbrowski, 274 pounds, 5-foot-4, and he got his education by writing into a firm on a matchbook cover. But what will we do about it? Nothing, because we're the new invisible man, the new whipping boy, and we still think the measure of a man's what he does and how he takes care of his children and what he's doing in his own home, not what he thinks about Vietnam.[13]

But a more reasoned perspective on the conflict between the Poles and the blacks is expressed in a feature article published in the Chicago *Tribune*: "Polish leaders indignantly deny the frequently made accusation that their group is antiblack. 'The conflict between the Poles and the blacks, where it exists, is neither basically racial nor ideological—it is simply economic,' asserts Joseph Bialasiewicz, the wise and able editor of the Polish weekly, *Polonia*. 'Poles and blacks,' he continued, 'are victims of discrimination and they compete often for the same low priced homes and for the same jobs.'"[14] Both groups felt the brunt of economic and social pressures.

Unlike the blacks, Poles were not locked into the Democratic party and therefore could not be taken for granted by machine leaders. Though Poles normally delivered huge majorities for the Democratic ticket, they still proved capable of bolting, especially when a fellow Pole ran against a non-Pole. I became aware of this mercurial quality when Benjamin Adamowski led a "Polish revolt" against Richard Daley in the 1955 Democratic mayoralty primary. And, in 1960, with the help of a thumping majority from the normally Democratic Polish wards, converted Republican Adamowski did win the key position of state's attorney. Running again for mayor in 1963 (as a Republican), he scored a sizable triumph over Daley in the Polish wards despite the mayor's staunch backing by the Polish-Democratic ward leaders. Ethnicity counted. When a Polish candidate opposed the party's choice, even Polish leaders could not overcome their constituents' strong ethnic preferences for fellow Polish candidates.

Like other observers of the Chicago political show, I was well aware of the party's struggle to maintain support from both Poles and blacks. To achieve the state nomination, I would have to cultivate both groups, and could ill-afford to antagonize either. For this reason, it was critical that I focus on general, social-welfare matters and emphasize education. Under no circumstances could I get into specific, inflammatory issues such as busing or housing, for either way, I would alienate a crucial Democratic voting bloc. Both groups could wield a veto against any candidate they found offensive.

Although I was later to find out that the machine did not worry overmuch about the black vote (and that, in fact, the black vote had diminished by the late sixties), in 1969 I overestimated its importance. Since I already had met and worked politically with several black leaders, I thought I might have a chance at winning the backing of this ethnic group.

Earlier in their history, Chicago's blacks had aligned themselves with the party of Lincoln, an identification that continued for many years mainly because of two factors: To begin with, they felt unwelcome in a party that was dominated by white ethnics; further, in the 1920s they found a champion in demagogic Republican mayor "Big Bill" Thompson, who, throughout his career, made strong and overt appeals for black support. When the Democrats accused the Republicans of pandering to black voters, Thompson endeared himself to the black community by replying, "The black finger that is good enough to pull a trigger in defense of the American flag is good enough to mark a ballot."[15] The voting returns vindicated Thompson's tactics he received an estimated 91 percent of the black vote in 1927.[16]

In the 1930s, the introduction of New Deal social-welfare policies brought relief to blacks, who, as a whole, most noticeably constituted Chicago's economic have-nots.[17] When Democratic Mayor Ed Kelly began to cultivate them, blacks turned to the Democratic party in increasing numbers, an affiliation marked by three significant events in the Kelly era. First, a black Democrat defeated the supposedly unbeatable Republican Congressman Oscar DePriest (also a black) in the 1938 congressional election. Second, 73 percent of the blacks voted for Mayor Kelly in 1935, in contrast to the mere 16 percent who had supported Democrat Cermak four years earlier. Third, Kelly enticed Republican William Dawson and other top black leaders into the Democratic organization.

Dawson, with patronage secured from Kelly, built a powerful Democratic machine in his Second Ward and then extended his power to the other black ward organizations. According to James Q. Wilson, Dawson knew how to deal harshly and decisively with his rivals without creating lasting enemies.[18] He was also instrumental in launching Richard Daley's mayoralty career. In 1955, my first year at the University of Chicago, Dawson helped lead the move to dump incumbent Mayor Martin Kennelly in the primary, then produced a margin of 125,000 votes for Daley in the closely contested mayoralty election. Although a loosening of firm white-ethnic machine ties occurred during the Daley era, Dawson's black submachine did not suffer this fate. It consistently delivered tremendous margins to machine-endorsed candidates, both white and black. In fact, in the black wards there was seldom more than a 1 percent difference in the number of votes delivered for the candidates on the Democratic slate. In the white wards, however, black candidates often fared poorly.

An interesting state senate race in the south-side Second Congressional District where I had lived at one time illustrates the reliability of the black vote. Abner Willoughby, a black liberal, decisively defeated Jewish Marshall Korshak in Hyde Park, an area populated largely by white professional people and the University of Chicago community. In the black areas, however, Dawson's organization brought about a complete reversal—there, Korshak trounced Willoughby and more than erased the deficit he suffered in the Hyde Park area.

A major ingredient of Dawson's development of the black submachine was his attention to recognition politics, specifically his emphasis on race pride.[19] Dawson worked hard to achieve notice for individual blacks and for the black community as a whole; and the machine was only too willing to bestow honors and acknowledgment that required no expenditure of substantial political capital such as jobs, contracts, or the like.

The black clergy were the principal beneficiaries of the machine's recognition. They were frequently called upon, for example, to give benedictions at the myriad political functions the machine hosted for visiting dignitaries such as United States presidents. Prominent among these black clergy was the Reverend Joseph Jackson, president of the 5 million-member National Baptist Conference and pastor of the mammoth Mt. Olivet Baptist Church. The machine accorded the Reverend Jackson personal recognition of various sorts, and he, on his part, constantly urged his congregation, which was the largest in all Chicago, to support the machine.

Another black minister, the Reverend Corneal "Deacon" Davis of the Quinn Memorial Chapel, worked actively in politics. "The Deacon," a long-time state legislator, served on many influential committees and, as a member of the Democratic state central committee, possessed high political status. Governor Adlai Stevenson II considered Davis, a flaming orator, his favorite speaker and on many occasions brought his three sons to the Illinois statehouse to hear "the Deacon" perform. Both the state and county central committees used Davis for benedictions and also featured him as a speaker at many major political events. The Reverend Davis and the black community felt additionally honored when Adlai Stevenson III launched his campaigns for state treasurer and U.S. senator at Davis's Quinn Memorial Chapel, in the heart of Chicago's black area.

The machine's effective use of recognition politics secured the cooperation of prominent black leaders and served also as a source of pride to the black community. As Edgar Litt points out, a machine cannot extend material rewards all the time and to everyone without going bankrupt—the machine's recognition politics, which could reap benefits at little or no cost, were necessary.

But material benefits were, of course, most fundamentally important to the black community. As the relative have-nots in Chicago, the group with the lowest average income, blacks gave high priority to the machine's support of liberal welfare policies and public service programs. And they needed jobs. The aphorism, "The black is the last hired and first fired" offers a clue to the appeal of a political organization that made low-level jobs available. Beyond these fundamentals, blacks wanted higher expenditures for public education so that they could compete on a more equal footing for the many jobs requiring either high school or college diplomas. Blacks also needed training opportunities to avoid biased entrance standards formulated by white craft unions.

After Daley developed and solidified his power as mayor, black leader William Dawson's influence waned, but many of his former lieutenants increased their political stature. The late Colonel Kenneth Campbell, Twentieth Ward committeeman and alderman, well illustrated effective black political leadership during the Daley era. Campbell possessed an impressive background. He achieved the rank of colonel during World War II and often used that title as a civilian. A shrewd, quiet man, he earned a master's degree in business administration from the University of Chicago and, while a graduate student, operated the only major black automobile dealership in the United States.

Several years before I ran for office, when I was conducting interviews on school desegregation, one of the community leaders with whom I spoke was Campbell. I found his political headquarters to be the social center of his subcommunity. A large assembly hall (that doubled as a dancehall), a bulletin board containing annoucements of social events and job openings, modern conference rooms, and Campbell's own pine-paneled office told me much about the extent of his ward organization. Assisted by intelligent and articulate aides, he drew also upon volunteer help that included lawyers and college graduates who worked in well-paying downtown patronage jobs Campbell had secured for them.

I learned in the course of my visit that Campbell and his staff routinely rendered assistance to those needing to cope with the bureaucracy. Whether this involved helping someone break through the red tape of welfare, enter public housing, or find employment, Campbell's organization made itself continuously available to serve his constituents. Campbell stated it succinctly: "More and more, the role of the ward committeeman has become both an administrative and a psychological one. We spend a great deal of time listening to complaints and advising people. They need someone they can talk to who is genuinely interested in trying to help them, even if one can't always succeed."

Campbell often helped parolees find jobs and contacted public officials on behalf of people in difficulty. He made deals with judges whereby first-time offenders could join the armed forces rather than go to prison. He felt proud that nearly all of these boys straightened out while serving the military and that some even became professional or business people who, in turn, helped other boys in trouble with the law.

As I sat in his office that afternoon, Campbell took a phone call from a Chicago judge, and it soon became apparent that he was trying to convince the judge to let off an eighteen-year-old whom police had arrested for burglarizing a liquor store. Campbell noticed my embarrassment at hearing, firsthand, his effort to "fix" this case. When he had hung up the phone, he looked directly at me and said: "You look shocked that I would get one of my boys off. Now, let me tell you something: I once read that justice is equally available to everybody, rich and poor alike—just like the Ritz Hotel. Since my people don't have money to hire fancy legal talent, I have to provide an equalizer to give them a decent chance. I think it's a lot better to build good citizens than to sentence boys to jail, where they learn how to become hardened criminals.

"See these pictures on the wall? Two lawyers, a doctor, and a dentist. Each one had trouble with the law as a kid, and I kept them out of jail. Now they help counsel boys in the ward, contribute money, and bring honor to our community. I'm proud of what we've done for them and of what they're doing for our community now." Campbell paused for a moment and then added, "As a professor, you're supposed to have some intelligence. Are you going to tell me that I should refuse second chances? That I should cease my efforts to build good citizens?"

"No, of course not," I replied. "You've made your point."

Though Campbell expended much time and effort on behalf of lower-income blacks in his ward, he paid attention to the interests of the black middle class as well. The machine's responsibility for administering the city government included the selection of special panels of approved doctors, pharmacists, dentists, and optometrists who would receive the exclusive business of blacks on welfare. Because Campbell's recommendations of medical personnel for these panels were routinely accepted, black professional people had a palpable incentive to support the party with both votes and financial contributions. Another service Campbell rendered was making sure that black businessmen got cut in on deals with the city and that they were not harassed by building inspectors. And when ministers sought his help concerning the absence of adequate parking space for their congregations on Sundays, Campbell arranged with the police for churchgoers to double-park during services.

Campbell liked to involve himself in civic planning and community action and not only worked through established voluntary religious and social organizations but also developed his own politico-social block clubs at the grassroots level so that his constituents could feel they were part of the action. In addition, Campbell's organization published a weekly paper highlighting social events and free services available at ward headquarters. Campbell succeeded in making the machine/church alliance the vortex of community life. In exchange, he generated a great percentage of votes for his party's ticket in every election, a vital bargaining chip in his dealings with the leadership of the Cook County Democratic central committee.

The dominance-submission relationship of the Democratic machine to the black submachine is illuminated in the following comment by a white member of the machine's inner core, the "board of directors." Although made in the context of demonstrating how well blacks fared in Chicago, the statement reveals much: "Chicago is the best-run major city in America. It has fewer problems with minority groups than any other city. Daley has selected black leaders for the black wards who are loyal to the party and who, at the same time, have the respect of the blacks and can bring in a real strong vote. The important thing is that you don't have to worry about dangerous radicals among Chicago's blacks. The leaders of the blacks are Daley's people, and, as a result, he can control the situation through them."

I took it for granted that the support of the machine's black leaders would be an enormous and clear-cut bonus in my quest for the party's endorsement. Alderman Campbell was one of Daley's trusted lieutenants. In my heart—and conscience—I felt closer to the more liberal voluntary leaders of the black community, but the political dictates of seeking office often conflict with a candidate's other values. I could neither serve the school kids of the state nor launch my own political career until I actually acquired the nomination. People like Jesse Jackson could not help me. But political leaders like Campbell could. I wanted that nomination, and so I rationalized my conflict of values in favor of pragmatism.

In comparison with the Poles and the blacks, Jews constituted a minority within Cook County. But they were a distinct minority and were particularly important to my nomination bid, for if I could not pass muster with my own ethnic group, the machine too would pass me by. Having lived in Chicago, I possessed some factual knowledge of the historical relationship between Chicago's Jewish community and the Democratic machine. But beyond the facts themselves, I perceived an intimate connection between that political history and two traditional Jewish values—the concepts of *tsodokah*, or social justice, and *torah*, learning.

Jews have always believed ardently in the concept of *tsodokah* and from this foundation have become firm believers in liberalism— economic, social, and political. To effect social justice, personal charity is not sufficient, however; *tsodokah* demands of the government itself a genuine commitment to the improvement of the human condition.

In the wake of the great migration waves of the 1890s and early 1900s, American Jews felt a direct stake in economic liberalism. They stood only fourth in median income among the six groups of immigrants ranked by the Immigration Commission. So abject was Jewish poverty in Chicago during the 1930s that my Aunt Rose Rosenthal still talked about the Twenty-fourth Ward organization's Moe Rosenberg Matzoh Club, which distributed unleavened bread for Passover to the many Jews unable to afford this essential holiday food.

Economic deprivation motivated the creation of the first Jewish machine, on Chicago's west side, and during the New Deal era, the political effectiveness of the Jewish politicians was unsurpassed. Jacob Arvey and Moe Rosenberg ministered to economic needs so conscientiously that Twenty-fourth Ward residents outstripped all other 49 wards in the victory surplus delivered to the party ticket in the 1936 general election. Even after Jews fled the Twenty-fourth

Ward in the fifties, leaders Arthur Elrod and Izzie Horwitz used their white precinct captains (who had already moved to the north side) to elicit overwhelming margins of votes from the ward's new black inhabitants. To one of the early complaints that blacks, not absentee Jews, should run the political organization of this now solidly black area, a Jewish political leader responded, "We worked like hell to make this the best ward in the city. Why should we have to give it up just because blacks moved in and forced us to leave?" The concept of social justice might be said to falter where housing patterns are concerned. His defense of continuing Jewish control of such wards reveals this Jewish politico as far more closely identified with his machine fellows than with the traditional Jewish value of *tsodokah*.

I did not relish the idea that I desperately needed the support of this Jewish politician who deprived blacks of representation within the councils of the Democratic party. But if I spoke out against west-side Jewish leaders, they would unquestionably veto me. Once more, political expediency led me to remain mute.

Jews have made dramatic economic advances since the 1930s, leading all other ethnics in percentage of members practicing medicine and law, prospering in business, and enjoying the highest per capita income of any ethnic group. In short, Jews no longer have a strong need to champion economic liberalism as a matter of self-interest. And yet *tsodokah*-rooted economic liberalism persists among Jewish values. According to Andrew Greeley, Jews score significantly higher on measurements of economic liberalism than all other white ethnics and rank second only to blacks.[20] Jews still charge government with the responsibility for implementing policies that help people, particularly society's have-nots.

Jews differ politically from other ethnic groups in one vital respect: Even though they disproportionately occupy the higher reaches of the professional and income scales, they still identify strongly with the Democratic party. In all other ethnic groups, a significant correlation obtains between rising income and Republican identification, but among the Jewish followers of *tsodokah*, income does not dilute Democratic party support.

The concept of *torah*, or learning, constitutes another major Jewish value. Jews, throughout their history, have ascribed a high premium to reading and to studying the teachings of the great prophets and rabbis, and American Jews have identified closely with intellectual presidents such as Abraham Lincoln and Woodrow Wilson.

Particularly vital to Jews is the education of the young, as revealed in this passage from the Torah: "It is permitted to make a synagogue into a school but not a school into a synagogue, for a school is more holy than a synagogue." Jews, according to Greeley, exceed all other ethnic groups in their interest in reading and art.[21] And in Cook County, intellectual reformers such as Senator Paul Douglas, Governor Adlai Stevenson II, Senator Adlai Stevenson III, Congressman Abner Mikva, and Alderman Leon Despres achieved a wide following among Jews. That the machine would frequently nominate a person (Jewish or non-Jewish—it did not particularly matter) who represented the concept of *torah* constituted an appeal often sufficient to keep the independent-minded Jews supporting the party ticket. My Ph.D. symbolically cast me as a man of learning; and I was Jewish. Perhaps that combination would recommend me to the Jewish electorate.

Foreign policy considerations have kept many Jews voting Democratic. Not only had Democratic presidents championed the cause of Israel, but Cook County Democratic leaders provided demonstrable support by investing in Israel bonds, purchasing Israeli trees, and pronouncing ringing statements in behalf of Israel's role as a "defender of democracy." While the *tsodokah-* and *torah*-oriented Cook County Jews needed only minimally the material rewards that appealed to other ethnic groups, the machine's use of recognition politics with respect to Israel frequently created a positive impact on local Jewish consciousness.

Torah and recognition politics provided a tenuous bridge between the Jewish politician and the idealistic, issue-oriented members of Chicago's Jewish community. Despite their historical attachment to both the national and local Democratic parties, Jews, because of a deep commitment to social justice, often operated as mavericks—both outside and inside the party organization. At the turn of the century, many Jews worked fervently in the Socialist party, and during the 1960s they displayed much greater tolerance toward student militants than did any other ethnic contingent. Ardent reformers that they are, Jews constituted, by percentage, the most highly represented religious group in the camp of Eugene McCarthy's 1968 protest movement. And what was true nationally held true among Chicago Jewry at the time I was campaigning for office. Jews involved themselves actively in the Independent Voters of Illinois, an organization that often challenged the machine-slated Democratic candidates. Leon Despres, a Jew, was Mayor Daley's sharpest critic in the city council; Jewish also were many of Despres's key backers.

At first blush, it might have seemed prudent for the machine to write off this most skittish of all ethnic constituencies in the Democratic coalition. But the machine needed the Jews, independent tendencies notwithstanding. First, Jews registered and voted in notably higher percentages than did other ethnic groups. Particularly this was true in primaries, which usually drew a low voter turnout. Without the Jewish vote, not only did the machine risk an occasional defeat in local and congressional contests, but Jews could make the difference between winning and losing key patronage positions in the more competitive countywide general elections.

Jews flexed their collective political muscle in 1966 by helping defeat Democrat Harry Semerow for president of the Cook County board of commissioners after the machine dumped Jewish incumbent Seymour Simon. And in the 1969 election of Illinois constitutional convention delegates, predominantly Jewish wards on the north side and in the Jewish suburbs elected several independent candidates instead of those candidates backed by the machine.

The machine felt it imperative to recapture both the Jewish and non-Jewish reform-oriented defectors in the 1970 election. It seemed obvious to me that the machine's need for an independent-minded type on either the state or the county ticket who was Jewish (or who could at least attract these voters) boded well for my nomination bid. I would have to balance interests carefully, however—I must convince the machine that I could help achieve the goal of a "better living for all" by supporting patronage and by steering profitable supply contracts in the direction of the "deserving"; but, at the same time, I must impress the reformers as a well-educated proponent of social justice, efficiency, and good government. Though with respect to political leverage the Jews might pale in comparison with other Chicago ethnic groups, custom dictated that a prospective nominee be acceptable to his own ethnic base. Such acceptance would not guarantee slating; but rejection would make a veto inevitable. To avoid the latter, I would have to win over both the Jewish politicians and the "good government" forces of the Jewish electorate. I could not afford to alienate either group.

Had I known beyond a doubt in the fall of 1969 that I had the Polish, black, and Jewish vote in my pocket, rejection by yet another Chicago ethnic group would have meant certain defeat. A comment once made to me by a politically sophisticated Jew says it all: "Every Chicago political leader is Irish—or wishes he was Irish." In the final analysis, my political fate rested with this most powerful of all machine elements. Despite their relatively small numbers, the Irish politically dominated the Chicago ethnic coalition because of their skill as broker-mediators among the party's ethnic factions. How and why the Irish came to play this role, and play it well, may be more fully understood if we trace briefly the political history not only of the Irish in America but also of their forebears in the British Isles.

Historical events in Ireland itself account significantly for many Irish political characteristics found in the American city. Nathan Glazer and Daniel Patrick Moynihan have concluded that "machine governments resulted from a merger of rural Irish custom with urban American politics."[22] The operative concept, according to Glazer and Moynihan, was that formal government lacked legitimacy, whereas informal government represented the people much more justly. Noted historian William E. H. Lecky has enumerated and described in condemnatory detail the immeasurable hardship and degradation inflicted upon Irish-Catholics by the penal laws created by the eighteenth-century English and enforced by Irish-Protestant appointees. From the inequity of these laws, there was no institutional source of relief to which the Irish-Catholic could turn:

> All the influence of property and office was against him, and every tribunal to which he could appeal was occupied by his enemies. The Parliament and the Government, the corporation which disposed of his city property, the vestry which taxed him, the magistrate before whom he carried his case, the barrister who pleaded it, the judge who tried it, the jury who decided it, were all Protestants. . . . [Irish Catholics] were educated through long generations of oppression into an inveterate hostility to the law, and were taught to look for redress in illegal violence or secret combinations.[23]

But when violent resistance, often through underground organizations, proved futile against the institutions that dispensed only injustice to them, the Catholic Irish learned to go around them. The equalizer was "interest"—magistrates who could be bought and favors that could be bartered. The English-appointed, Irish-Protestant minority, who, from the sinecures of government and corporate office, controlled the other three-quarters of the population, engaged in abuse of office and misappropriation of public monies in multifarious ways. This corruption could be seen plainly by townsman and countryman alike, historian George Potter tells us: "He might not know what his bartered vote led to in the English Parliament in faraway London, but he knew for a certainty that the new road was a 'job,' in which the local magnates had not-too-clean fingers. It is not without pertinence that the word 'jobbing,' the turning of public trust to private advantage, had its widest circulation, if not its origin, in Protestant-Ascendancy Ireland. . . . Public works went by favor, not by merit or necessity."[24]

Thus, through the hard school of experience, as well as by the flagrant example of his oppressors, did the Irish-Catholic become an inventive (and circumventive) adept in the purchase of "interest." Thomas Brown captures the essence of the philosophy of interest: " 'I'll have the law on you' is the saying of an Englishman who expects justice, but 'I'll have you up before his honor' is the threat of an Irishman who hopes for partiality."[25] Personalized politics became the mode by which impersonal and abstract law could be reduced to a manageable human scale. Potter says: "The Catholic Irish used all the native ingenuity of the race to oppose and thwart the 'landlord's law,' but the law itself they loved, sometimes as a game, sometimes as a challenge to wits, sometimes for the majesty denied to them as a people and, above all, they loved it because it centered in human relations and personality."[26]

This legacy, the politics of survival, perhaps could be likened to a cultural genetic code that made it instinctive for the Irish-American politician to bend the rules to his own advantage and to devise such stratagems as would assure the equal odds he could not trust the formal institutions of society to offer him. Glazer and Moynihan note: "There was an indifference to Yankee proprieties. To the Irish, stealing an election was rascally, not to be approved, but neither quite to be abhorred."[27] Out of the individualized, personalized politics of interest (or of rascality) in the homeland, the transplanted Irish contrived an informal political bureaucracy that eventually would become semiinstitutionalized in the American big-city machine. Such a bureaucracy, created and controlled by themselves, would allow them to stamp their imprint on politics in the new country, rather than simply to fall into line and follow the norms of the American political establishment as they found it.[28]

The Federalist-sponsored Naturalization Act of 1870 and the Alien and Sedition Act of 1878 impeded further Irish immigration and helped politicize Catholics against the entrenched Protestants. This polarization intensified during subsequent decades, when the Know-Nothings and their Republican successors stoked the flames of anti-Catholicism and thus provided an even stronger incentive for Catholics to join the opposition Democratic party. Andrew Jackson's Democracy not only welcomed Irish-Catholics but also encouraged them to assume the mantle of urban leadership. Ensuing waves of Irish immigrants, fully appreciating the availability of immediate naturalization, jobs, and compassionate help, gladly gave their votes to their Democratic benefactors.

The Irish possessed distinct advantages for achieving governmental and urban leadership in cities like Chicago. To begin with, as the Catholic group most proficient in the English language, they could represent other ethnics with the established Protestants. Furthermore, the majority of Irish politicians owned saloons—an opportune position for building effective political organizations. These saloon keepers published their own newspaper, *Mixed Drinks: The Saloon Keepers' Journal*, which often featured political stories. A prominent Irish politician-saloon keeper, Joseph (Chesterfield Joe) Mackin, boss of the First Ward, introduced the free lunch in Chicago by offering an oyster with every beer sold in his tavern.[29] Johnnie Powers, another crafty Irish saloon keeper-politician, adopted the Italianate name of Johnnie De Pow when the ethnic balance of his Nineteenth Ward changed from Irish to Italian.

Michael "Hinky Dink" Kenna, the most prominent saloon keeper-politician of his era, functioned as political captain of the saloon district and, according to Lloyd Wendt and Herman Kogan, "organized the 'saloon hangers-on' as a corps of assistant precinct captains to make door-to-door calls and offer promises of free beer and lunch."[30] Events of the depression of 1892 illustrate Hinky Dink's political astuteness:

[G]reat hosts of the unemployed roamed the streets begging jobs and food. The city-hall corridors were thrown open and each night 1,500 of the unfortunate slept there, depending for their food on saloon free lunches. Hinky Dink fed more than any other. In one week, at the height of the misery, he cared for 8,000 destitute men. . . . Kenna's activities that winter were those of a Good

Samaritan, but they also gave him an idea. Every one of these men, however impoverished, could vote. There was always a plentiful supply in Chicago, come panic or prosperity. It would be simple, and inexpensive, at election time to house and feed the multitude, and instruct them in the principles of franchise.[31]

The Catholic Church's rigid power structure, authoritarian relationships, and emphasis on chain-of-command supplied the Chicago Irish and their urban counterparts a model for a viable political organization. As Edward Levine states, "Since these were the only organizations with which the Irish had contact and to which they had access, each [the Church and the political party] reinforced the character and correctness of the other."[32] The Irish were barred from the councils of business and from the Protestant establishment, and political dominance thus gave them a power lever that other leaders must recognize and respect. Levine describes the importance to the Irish of this political prominence:

> [T]hey had the deep, abiding satisfaction of knowing that they had fought for and won political power which brought them, if begrudgingly, the status of political equality from those who otherwise despised them. Excluded as undesirables from the other major arenas of society, the Irish had with continuing success invaded and entrenched themselves in city politics, for them the most exciting of all sectors of urban life.[33]

The foregoing historical overview suggests that the early Catholic Irish in America saw their economic and social survival as dependent upon political involvement, which, in their skillful hands, became political control. Just as legislative bodies do not willingly reapportion themselves (in John Locke's words), so, too, the controlling Irish did not voluntarily relinquish their power. Beyond its material benefits, to them power politics was a game, all the more enjoyable because they made up the rules; and over the decades it became a profession, all the more profitable because they frequently could determine the qualifications and attach their own ethical standards. Protection from discrimination and the opportunity for steady employment formed powerful incentives for these people to form a machine and for subsequent generations to join it. A parallel between the political development of Irish-Americans and the more recently raised political consciousness of blacks is obvious.

Irish party leadership in Chicago carried over into formal government. During my tenure there, I learned what longterm residents already knew, that Irish ascendancy was virtually complete in the key city and county bureaucracies, the court system, the sanitary district, and a host of other governmental units possessing status or employing large numbers of people.[34] That the Irish made up less than 7 percent of the population but controlled an enormously larger percentage of the best jobs, especially the policy-making positions, attested sharply to their knack for achieving and maintaining political power.

The desire to reward other Irish does not tell the full story; the desire to preserve what they had labored (and schemed) to harvest tells more of it. From a protective point of view, an Irish official such as state's attorney could be relied upon not to prosecute the machine for vote fraud. From a facilitative point of view, an Irish clerk of the county court could be counted on to distribute the hundreds of patronage jobs at his disposal where they would do the organization the most good. According to one influential Republican, "The Irish play for keeps. And they put Irish in key slots because they think they can trust other Irish better than they can a Pole, black, Jew, or Italian to place the interests of the machine first." What must be added, and what was frequently withheld by machine critics, is that the Irish discharged their responsibilities in a manner generally commanding the respect of other ethnics. Although larger ethnic groups grumbled about not receiving amounts of patronage or prestige commensurate with their numbers, they nevertheless gave the Irish high marks as effective leaders. Levine comments, "There have been all sorts of Irish bosses, but an Irish tyrant is unheard of."[35]

The justness of Irish "rule," then, was that quality above all others that earned them the respect and cooperation of other members of the ethnic coalition. The historical struggle of the Irish had bred in them a hatred of political oppression that translated into a sense of fair play and a belief in the abstract moral principle of political justice—an effectual voice in the political process—as an end. But also throughout that history the Irish were forced to become realists, a requirement that nurtured in them a functional philosophy made up of two primary tenets—pragmatism and expediency. Pragmatism and expediency were the means by which the Irish won for themselves not only political equality but the social and economic equality that issued from it. From the point of view of the Irish, those same means were available to any other ethnic group who could learn to use them well enough to beat the champions at their own game. Any suggestion that a mayoralty primary could be won in Chicago against a machine that was fueled by perpetually flowing patronage and whose product was diversified self-interest would have elicited some measure of disbelief from the Irish politicians I knew, or knew of, in the sixties. And it would be more than a decade before Harold Washington's victory would prove them wrong. But at the time of which I write, the ramifications of pragmatism and expediency in the political life of Chicago's Irish leaders were evident when one notes the qualities for which other ethnic groups admired them and the values the Irish themselves held and cherished.

One of these values was loyalty. Politically, this meant that once a politician made a commitment to a fellow politician he was obligated to stay hitched. In 1970, the Democratic Cook County central committee stripped Forty-third Ward committeeman Edward Barrett of his stewardship because of poor election results in his ward. In view of his long years of loyal party service, however, the committee later permitted him to run again, this time for the lucrative post of county assessor. The machine might demote, at least temporarily, a member whose performance fell short of its rigorous criteria, but it did not drum him out of the regiment. It continued to reward Barrett and others like him with political office. But if the party remained loyal to its members the reverse also obtained, that when a machine member lost an intraparty contest, he was expected to fall in behind the others and support the victorious person or faction. This sort of loyalty strengthened the party's effectiveness in the subsequent election. And in the public arena of party performance, it constituted a reflection of a quality upon which the Irish politician placed the highest value in his personal dealings with other politicians—that of integrity. One might waffle on one's word to an outsider, but when given to a machine fellow that word represented an ironclad, inviolable oath.

Compassion, and its externalized form of charity, was a second quality the Irish valued and for which they received respect from other ethnic groups. Although not ideologically oriented and seldom advocating great societal changes, the Irish nevertheless embraced the duty of rendering personalized assistance. This tradition among Chicago's Irish traced its roots to early saloon keepers such as Hinky

Dink Kenna, who gave free food and lodging as a part of the exchange relationship that produced votes. But charity also possessed another political dimension. Effective political leadership demanded a readiness to forgive those whose foibles prevented them from measuring up to the personal standards of the leaders. A favorite Irish expression, quoted by Levine, captures the essence of this leniency: "You're too big for petty vengeance."[36] Levine notes that the Irish tend "to be charitably disposed toward most of the moral and situational shortcomings of others. However, the line is sharply drawn for apostates, heretics, and for marital infidelity, and it is not blindly or universally extended. It generally, though not exclusively, characterizes attitudes, judgments, and actions concerning other Irish."[37]

The case of powerful Thirty-first Ward committeeman Tom Keane provides an example. In 1974, Keane was sentenced to prison for mail fraud, but the Irish-led machine refused to disown him. First, they supported his wife's election bid to retain his seat as a city alderman; and, second, the ward headquarters accepted weekly collect calls from the incarcerated Keane to keep him up to date on what was taking place. The machine wanted, of course, to retain control of the aldermanic post, but it need not have slated Mrs. Keane. Another, experienced member of the Irish political family might have constituted a more expedient choice had self-perpetuation been all that mattered.

A third value evidenced by Chicago's Irish was respect for tradition. The Irish felt attracted to politics partly because it was a family (and, certainly, a cultural) heritage, wherein each new generation became socialized into political careers. Many Irish-Americans active in Chicago politics came from families with a history of political involvement. A prominent Irish leader told me: "I was raised in politics. From the time I was six years old, my dad took me to rallies; and after I was ten, I helped him pass out campaign flyers door-to-door and sometimes canvassed with him. When I was sixteen, my uncle developed a heart condition, and I would cover all the apartments above the first floor. It never crossed my mind that I would do anything different than my dad and uncle. I just figured that I would be in politics and work for the city like they did." This is not to suggest that political nepotism itself earned the Irish the respect of other ethnics—it in fact more often produced bitterness.[38] But the cohesiveness of the Irish and their perpetuation of the tradition of political involvement within kinship alliances and communities elicited envy among those who could not achieve such within their own ethnic groups.

Winnability constituted another significant attribute for which the Irish were respected by other ethnics. For if candidates could not win, then the party ultimately would sacrifice the dominance, the recognition, and, most importantly, the patronage dependent upon occupying elective office. As the late state chairman Jim Ronan said, "We would rather run somebody we don't like who has a good chance of winning and helping the party than somebody we do like who might blow the election for us." To win, the machine had to select a ticket that appealed to various voting segments, attracted the machine's precinct captains, possessed ethnic balance, raised sufficient campaign funds, and earned media support.

Enter the pragmatic Irish. As the one ethnic group eliciting general trust, they functioned superbly as broker-mediators. Although others occasionally objected, they respected the Irish tactical ability to fashion slates and win elections through shrewd campaign strategy. Basic to the Irish politician was his willingness to compromise, a quality probably derived from his forebears' efforts to deal with the eighteenth-century counterpart of the slum landlord and from the subsequent adaptability and pragmatism honed in America. The Irish politician generated confidence as one who could work out deals, whereas other ethnic groups, in contrast, had to concern themselves overmuch with soliciting recognition for themselves. Because the Irish already enjoyed high political status, they could minimize the quest for recognition and with easy self-assurance offer themselves for psychological as well as material leadership. Thus established, the Irish were free to go about the business of winning elections and running a government that indeed provided a better living for members of the machine, from the leadership down the ranks to those who labored in the precincts.

The Irish, then, remained the single most powerful ethnic contingent in Cook County. Their long and passionate love affair with politics, the sophistication they brought to the grand game, and the power they wielded made them an awesome tribunal for any aspiring politician to face. In 1969, I knew that my nomination decision ultimately would take place in an Irish-dominated court that would judge me by Irish norms. I would have to prove myself to them on

organization members, they usually went to individuals of lesser standing, such as assistant precinct captains and party supporters.

Skilled workers could choose from a variety of jobs. Operating a park district or any one of many other governmental subdivisions required a work force of competent secretaries and clerical workers. In addition, governmental units demanded trained workers in the trades and required a significant number of electricians, carpenters, painters, plasterers, and other craftsmen. But the machine also permitted a better living for professional people. Any large metropolitan area requires scores of attorneys for day-to-day legal decisions and accountants for the extensive functions of agencies and departments. Furthermore, a modern city employs engineers in the city waterworks and sewage disposal operations, in planning and constructing streets, highways, and the entire arterial system throughout the county. In short, a polity as vast and complex as metropolitan Chicago necessitated an enormous amount of expertise.

Regardless of the skill or professionalism these jobs entailed, one patronage feature predominated: the individuals filling them usually received better compensation than they could find in comparable jobs outside the government. Moreover, their fringe benefits (particularly retirement plans) normally surpassed those in the private sector; and what amounted to almost a lifetime employment guarantee provided job security often lacking in private industry. Technically, these jobs came under civil service, but the city filled many of them on a temporary basis, with reappointments at 120-day intervals over periods sometimes exceeding 25 years. On the whole, civil service in Chicago functioned only symbolically.[1]

The Cook County government also operated on an informal basis. I vividly recall sitting in the office of Dan Ryan, president of the Cook County board, in June 1958. I was waiting to see Izzie Horwitz about a summer job and noticed a dozen other young men clutching letters from their ward committeemen. Upon taking their letters, the administrative assistant referred them to waiting jobs. The ward committeemen thus acted as informal employment agents for constituents seeking local government jobs. Also operating through informal channels, but on a larger scale, were various entrepreneurs. Some sold insurance for companies expecting to profit from business with the city or county, companies that often preferred dealing with party loyalists. Others worked for equipment dealers, building supply houses and the like, their principal task being to engender good will with public officials and promote government purchases from their companies. These political operators usually did little formal work; their sole function was to arrange contacts that facilitated lucrative deals. Thus, business also benefitted from the "better-living" provisions the machine created for its individual members.

Business interests received other rewards for their loyalty. The machine accommodated businesmen through special tax assessments, appointed them to important boards, or sought them out as advisors in specific areas of expertise. These mutually profitable relationships between business and the party posed a dilemma to the Cook County Republican party. Local Republican politicians found it difficult to convince Republican businessmen to support their candidates against members of the Democratic organization.

For some people, a better living meant not a better job but the psychological rewards available to devoted members of the organization. An invitation to a dinner for the president of the United States or a trip to Springfield for Democratic Day at the state fair were coveted prizes well worth the time, effort, and dedication the party demanded of those who enjoyed its favors. Status seekers relished the chance to visit political headquarters on a Saturday morning and rub shoulders with "the boys," to join a poker-playing group, or to party with the political elite of the neighborhood.

The organization was consistent in providing a better living for its friends, whether that meant a better job, public recognition, favored treatment for business and industry, or responsiveness to the city's churches. But the machine's ability to continue its payoffs—the patronage jobs, the honors, the favored treatment, the deals—hinged upon its ability to win elections. Because these blessings flowed from the power of political office, the machine could perpetuate itself only by controlling most city and county elective posts. And when the operation occasionally faltered at the county level, state offices provided alternative patronage plums.

The state superintendent of public instruction, the office I sought, controlled more than 1,000 patronage positions, and many were nonprofessional. For the young people who craved jobs in Springfield, as well as for others seeking them in Chicago, the machine needed a superintendent who was dependable on patronage. I therefore needed to prove my reliability in the vital area of jobs. To offer such proof, I developed the following strategy: I would advocate "loyalty and competence" as my bench mark for future patronage. A stamp of approval from the appropriate leader in each domain would confirm a job-seeker's loyalty. I, however, a professional educator, would determine competency. A Republican or independent would be hired only if no competent, loyal Democrats availed themselves.

The greatest assurance of a political machine's repeated electoral success is strong and workable discipline. The Cook County organization could not tolerate members who acted independently, because such people jeopardized success at the polls and the organization's ability to fulfill its promises. On the other hand, the machine did allow argument—its leaders often spoke bluntly with each other and generally did not inhibit themselves. But once the party reached a decision, it expected everyone to fall into line. This did not always come easy, for sometimes what best served the organization ran counter to individual, personal values and ambitions. But successful machine members learned to put their political family first.

Early on, I myself had begun to weigh the risks of standing up for personal principles or ambitions irreconcilable with the way the machine did business. If I displayed tendencies toward independence, my career could get derailed before it got started. I had heard some references to members of the machine who had found themselves thus caught between principle and ambition, but it was a slatemaking decision made some two years after my campaign that most dramatically illustrates the problem. A prominent machine member with whom I was having a conversation on the subject of party discipline pointed to Roman Pucinski as a classic example of the sometimes agonizing conflict between self-interest and obedience to party decisions.

Pucinski, a former reporter for the Chicago *Sun-Times* and an important ward committeeman, had served in the U.S. House of Representatives for fourteen years. He had served well, too—his performance had satisfied the machine, the voters, organized labor, and the media. For this very reason, the organization decided that Pucinski should oppose Charles Percy for the U.S. Senate seat in 1972. He was their best hope. But this decision frustrated Pucinski in the extreme. A member of the House Committee on Health, Education, and Welfare, his seniority had earned him the chairmanship of the subcommittee on education. Shortly before the slatemakers made the decision formal, he told a friend, "Now that I'm chairman, I see a real possibility of making changes and upgrading American education." He did not want to miss this opportunity.

Moreover, his district's Polish majority greatly respected their congressman; as a senator, and thus representing the whole state, Pucinski feared losing the rapport he had established with the people in his own district. Finally, he had to worry that Percy would trounce him. Pucinski did not want the dubious distinction of losing by the biggest margin in Illinois's history of U.S. Senate races. Percy, conqueror of the reputedly invincible Paul Douglas, was an outstanding campaigner. In addition to Republican and much liberal Democratic backing, he could count on support from blacks because of his voting record. Pucinski had good cause for concern about the outcome of a contest with Percy.

But, as an organization man, Pucinski understood the machine's problem: the Democratic party was in trouble with Polish voters, who wanted a Polish name at the head of the state and local ticket. The office of U.S. senator appeared near the top of the ballot, and, with Pucinski's name in that position, the party would surely get most of the Polish vote for the other important offices.[2] The leadership slated Pucinski.

In almost any other situation, a U.S. congressman could reasonably have refused to make this effort. Pucinski told a friend, "Damn it, I don't want to run—believe me, I honestly don't. But I've profited from the organization, and if 'downtown' says I'm needed to help with the Polish vote, then, damn it, I'll run!"[3] Pucinski ran. He not only lost by a wide margin, but, no longer a member of the House of Representatives, he lost some of the status and prestige he once had possessed.

"If you play ball with the machine and accept its favors, then you automatically become its captive," organization opponent Leon Despres once observed. But that remark did not fully describe the relationship between the machine and its supporters. The party was also quick to reward its loyalists. In 1959, the Daley machine competed with downstater Paul Powell in selecting the speaker of the Illinois house. Sam Shapiro, a legislator from Kankakee, supported the Cook County choice even at the risk of incurring the enmity of the downstaters; and Daley did not forget to show his appreciation for Shapiro's help. He saw to it that Shapiro was slated as lieutenant governor in 1966 and as governor in 1968. Such rewards were essential to discipline, because machine cohesiveness depended as much on rewarding cooperation as on punishing dissidence.

Thus, party leaders tried to make it easy for supporters to accept machine norms. The sacrifice of Congressman Pucinski formed the exception, not the rule; ordinarily, the organization took into account the ambitions and needs of the people upon whom it depended. But in a city composed of several sizable ethnic groups whose individual members remained tied together by their common cultural background, winning elections often depended upon slating an ethnically balanced ticket. And when the party needed an attractive Polish candidate, Pucinski had to play the sacrificial goat.

Party discipline enabled the organization to maximize its potential. During the Illinois constitutional convention in 1970, this discipline showed. The delegates apparently checked with "downtown" during weekends at home, for, when they returned to the convention, they voted overwhelmingly on the Chicago side of those questions affecting Chicago's interests.[4] (On provisions irrelevant to Chicago, some delegates voted one way, some the other.) The Chicago Democratic organization got almost everything it wanted from the convention, even though it did not constitute a majority. Its success issued from its delegation's superior discipline in comparison with that of others. At the close of the convention, Mary Lee Leahy, a fiery independent, placed matters in perspective: "I can never be a Democrat," she said, "because of the discipline required and the lack of individual freedom and initiative for party members. But I can never be a Republican either, because the Republican party has no guts."

Sometimes the machine would exhibit great patience until an opportunity to discipline those who had strayed presented itself. From the time I was a University of Chicago graduate student in 1954, I had watched with interest the rising political career of my Hyde Park neighbor, Abner Mikva. Mikva ran for the U.S. House of Representatives against machine opposition, lost the election, but, undaunted, ran again, this time with the acquiescence of the organization, who realized it could not stop him. Mikva won this election but then proceeded to play a decidedly maverick role in Congress. When the 1970 U.S. census made it obvious that, through reapportionment, Illinois would lose a Democratic congressional seat, the machine "apportioned" Mikva out. He later moved to a new district, predominantly Republican, ran in 1972 and lost, but then won narrowly in 1974, 1976, and 1978. But since his 1972 defeat had cost him his seniority in the House, in its own way the machine ultimately made him pay for his political deviancy.

A ranking party member, who liked to praise the quality of the Democrats' discipline, told the following story about independent-minded Adlai Stevenson III. Young Adlai approached him one day complaining that he could not accept many parts of Governor Otto Kerner's program. Stevenson just did not see how, in good conscience, he could vote for all of it. My informant had replied:

"Adlai, sixteen or seventeen years ago, when I was in the legislature, I went to Dick Daley—he was your dad's legislative liaison, you know—and I said, 'Dick, I'm having a great deal of trouble accepting this entire package of Governor Stevenson, and I can't see my way clear to vote for all of it.'

"Well, Daley thought a moment, and then he pointed out that the governor had a good program overall, but that if I went off on this part that I didn't like and another fellow took off on another part he didn't like, we'd end up without getting anything through. Daley made it clear to me that we were all going to have to stick with the governor right down the line, or else we wouldn't have any program at all.

"Just like Dick Daley asked me to support your father's program when he was governor, Adlai, I'm asking you to support Governor Kerner's program now. Sure, everyone wants to be independent, but it just isn't possible if we expect to get our program through."

Sometimes, the machine could bring recalcitrants into line with this kind of reasoning; but it could more easily prevent disciplinary breeches by accurately assaying key party members and anticipating where they were likely to cause trouble for party strategy. In 1948, the Democrats were in disarray, with chances for victory looking grim. But when Jacob Arvey approached Paul Douglas and Adlai Stevenson II, both indicated their willingness to run for office. Douglas and Stevenson were well-educated, polished, and altogether exceptional men who commanded enormous respect, and the organization was delighted at the prospect of their names heading up an otherwise lackluster ticket. A problem arose, however: Douglas wanted to run for governor, and Stevenson favored a seat in the U.S. Senate. But Douglas had played the maverick as alderman of Chicago's Fifth Ward, and the party could better serve its own interests if Stevenson ran for governor and Douglas for the Senate. Stevenson balked at the idea but eventually yielded to party pressure. Following the successful election, Douglas was safely out of the way in the Senate where, burdened by great national and international issues, he could not exert strong influence in local politics.

The party insisted that its candidates for those elective offices controlling substantial patronage accept discipline; but even for these offices, the organization occasionally had to slate a maverick. That happened only after the party's careful evaluation of the situation had determined that, with his name at the top of the ticket, his vote-getting record would sweep in the party's lesser-known candidates. It was a simple matter of weighing the risks—the loss of control of one important office against defeat at the polls for substantially all the positions on the ballot. Thus, the sometime presence of independent-minded nominees such as Paul Douglas, Adlai Stevenson II (and, especially, his son), or, in 1974, Paul Simon.

But when a lesser luminary ran, he had better not deviate. Bill Clark's 1968 campaign for the Senate exemplifies the subtleties of party discipline. Clark, the erstwhile state legislator, senate majority leader, attorney general, and son of a former party leader, exuded winnability, that quality most beloved in any candidate. The Clark people thought they had an understanding with the party whereby they could develop issues freely and run Clark's campaign as they saw fit. But when Clark chose to run a dovish campaign on the issue of Vietnam at a time when Daley and the machine had lined up with the hawks (Daley, a few years hence, would reverse his position on Vietnam), the party hierarchy took offense. Later, one of Clark's spokesmen said disgustedly, "The only indication we ever had that something was wrong between us and the people at the top came by way of the daily news reports. Mayor Daley never called Clark in and chewed him out or even mentioned that he thought Clark's campaign style was an affront to the organization. But we kept reading in the newspapers about Daley's unhappiness with Clark."

Clark soon discovered that he could raise funds neither from the usual political sources nor from organized labor. The machine had signaled its displeasure to these ordinarily generous contributors. In the critical days before election, Clark's campaign foundered on the adverse publicity and the resulting financial drought. His campaign people had put together some excellent television commercials at a cost of $35,000, but no one would step forward with the money needed to televise them.

After the election, the Clark incident became widely known among the party elite, who frequently cited it to remind aspirants for political office of what happens to those who disregard party discipline. Clark, short of funds though he was, lost by less than 1 percent of the vote to the durable Everett Dirksen. But, in spite of that impressive showing and of Clark's prior string of electoral successes, Daley and his cohorts ostracized him, and the machine did not slate him again. One leader remarked, "The message to future candidates was loud and clear: 'Go off on your own, and you'll have political hell to pay—Bill Clark will be your fate.' " A winner is hard to keep down, however, and Clark, finally breaking the machine's immobilizing grip, defeated machine-endorsed Judge Sam Powers in 1976 for a seat on the Illinois Supreme Court.

Illinois Republicans envied the Democrats' discipline—"It makes everything so much easier," a former Republican county chairman sighed. With some bitterness, he continued:

"We had a candidate for mayor once who was a definite liability. It was hell going around Chicago's northwest side trying to sell that guy as a Republican. When asked if he'd support the Republican ticket, our candidate said he would think it over. When asked if he would support President Nixon, he said he'd have to think that over, too. And that was at the height of Nixon's popularity in 1971.

"It's a hell of a note when you can't get your own candidate to agree to support the Republican ticket or the Republican president, and it makes it pretty damned hard to go out and tell Republican voters that we've got a good Republican candidate whom all of us should get behind and support. It's a damned travesty to be in that position. But, anyway, Governor Oglivie pushed for this character, and he made a joke of the mayor's race. And that's the difference between us and the Democrats—they've got discipline, and their candidates show it."

The Republicans correctly identified the key to the Democrats' repeated success as their ability to muster their troops and present a united front for the good of the organization. With the Republicans, it often boiled down to every man for himself; and, unless that man possessed charisma or could wage an extraordinarily sharp campaign, he was not going to triumph over an opponent backed by the entire Democratic organization. The Republicans could, and did, win in Cook County when they produced a candidate indisputably the better choice, but that seldom happened. When the candidates were evenly matched, the superior discipline and organization of the Democrats usually enabled them to chalk up a victory on election day.

The Democratic machine's strong, workable discipline and its single-minded dedication to the concept of a better living for its members had to be, I felt, the focus of my Chicago strategy. I would have to sell myself as a hard worker and a winner, as a definite asset to the ticket. An organization committed to a self-perpetuating financial prosperity demanded dedicated campaigning. Moreover, I must present myself as compatible with machine policies—a candidate loyal, supportive, and absolutely free of maverick tendencies. In order to prove myself in all these respects, I specifically needed to win the support of those key party leaders who ran the wards and precincts of Chicago, the ward committeemen. I would have to cultivate them assiduously, were I to win the nomination prize.

The primary gatekeepers of a "better living" were the committeemen from each of Chicago's fifty wards. And because the machine's ability to score victories depended on success at the ward level, each committeeman was crucial to the operation of the whole.

Unsalaried though their job might be, the ward committeemen tended to devote the greater share of their time to their political obligations. The incidental benefits of their political position made their labors in the ward both possible and worthwhile. Many ward committeemen were lawyers or businessmen whose firms and companies relied on their politically influential member for assistance in dealing with city hall, a service that kept the firm on the city payroll but freed the committeeman from the day-to-day work at the office. Some committeemen held a second elective office, serving on the city council or county board or in the state legislature; a few even occupied seats in the U.S. Congress while heading up a Chicago ward. Other committeemen were ensconced in good jobs with city agencies. In addition, the committeemen frequently were privy to inside information, for example, land development and proposed construction, that they could turn to private advantage. Material rewards such as these prompted their political involvement in the Cook County organization.

Of course, men and women who defined the first duty of an elected official as public service deplored a system that encouraged political participation by offering a quid pro quo arrangement. One such was former Alderman Leon Despres, an outspoken critic of the machine who represented Chicago's Fifth Ward. Occasionally, I would drop in on my "philosopher-king" alderman; while I did not agree with some of his reformist arguments, I delighted in the cogency with which he made his case. More importantly, even though he functioned as the machine's foremost critic, his understanding of its operation stood second to none.

I once asked him, "Len, don't you agree that the machine cuts through the bureaucratic red tape that big-city residents have to cope with?"

"Well, maybe. But the machine member is mostly interested in the patronage—the advancements and the cuts in the deals; and he's not particularly interested in the quality of services for his ward. He relies on the patronage machine to elect him, and after he's elected he tends to concentrate his attention on the partisan aspects of politics, rather than on his duties as a public servant. He may even feel the voters are nuisances and may have elaborate devices to avoid seeing them. Many committeemen do. Many of them refuse to see the voters and insist they see the precinct captains. So, for many of the machine committeemen, there isn't even a demand for services. Do you have any idea how many patronage jobs there are in Cook County?"

I shook my head.

"About thirty-five thousand. Of course, for some, the living isn't very good—it's at the edge. But the closer you get to the center of the machine, the better the living. Every ward committeeman is close to the center and either enjoys a handsome living off politics or is on the escalator toward enjoyment of a handsome living. And he'll go right on up unless he does something stupid and has to drop off. Now, that kind of living is what the machine personalities are interested in."

While respected liberals such as Despres are critical of the committeemen, other, equally respectable liberals such as Senator Paul Douglas have acclaimed them for their role in promoting the democratic process:

[T]here is a great continuing need for the ward political organizations and leaders, and it would be a great loss were they to disappear. For they are the vital cells of democracy. Democracy is not self-operating. It needs parties to stress issues and carry them to the voters and then to get out the vote on election days. There are comparatively few localities where this can be done on a purely intellectual level. It can best be done by friends and neighbors who, by acts of kindness, have already proved their concern and liking for the man or family in need of help.[5]

Douglas goes on to make the case for the ward organizations and for personalized and informal (that is, *Geimeinschaft*) solutions to problems induced by life in a highly complex, industrialized (that is, *Gesellschaft*) society:

> [The ward organizations] commonly are . . . good neighbors. This is especially important when the citizen has to deal with the local, state, or national bureaucracy. The bureaucrat often becomes cold, impersonal and dilatory in his dealings with the citizenry. Protected by civil service, the public functionary, feeling secure himself, very frequently does not identify himself with the plight of the citizen who approaches him, hat in hand. Sometimes he is afflicted with "the insolence of office" and compels the patient suppliant to accept slurs and petty cruelties.
>
> A political organization, in order to win votes, must be an efficient service organization and by the very nature of its being must try to be helpful.[6]

I knew that the most powerful ward committeemen would provide my surest access route to Mayor Daley; and one who could really help was Vito Marzullo, my father-in-law's political friend who ran one of Chicago's strongest ward organizations.

My conversation with Marzullo was enjoyable, he orchestrating it as more or less a solo performance and my own occasional, respectful questions and comments functioning as mere counterpoint. He reminisced about how he had gotten started in politics and how, over the years, he had developed strong attachments to the people in his ward, seeing no conflict between his duty to them and his pursuit of personal success within the organization.

"Mel, let me tell you someting—it's just like it says in the Bible: You cast your bread on the water, and it comes back to you many times. If you love people, and if you do right by them, everything else just takes care of itself. That's been my whole philosophy, and things have worked out fine. Now, here's an example of what I mean:

"The other day, I attended a funeral over at my son's funeral parlor, and this middle-aged man comes up to me and says, 'Alderman Marzullo, you don't remember me, but you gave me a break once many years ago, and I want to thank you for it.' Then he went on to tell me how, as a young man, he'd been picked up by the police for some minor offense. They hauled him into the station, and I guess one of his relatives or friends called me, because he gives me credit for preventing him from being booked and having a police record to contend with the rest of his life. Well, I've stepped in and helped out a lot of young guys who got mixed up with the law, and most of them profited from their experience and have gone on to lead good lives. So, when this man comes up to me at the funeral and thanks me for helping him out of a jam years ago, I just couldn't remember having done anything special for him. But the important thing is that *he* remembered. That's the kind of thing I treasure. Whatever I did for him, I did it because he needed my help, and I didn't have no thought about gaining votes or anything like that. But all these years, that man's been grateful to me. And you can be sure he's spread a lot of good will toward me. He's told other people that Vito Marzullo is okay.

"I could give you hundreds of instances like this one. These are the types of things a man does because he loves people. You don't do them because you're worrying about politics. I love people, and it makes me feel good when I can do favors for them. Everybody in my ward is like a member of my own family, and I consider myself personally responsible for them. So when I'm out doing things for them, it's because I enjoy it, not because I think it's going to make me any political gains. But, sooner or later, whenever you do a favor, it comes back to you."

Admittedly, Marzullo was not the prototype of today's well-schooled ward committeeman. A holdover from another era, he continued to manage his ward in the personalized style that predated the advent of institutionalized social conscience and public welfare programs. Marzullo immigrated from Italy and settled in Chicago at a time when, in an otherwise hostile society, the Democratic organization offered friendship and hope to the poor and the foreign-born. He joined the organization because, to surmount the obstacles of discrimination and poverty, he needed help; he remained a member because he prospered and because in his opinion the organization was the most reliable source of assistance for his people.

Marzullo was responsive to his constituents, whose appreciation took palpable form in election returns from his ward that kept the central committee satisfied. As for Marzullo, he enjoyed a better living than he could hope for outside the machine.

"It works like this," Marzullo says, "I help the people, and they help me, and the organization helps all of us. Now, some people think there's something bad about that arrangement, but I don't know where any of us would be if the organization hadn't backed us up all these years.

"I remember when I first came over from the old country. There was a lot of hate—a lot of downright meanness. The orthodox Jews used to be pretty thick around here, and their custom was for the men to wear long beards. Some people thought it was a good joke to pull on their beards and call them names. There used to be a lot of name-calling.

"And people like me, we were dagos and wops. And they called the blacks no-good niggers. But the Democratic party showed love and respect for all the people, regardless of their backgrounds. The organization helped people find jobs and saw to it that their kids had a doctor and kept some of them out of jail, but even more important, we helped build love and respect for America.

"When I look around now, I can still see hate in people, but I don't see people calling each other names the way they used to do or fighting among themselves because of their religion or their nationality. I think this is the greatest advancement that's come about. This is a big accomplishment we never could have done without the Democratic party."

Social and political reformers did not deny the machine's contribution in helping assimilate immigrants into the mainstream of American society, a socializing function the machine continued to perform for Chicago's new arrivals from the rural South and Puerto Rico. But the reformers were angered because they felt this contribution had been so costly for the people and because the power of the ward committeemen to control voting behavior (by bartering friendship, assistance, and jobs for votes and cooperation) impeded the development of social awareness and frustrated free political expression. Marzullo saw no merit in these accusations, however: "These do-gooders are a minority," he said. "But I tell them where the hell to get off. I tell them to come on and oppose me in any election, but they almost never do. If they did, I'd beat them fifteen to one every time. But they don't play fair. They don't go by the rules."

My ethical problem with politics persisted. I disagreed with Marzullo's view of political dissidents; yet I would need his support later.

Vito Marzullo had developed his effective organization around his ward's ethnic identification and socioeconomic needs, and his success was linked to a common background he shared with the ward's residents. But in wards lacking these homogeneous characteristics, usually only the Irish could appeal to sufficient numbers of the electorate to win the committeeman's post and successfully manage the ward organization.

Thomas Arthur (Art) McGloon, Thirty-seventh Ward committeeman from 1964 to 1970, well exemplified the special flair of the Irish for Cook County politics. McGloon's smile and warm manner were two of his major assets, enabling him to establish instant rapport with people from all walks of life. I had liked him from our very first meeting, and, because he was my father-in-law's ward committeeman, I counted heavily on securing his support.

McGloon had been socialized into politics within his family, his father having served in the Illinois legislature from 1915 to 1917. The elder McGloon resumed his education at the end of his term of office by attending evening high school and then the Kent College of Law.[7] Young McGloon hoped to emulate his father, but, in his own opinion, did not wholly succeed. "My dad was far above me," he once said. "I can never amount to a patch on his pants."

McGloon began his political career in 1945, following a stint in the army. After he returned from the service, and having made up his mind to work for the party, he asked his ward committeeman, Bill Lancaster, for a job. McGloon had already earned his law degree, so Lancaster had no trouble finding work for him. The county hired him as an assistant public defender; and, in addition, Lancaster appointed him captain of one of the ward precincts, work that challenged McGloon's political virtuosity. The residents, primarily conservative middle-class people of Scandinavian descent, voted a strong Republican ticket. McGloon set about the task of political persuasion and gradually converted the precinct from strongly Republican to strongly Democratic.

In 1958, the party slated McGloon for the state senate, an election that he won; but, as a member of the Democratic minority, he soon encountered hardships in his legislative job. Promoting his constituents' legislative requests proved more time-consuming than he had anticipated, and so, after winning reelection in 1962, he asked to relinquish his precinct work. Paul Corcoran, Lancaster's successor as ward committeeman, sorely regretted losing McGloon's talents, but agreed to let him step down.

McGloon did not remain outside the ward organization very

long, however. When Corcoran died in 1964, the ward precinct captains urged McGloon to take over. McGloon demurred. He wanted to devote more time both to his senatorial duties and to his successful law practice. He suggested alderman Tom Casey for the job. But Casey, echoing the precinct captains, thought McGloon better suited for maintaining a strong ward organization, one that could marshall the votes necessary to ensure continued support from Mayor Daley and the county central committee. And that support was crucial to the ward politicians' need to protect their patronage jobs and their prospects for advancement. McGloon rendered valuable service as a prestigious state senator, but he now was needed in the ward, to which everyone agreed he should give first priority.

McGloon acceded to these entreaties and pressures to run for committeeman. Corcoran's death, only ten days before the primary, had left no time to post names on the ballot, necessitating a write-in campaign. The ward organization produced a drawing of the voting-machine ballot that featured a hand holding a pencil inscribed with McGloon's ballot number and name, then distributed 25,000 such pencils. The campaign yielded highly successful results: the organization garnered 9,800 write-in votes, which is a record unmatched by any previous write-in candidate in any Chicago ward.

Now, ordinarily, uncontested primaries were rather dull affairs and offered little general interest. Certainly, members of the organization had no reason to question the presumption that McGloon possessed unusual strength in the ward and would easily win the committeeman's post for the Democrats. But McGloon and the ward organization were also running in another "constituency"—the Cook County central committee, headed by that most astute of election analysts, chairman Richard J. Daley. McGloon and "the boys" wanted a massive, record-breaking write-in vote to prove to Daley and the committee that the Thirty-seventh Ward wielded heavy political clout. That McGloon accomplished this in a predominantly middle-class constituency established incontrovertible evidence that strong leadership and highly effective organization were hallmarks of the Thirty-seventh Ward.

McGloon's performance as ward committeeman earned him increased respect from Mayor Daley and the central committee as well as from fellow members of the Chicago delegation to the state senate. A promotion soon followed. In January 1965, the Democratic senate caucus honored McGloon by selecting him minority leader. He gained stature in this new role and served Chicago's interests well in the legislature. His dual positions of ward committeeman and state senate leader mutualy reinforced his strength in both posts.

During McGloon's tenure as committeeman, the Thirty-seventh Ward consisted largely of a middle-class population of higher socioeconomic status than most Chicago wards. McGloon understood that even middle-class people have problems that the ward organization can solve. In a conversation I had with him, he emphasized these services:

"I always place particular emphasis on services that can actually be seen by the people's very own eyes so that they know firsthand what is being done for them. And it pays off in votes for the Democratic party. I always make sure we take care of the streets, fix the curbs and sidewalks, prune the trees, see that the trash is always picked up, the lights are always working, the garbage is removed regularly and the alleys are kept clean. Alderman Casey and I were able to pick our own man as ward superintendent, and since he is not a carry-over he is very anxious to please us and always sees to it that his men perform an unusually good job.

"I also make it very clear that in those sections of the ward where people don't seem to work as hard at keeping things up and making their block look good, I still want the workers to make sure that it is appealing to the eye, even if it takes extra work. I feel that we all live in the same ward, even if not in the same section, and I want our ward to be a showpiece for the rest of the city."

Aside from his concern about the visual appeal of the ward, McGloon performed other community services. He secured Illinois state scholarships for children of constituents for example. Whenever he, members of the organization, or other citizens noticed a need for stop signs in the ward, McGloon immediately ordered their installation. He responded with similar alacrity by ordering the placement of adequate traffic caution signs in the area of new schools or playgrounds. When necessary, McGloon brought specific constituent problems to the attention of the appropriate people "downtown." McGloon attributed these fruits of success to hard work by the ward leadership: "The fact that [Tom] Casey works hard at the job of being alderman, that I work hard as a ward committeeman, and that I am a legislative leader who can get things done in Springfield for various groups and departments in the city—all these contribute to extra-good services for the Thirty-seventh Ward. It is a real advantage to be able to make calls directly to department heads who often need help in Springfield. They are only too glad to cooperate."

As the top-ranking Democratic state senator, McGloon reaped many honors. These included Most Valuable Legislator, Celtic Public Official of 1968, Catholic Labor Council Award for Leadership, Order of the Celts Award for Public Service, and Bonds for Israel Award of Honor, this last an illustration of other ethnic groups' high regard for him.

Watching committeeman McGloon finish a campaign proved a highly instructive experience for me when, on the night of the 1966 general election, he invited me to sit next to him and observe the functioning of his ward headquarters. First, the neighborhood caterer delivered a dozen or so decorated trays of food. A plentiful supply of beer, scotch, bourbon, and soft drinks also had been stocked. In the back half of the large headquarters, the ward's accountants, who held local government jobs, operated the calculators. Their task was to keep a running ward total of every election contest so that McGloon would have current figures for all of them.

During the evening, friends of the organization dropped in to socialize and partake of refreshments. Alumni of the Thirty-seventh Ward were in evidence as well. Gruff-talking Judge Emmett Morrissey, who was dressed like a factory worker in his plain slacks, zippered jacket, and soft cap bellowed out one story after another. Judge Harry Iseberg, like Morrissey, a former precinct captain, appeared very much the judge in his conservative suit. And an affluent-looking former precinct captain regaled a few listeners with his personal Horatio Alger story: "I got lucky and made some money, and the wife decided we should move to a ritzy suburb. My new neighbors accepted me okay as an Irish-Catholic. But when I told them I was a Democrat, it shocked them. And when I told them I used to be a precinct captain in the Thirty-seventh Ward, it blew their goddamned minds. They still can't get over it!"

As the evening wore on, the Thirty-seventh Ward's multi-ethnic precinct captain's army came trooping in, voting machine results in hand. There were Italians, eastern Europeans, Greeks, Jews, and Irishmen with the educational level ranging from grade school to law degrees. For while the Thirty-seventh Ward might consist primarily of middle-class voters, the ward organization itself ran the gamut, and neither ethnicity nor social class served as reliable predictors of individual precinct achievement. But the Thirty-seventh Ward was by no means an organization of equals; committeeman McGloon was very much in charge. He decided who would lose patronage jobs and who would receive promotions by the single criterion of how well each had performed in his own precinct. But guesswork did not enter into it. Each man knew McGloon's standards in advance, and each knew how he would be judged. Committeeman McGloon would render political justice according to the measuring rod of precinct delivery.

McGloon sat at a table near the entrance. In front of him lay a notebook listing all the ward's precincts as well as their captains' estimates for each office. He recorded the vote figures as they came in and then made a note of deviations above or below the original predictions. It was interesting to observe the interactions between McGloon and the precinct captains, which varied according to the vote totals they handed him. He gave particularly hearty greetings to those whose precincts produced favorable results that came close to the original estimates.

Noticing the accuracy with which most captains predicted their precinct outcomes, I asked McGloon, "How would you react if a precinct captain brought in a tally much higher than his original prediction?"

"It would indicate that he hadn't carefully canvassed his precinct," he replied.

"That's a lot of pressure on these captains, knowing that their jobs may be riding on how well they do in their precincts," I remarked.

"It's nothing compared to the pressure I have to face," he said. "After this is over, I have to take the results downtown and see Daley. I had to give him my estimates, which he'll compare with my ward's production—and tonight the results aren't very good."

McGloon had reason to worry. Early in the evening, it had become obvious that the Democrats faced a crushing defeat for most county and state offices. The most important patronage office, president of the Cook County board, showed Republican Richard Ogilvie and Democrat Harry Semerow engaged in a tight race in the Thirty-seventh Ward. McGloon was disappointed, since he normally registered large victory margins. Moreover, although ward committeemen placed major emphasis on the local, patronage-rich offices, they felt sad and despondent because Charles Percy was defeating Senator Paul Douglas. While Douglas had not been "one of the boys," they nevertheless respected him greatly as a senator and as a man of integrity, who consistently rated the precinct captains as the backbone of the Democratic party. But that night Douglas could not eclipse the rising star of Charles Percy.

Though 1966 was not a very good year for the Democratic party in Illinois or for Chicago's Thirty-seventh Ward in particular, Art McGloon, in the years that followed, continued to convert his triple talents into personal success. On the basis of his records as ward committeeman, senate leader, and successful lawyer, in 1970 he became a justice of the Illinois Appellate Court, the state court second only to the Illinois Supreme Court in prestige. As one watched McGloon on the bench, one felt that he embodied a strong argument against the Bar Association's desire to remove the selection of judges from political considerations. It was apparent that, in McGloon's case, coping with real people and working out solutions to difficult problems in both ward politics and in the legislative process contributed to the sense of humanity he displayed on the bench.

Art McGloon gave vivid testimony that the machine's strength was not confined to the impoverished inner city wards. McGloon, like other Irish leaders, demonstrated a remarkable ability to win the respect and strong backing of his ethnically heterogeneous precinct captains. He welded them into a first-rate organization that engaged in an apparently profitable exchange relationship. It rendered vital services and favors for the voters and received grateful votes in return. This laid the foundation for yet another exchange relationship. The Thirty-seventh Ward delivered Democratic margins for the county machine, and the machine rewarded members of the Thirty-seventh Ward organization with a much better living. In the case of McGloon, yet another exchange relationship existed. His achievement in the ward served as a political base that led to senate leadership and eventual slating for the Illinois Appellate Court—roles he performed with marked success.

Sitting next to McGloon on election night provided a significant future ramification for my political career. I took mental notes, and upon returning to Carbondale, I wrote to McGloon thanking him for his tutelage in my political learning process: "If the great teacher is one who dispels ignorance and opens a door to new vistas of knowledge, then you are a politics professor without peer. My deepest thanks for providing me with a learning experience unmatched by anything I have ever encountered. Thanks to you, I will now become a much better politics teacher." McGloon must have appreciated my letter; he wrote back that he very much enjoyed teaching me the ropes and that he would always be available to help me. Neither of us could foresee the key role he was destined to play three years later in deciding the outcome of my nomination quest for state superintendent of public instruction.

The success of ward committeemen like Art McGloon and Vito Marzullo depended ultimately upon the men and women who directly managed the ward's many precincts. As the party's link with the voter, the precinct captain provided a personalized connection between the machine and its constituency. Consequently, the slatemakers not only tried to gauge a prospective candidate's appeal to the voters, but they also asked: How well does he relate to the precinct captains? Can he really arouse and galvanize these front-line troops?

As a student at the University of Chicago, I had worked in a machine-directed coalition on behalf of Barratt O'Hara, who sought to regain the Second Congressional District house seat he had lost in the 1952 election. Because of the rabidly racist campaign of O'Hara's opponent, our hard work on O'Hara's behalf produced a strong sense of camaraderie among us. One of our frequent pastimes consisted of analyzing the personalities of that year's Democratic candidates. The following remarks illustrate the opinions that various precinct captains offered:

"Sam Lipchik is a hot shot. He judges himself as being a do-gooder and a big independent, but then he comes around and expects us to bust our ass for him. What a two-face! I'll be damned if I make any extra effort for him!"

A more positive view prevailed regarding Senator Paul Douglas: "He's a brilliant man and honest to the core. But he's no snob. Ever since I met Senator Douglas thirteen years ago, he's always called me by my first name. I love that guy, and I'd do anything to get him reelected."

From my experience with them, I judged that, in general, the precinct captains fell into two categories—the salt-of-the-earth, who had limited formal education, and the well-educated, who earned his living in the professions. Few candidates could hope to appeal to both types. Senator Douglas had that rare knack, and because I took him as my model, my goal was to convince the slatemakers that, of all the prospective nominees, I had worked most closely with both kinds of precinct captains, respected them, understood them, and thus could best arouse them to work hard. It was the precinct captain, dealing directly with the voters, who ultimately determined success or failure, and the machine noted carefully those factors that caused captains to go the extra distance and make the extra push beyond political payoffs. Selecting nominees who could motivate the captains ranked high among the machine's priorities.

A prospective nominee could not claim to understand the machine unless he realized that it sustained itself largely through an exchange relationship with ordinary men and women in the electorate. In return for their votes and financial support, the organization provided them with services and looked after their needs. To accomplish this, the precinct captain functioned as the key figure in maintaining good relations with the people and was charged with the duty of delivering the reasonable services they asked for. The cogwheel of the party, he represented the organization in dealing personally with the everyday problems voters confronted.

One of the major problems affecting residents of a large metropolis like Chicago is their loss of a sense of community, particularly those who had severed their ties with their respective ethnic groups. Big cities are impersonal, and the people living in them can easily feel that no one knows or cares about them. This feeling gave Chicago's precinct captains a chance to perform a valued service, to offer themselves as friend to the new resident, the widowed, the elderly, and those who, for other reasons, felt alone and frightened in a city of 4 million self-absorbed inhabitants.

These victims of loneliness and fear live scattered throughout all parts of every big city. This was true of Chicago as well, but the people most threatened by its aloofness concentrated in its less affluent precincts. In addition to their poverty, earlier in Chicago's history they were likely to be handicapped because of little or no schooling or because of unfamiliarity with the English language. More recently, as members of a minority group or as immigrants from the rural South or Puerto Rico, they found the ways and manners of the city incomprehensible. These people, more than most, needed friendship and assistance from their precinct captains; and the organization took care that the captains of low-income precincts were equipped to handle the problems of the families residing there.

Ikey Grosnyk was the prototype of the effective captain in precincts where the poor and near-poor lived, and his success was attributable to his ability to empathize with his clientele. Grosnyk grew up in poverty, and although the demographics of Chicago's poverty neighborhoods had changed somewhat since his youth the values of the inhabitants had not altered. The Irish and Italians, the Jews and the Poles had moved one or more levels up from poverty, but the new denizens of their vacated tenements—blacks, Latinos, and the remnants of the European ethnics left behind in the struggle for prosperity—still grappled with the old problems: a lack of money and an inability to understand the system.

Grosnyk helped these people sort out the complexities of society. He shepherded them through the red tape at the housing agency and the public assistance office. He arranged job contacts and sometimes went directly to the ward committeeman to initiate a well-placed call that halted an eviction or elicted money to pay a past-due utility bill. He was sometimes on hand shortly after a death, ready to step in and make the arrangements at the local funeral home. He would obtain legal assistance for those who needed it but who lacked the money to hire a lawyer, for every ward in Chicago had lawyers on call to provide free services to needy members of the electorate. The precinct captain was capable of many things, from getting the streets and sidewalks repaired to acting as a substitute father for boys from broken homes, and the residents of his precinct brought him all kinds of problems. He helped them willingly, and he knew whom to contact. If the foregoing description of the precinct captains' role seems overly altruistic, it should be remembered that he received votes in return.

"The whole secret of politics," Grosnyk told me, "is knowing how to play 'drop it.' 'Drop it' means you give something away, but you do it with finesse and skill. You do it real naturallike, so that you don't make people feel ashamed or nothing like that—it just sort of 'drops down,' naturallike. Now, I find out a guy likes baseball, for instance, and by and by, I says to him 'How'd you like to have a couple of tickets to the Cubs' game? I get them every once in a while.' He says, 'Sure would.' And I go out and buy two tickets, but I make out that I got them free, because he'd feel real bad if he knew I had to buy them out of my own pocket. But the few bucks I paid for the tickets pays me dividends later on in having some good loyal supporters—him and his wife and maybe some kids in the family old enough to vote. The main thing is, I've given away the tickets to him without lowering his dignity, because he doesn't think I'm engaging in any charity, where I go digging down in my pocket for the tickets.

"You can play 'drop it' in a lot of ways, with liquor, favors, or just whatever it be. But 'drop it' is the important part of politics. If I'm in a drugstore and a couple comes in, and it's a real hot night, I says to him, 'What kind of ice cream do you like? What kind of ice cream does your wife like?' Well, it's a natural-type thing, and the soda jerk gets the ice cream out, and we all sit down and have ice cream together. That's a cheap and reasonable way of playing 'drop it,' but it's very natural, see? That's the whole secret.

"I used to often take twenty kids out to Riverview Park. They'd have a good time. I'd get big strips of tickets through Charley Weber and the organization, and then I'd get three women to go along as sort of guides to watch out for the kids. I'd give them about twenty bucks so that they'd have money for refreshments for the kids. That's another way of playing 'drop it,' but it's nothing crude, and it makes everybody happy."

Although Grosnyk was a specialist in handling problems affecting Chicago's poor, he was alert for any situation that offered a chance to demonstrate the organization's efficacies and win over another loyal supporter for it. I asked Grosnyk, "I can see how 'drop it' would go over real big with the poor, but can you play it with middle-income or rich people?"

"Sure. Now, a lot of people think that the only way a party organization can operate is to help out the poor, but that's a lot of rot. Everybody has something the party can appeal to. I remember I went up to a guy once, and he says, 'Why should I vote for you guys? There's nothing you're gonna do for me.' I says, 'Try me out. Ask me for something you need.' He says, 'Well, I'll tell you, I've got a boy who's gonna be out of high school for two weeks during the Christmas holidays. Can you give him a job?' I said, 'I think I can.' I got him a job working for the election commission for the two weeks, and he made a real good salary. It helped him save up for college the next year. Well, the old man hadn't been much for supporting us in the past, but him and the wife were always dependable voters after that. You don't have to be poor to appreciate 'drop it.'"

Proselytizing a Republican added spice to the life of Ikey Grosnyk and his kind. Grosnyk did not spend much time on schemes for carrying it off, though, because trying to nudge a Republican into the Democratic fold was mostly a waste of time. But, once in a while, a made-to-order situation fell into his lap. During one of our conversations, he described such a case:

"There was this woman in my area who was given a rough time about her rooming house that she'd remodeled at considerable expense. The inspector came around and told her she couldn't rent out the rooms because she didn't meet some building code technicalities. Well, she went to see the Republican captain about it, and he told her it was all my doing—that I was the one who caused that. She came in here to see me and really raised hell. I told her I'd had nothing to do with it and that he was just trying to make me look bad, and I told her I'd see to it that something was done about it. I went downtown and talked to the right guy in the inspector's department, and they decided to give her the okay on it because, basically, it was a safe structure. Anyway, she was very happy about it, and when I was talking to her later on she puts a twenty-dollar bill in my pocket. Well, I grabbed her wrist, and I about broke it, and I told her, 'If you ever do anything like that again, I'll actually break your wrist—I'll break both your wrists. I've never taken a nickel from any of my people, and I'm not gonna start now.'

"What I did expect, though, was for her to make sure that her and her roomers voted in future elections. And I said to her, 'Don't just tell your roomers to vote. I want you to actually bring them to me in person and see that they vote.' And after that, she always did. So, you see, that was worth a hell of a lot more than her twenty dollars, and I got all that by knowing how to play 'drop it.' I also told her that down at the inspector's office they liked real fine cigars, and what she might do was not to give them any money, but to go down there with one of those boxes that costs around twenty bucks. And she did, and that made everybody happy. I can multiply this incident many, many times, and that's the difference—that's why I'm an outstanding precinct captain."

The organization's strength was in its good rapport with people, and maintaining that rapport was the precinct captain's first and most important duty. His ability to execute clever stratagems such as "drop it" and his discerning eye for probable converts to organization politics were valuable assets in the performance of his job, but a great deal more was involved in running a productive precinct. A productive precinct, one in which the precinct workers maximized the Democratic vote, resulted from the precinct captain's long hours of dedicated hard work. When I asked Grosnyk if "drop it" was the major reason for the organization's success, he replied quickly:

"The real thing that makes us a great organization is that we believe in old-fashioned hard work. It just takes a lot of elbow grease and personal interest in your people. That'll do the trick. Now, when it comes to winning elections, I'm a real pro. Before the election, we have to make a report to the committeeman on how our vote will turn out, and the committeeman then gives his estimate to the mayor. Well, I don't live in no controlled precinct, you know, and I really have to work to find out who's for us, who's against us, and who's undecided. Then, after I find out, I keep going back to those undecideds, and I work on them right up to the very end. And when I turn in my totals on election night, and my committeeman takes a look at them and then takes a look at the chart he has right there in front of him with my estimate on it, I can tell you that out of four hundred voters in my precinct I never miss that estimate by more than five. A lot of times I'll hit it right on the button.

"Some captains used to get real upset because some of the independents would come in and campaign. They wanted to call the cops and have them locked up. But I said they had a right to campaign and to give them a chance. We can certainly stand the competition."

Such confident talk may misrepresent the facts of the precinct captain's life, however. Actually, Grosnyk was always concerned about competition and seldom complacent. In addition to the sheer hard work of keeping up with the people and their problems and marshalling their votes, he had to be conversant with the election laws and, sometimes, able and willing to bend them a little in favor of the organization.

"Mel, you're in political science. Well, let me tell you something you'll appreciate. I always knew what the election law was, and it came in very handy," Grosnyk said. "I'm a technician, and that makes me an effective precinct captain. I know exactly what the law says and how it's interpreted. I know the difference between 'instructions' and 'assistance,' for instance. Now, in order to receive 'assistance,' you have to be physically disabled—like handicapped, or something like that; and then we can go in there and actually pull the lever for people. But, when they receive 'instructions,' what we do is we make sure they know exactly how to vote. Well, I always make sure one of our people goes in there to give the instructions and to notice how a guy votes. If he votes right, I get the nod. But if I get a shake of the head, I know the voter double-crossed me; and if that happens, I make a note for future reference. Mel, do you know how else you can tell their vote?"

"No, Ikey."

"Well, you can also figure if they're voting right by watching their feet. If they're doing the job and voting the straight Democratic ticket, they stand in one place and pull that party lever. On the other hand, if they're walking all over the damned place, then you know they're splitting their ticket on you."

Circumstances sometimes demanded greater discrepancies between election laws and polling practices, although for the most part the days of blatantly illegal elections were in the past. Occasionally, a Republican judge could be "bought" on election day because he lived off the largesse of the organization all year long. At other times, the party precinct workers were left to their imaginations and to the possibilities of a propitious moment.

"Ikey, just how possible is it to rig elections at the precinct level?"

Grosnyk equivocated. "Mel, there are a lot of guys who think we're a great organization because we pull off shady stuff. That happens some, but a lot less than people think. Now, it used to be that you could stuff ballots. But if you were going to do it, you sure had to have enough names in the binder so that you didn't come up with more ballots than names. Well, if the guy serving as Republican judge was on your side, then you were okay—you got cooperation. But a lot of times you couldn't get your own man in there because the Republicans would find a bona fide Republican to work as a judge. Then you'd have a real problem."

Modern technology—the voting machine—had narrowed the precinct captain's opportunities for running up the Democratic vote on election day. The threat of losing the organization's friendship still brought wavering voters into line, however, and payoffs and bribes could still buy cooperation.

Ikey Grosnyk served the machine with real devotion. For him it was a way of life:

"I was a fresh, immature adolescent who lived on the northwest side of Chicago. I didn't amount to nothing when I was a teenager. You know, I went into politics as a degenerate, good-for-nothing young punk. Politics straightened me out. When I was twenty-two, they put me on as a clerk just to count votes, and I started to learn the inside of politics."

The promise of a better life brought people into the organization, and the fulfillment of that promise secured their loyalty. There were abundant rewards for the faithful. A precinct captain, like Ikey

Grosnyk, usually had a well-paying job with the city and plenty of side deals, too.

"Can you actually support your family on a city salary?" I asked him.

"Come off it, Mel. You know better than that! The salary alone can't do it. You need to provide extra service. Now, when I worked down at the License Bureau, and when some person came in and they needed a favor done, I'd say, 'Hmm.' And then I'd pause a while, he'd look at me, and I'd say, 'Hmm' again. You know what a hummer is? People say they don't know, but they do. Let's say you go in to see a specialist, and he holds up an x-ray, and he says, 'Hmm.' Well, all that time, while he's saying, 'Hmm,' the price keeps going up, and it goes right out of sight. And that's the way it was at the License Bureau. I'd start 'humming,' and what it meant was that the price for that favor was going up all the time.

"Remember when you and your girl came in for your marriage license? The clerk recommended a certain lab because it was cheaper, better, and quicker. We also gave you a card for that lab, and on the back of the card there were some initials. That's so they'll know over there at the lab who to give the dollar kickback to. They keep track over there, and once a month we get referral money. The important thing is, never take a dollar from the public till. That would be dishonest. And that money I get goes for a good cause. I couldn't send my two kids to college on just my salary. Certainly, no one's against education. Doctors and lawyers recommend good specialists all the time and take kickbacks. I just do the same thing. I make referrals to specialists."

"How would you evaluate your many years in politics?"

"As I look back over my career, I wouldn't have had it any other way. There are a few things I'm not especially proud of; but I can take great pride in helping hundreds of people, and many of them were in desperate situations. And I'm proud of my part in helping to elect great men like Mayor Daley, Senator Douglas, Governor Stevenson, and young Adlai. I've profited personally, all right; but what's more important is, I've helped elect all those great men who really know how to help people."

Precinct workers like Ikey Grosnyk had almost unlimited faith in the organization's ability to provide the poor with a better living. That faith, together with other assets, their insight into problems affecting the poor, their willingness to devote long hours to precinct work and to overlook the law, equipped them uniquely for work in Chicago's low-income neighborhoods. Elsewhere in Chicago, circumstances were different, and the organization used other means to promote its exchange relationship with the voters.

A large segment of Chicago's population required very little in the way of individual attention. For these people, maintained and well-lighted streets, regular garbage collection, and the availability of good fire and police protection were ample evidence of efficient city government. The city of Chicago performed such services very well in the middle-class neighborhoods and gave those voters reason enough to return the Democrats to office, election after election.

Other voters expected more, however. For them, the organization was still personified in the precinct captain. They looked to him for attention and favors, and they expected him to woo their affections and support. Professionals, particularly lawyers, often served the intermediary function of promoting the exchange relationship between the organization and Chicago's middle-class voters. Most of them grew up in the neighborhoods they served and knew the residents well. Often, they belonged to the predominant ethnic group in their precinct. Many worked hard for their education, holding jobs during the day and attending school at night. Now they had the responsible positions in city government and were knowledgeable in important policy areas such as housing, civil rights, or land development and zoning. Their names appeared in the newspapers, and they had about them an aura of immense respectablity, even stature, when they approached old friends in their role of precinct captain.

The local-boy-made-good had a distinct advantage in handling his precinct work, but he would not continue to hold the people's respect and admiration, or their votes, unless he could generally satisfy their expectations. Frequently, conversation was all his constituents wanted. They were pleased when he inquired about their health, their children, and their businesses, and they were gratified when he solicited their opinions concerning crime control, taxes, and the high cost of living. The effective precinct captain willingly gave of his time, but, in addition, he had to be prepared to give advice. Sometimes, he was asked perplexing questions. His people wanted to know what would be done about inflation or the energy crisis or unemployment. More often, they wanted to know how to qualify for a small business loan or for financial aid for a son or daughter about to enter college. At other times they needed help for a child in trouble or accounting advice on a tax problem.

The precinct captain provided his constituents creditable information and sound advice. He introduced them to responsive personnel in government agencies and helped them obtain competent professional assistance to work out serious personal problems. In return, he asked them to support the Democratic party, not only because he had done them favors, of course, but because the Democrats deserved their support. He was articulate and incisive, and easily enumerated many valid reasons for voting the straight Democratic ticket. He pointed to advances of the working class under national, state, and local Democratic administrations and recited a litany of ethnic names in connection with important political positions in the Democratic party. He reminded Catholics that the only party to nominate and elect a Catholic for the nation's highest office was the Democratic party. He bolstered Jewish hopes that soon the Democrats would nominate and elect a Jewish president. His arguments were convincing, and when the voters in his precinct pulled the party lever, they were confident that their votes were votes for social progress and good government.

Although the precinct captain's work was hard, his job was hardly thankless, and, for this reason, many enterprising professionals exercised the privilege of heading up a middle-class Chicago precinct. Success in his precinct assured the professional of well-paid employment with the city and opened advancement opportunities to more influential positions. Recognition for promotion required more than a demonstrated ability for managing a successful precinct, however. The organization also demanded professional competence. Furthermore, once the professional gained the organization's favor by operating a first-rate precinct and demonstrating his professional capabilities, he then had to qualify for promotion on the basis of the quota system, biding his time until there was a vacancy for a member of his ethnic group. The organization would by-pass even the most deserving professional to maintain balance in its ethnic representation.

An elective or appointive position in the judiciary was a splendid reward for a capable lawyer, well worth long hours in the precinct in addition to time spent at the practice of law, and the opportunities were not necessarily circumscribed by the Cook County boundaries.

The organization's approval might open the way to a seat on the Illinois Supreme Court or, if there were a Democratic president, the federal district court. The judgeship offered an excellent salary, plus a generous pension at retirement, and substantial status and prestige besides. Chicago's many lawyers each were intent on staying on the right side of every judge. One had only to take up surveillance near the Loop any work-day morning to come to a full realization of the prestige of the judge's office. Soon, a judge would stroll in, and someone near at hand would recognize him. "Good morning, Judge," he would call out. Alerted, others would hurry to pay their respects. "Good morning, Judge," they would parrot. And then there was the privilege of dining at the special judges' tables in the Bismarck Hotel, and the thrill of dropping in at ward headquarters on election night (even though he no longer could officially campaign), where a judge was received with all the respect and accolades due an honored alumnus.

The prospect of such satisfying rewards attracted many bright, young attorneys to the machine, but others arrived by a more ordinary route—the simple necessity of making a living. Casimar Pikarski was one of the latter.

Pikarski had all the qualities the organization looked for in the men it selected for work in middle-class precincts. He grew up in a mixed ethnic neighborhood on Chicago's west side. His parents were among the first residents of the community, and Pikarski still lived there, only a few blocks from his boyhood home. He graduated from the local high school in the Depression years and, unable to afford regular college, enrolled in the DePaul Evening Law School.

"Cass, how did you get started in politics?" I asked the bright attorney with whom I had worked in the O'Hara congressional campaign.

"I was one of the lucky ones. I had a daytime job and was able to scrape together enough money to go to night school. In some families, every cent any family member earned had to go toward keeping the home together. I remember how it was around the old neighborhood. Proud men without work, begging for odd jobs and standing in bread lines. Then President Roosevelt started his New Deal programs, and those men started going off to work in the morning. At the end of the week, they'd have a paycheck, and that was important. But, more important, they had their self-respect."

Pikarski approved of President Roosevelt and the programs

initiated during his administration. "I'm a born Democrat," Pikarski said. "My parents perceived the party as an instrument of social justice for the Poles, and we were brought up to understand that good citizenship meant being a good Democrat. But my personal conviction in the party's concern for people results from having seen the changes that took place right here in Chicago under President Roosevelt's administration during the Depression."

After graduation from DePaul, Pikarski entered private practice, sharing an office with an older attorney. His hopes for building a successful practice soon dissipated under the realities of hard times. But, even though his new law degree was not paying off financially, the ability it signified did not go unnoticed.

"Emmett Healy started dropping by my office from time to time," Pikarski recalls. "He was just a precinct captain in the ward then. Later on, he moved on up to become a federal judge, but in those days he was just a darned good Irish lawyer with a lot of political ambition, and he happened to be a precinct captain in the ward where I lived. Anyway, he'd stop in, and we'd talk about the economy and how difficult it was to get a practice started when everyone was so broke. Then one day he told me he was considering running for alderman, but, being Irish, he worried whether he could appeal to the Jews and the Poles and the Italians in the area. He asked for my help in rallying the Polish votes. I respected him, and my practice surely wasn't demanding much of my time. Well, I went to work in his campaign, and he was elected alderman with a lot of support from the Poles. Later on, he came around to thank me. He mentioned there was an opening for a new attorney on the corporation counsel's staff, and when he left I hurried down to the ward office for a letter from the committeeman and then down to city hall to apply. I was hired on the spot, and that was the beginning of a rewarding relationship betwen me and Emmett Healy. He became my friend and mentor, and when he took over as committeeman in our ward, before he got the nod for a judgeship, I just naturally gravitated to a precinct captain's post."

Pikarski did better than a good job for the corporation counsel. He received citations for outstanding work in upholding and promoting standards and requirements of the housing authority. Later, when he was moved to the civil rights division, he was praised by the black community as well as by the organization for his relentless prosecution of white slumlords. Still later, after he went to work as attorney for the Chicago liquor commission, Pikarski built an enviable record by winning 93 percent of the cases he argued. Many of these involved the revocation of liquor licenses, a matter of such serious concern to tavern operators that Pikarski often found himself pitted against top-flight defense counsel.

"I always gave my cases top priority," Pikarski explains. "I never went into a hearing unprepared. I knew I wouldn't remain on the corporation counsel staff very long if I made the city look bad. I was well rewarded for my efforts, though—well satisfied with my promotion record—and I felt I had really arrived when I was given the opportunity to represent the city before the United States Supreme Court."

Pikarski was more than an astute lawyer, however; he was also a careful politician. Politicking was not second nature to him, the way it was to some, but he knew and observed the rules of the game. He knew enough to make friends with the local reporters, especially those covering city hall, but he also knew enough not to court the press. Too much favorable publicity of his own work could be politically risky if it diverted media attention from the mayor's contributions to good city government. "While I was the liquor commission's attorney, a decision was made to go after the taverns employing 'B-girls'," Pikarski recalled. "We cracked down hard and closed up a lot of them. It was the kind of thing that caught on with the public—really newsworthy. Someone told me a reporter for the *Daily News* intended to do a story on the tavern closings and that my name would be mentioned, and I also found out that the *Sun-Times* was going to editorialize the virtues of our efforts against the 'B-girl' operation. Well, I didn't lose any time calling my friends on those newspapers and pointing out to them the mayor's part in the proceedings. 'After all,' I told them, 'Mayor Daley has the legal responsibility for liquor control in Chicago. He appointed both the members and the attorney of the liquor commission and makes the final decision about closing any of those taverns we go after.' I insisted that Mayor Daley be given the credit he deserved, since we were only following the policies of the mayor. When the stories finally appeared, they gave me a lot of good publicity, all right, but Mayor Daley also was given a good press. I was pleased, especially since it broke right after the notorious 'cops and robbers' scandal, in which several Chicago police officers were convicted of robbing businessmen in the area. It helped restore the mayor's image as the head of a law and order administration and certainly showed that he was well in command of liquor control."

All of the time Pikarski worked as a city attorney, he also kept up with his work in the precinct, and, even though his wife helped, there was a great deal of work for him to handle. "It's easy to lose perspective," Pikarski admitted. "Sometimes, when I was engrossed in an important case, I'd be tempted to let the precinct work slide a day or two. But then I'd think of the risks. If very many of us were diverted from our work in the precincts, our neglect would soon start showing up in the results at the polls. To put it in blunt language, my job with the city depended on my success in the precinct.

"So I'd make time in my schedule to talk with the precinct residents. I'd listen to their problems and complaints and make a list of the things they wanted done. Those that I could handle, I'd take care of. Others, like installing a new traffic signal near one of the church schools, I'd take to the ward committeeman, and he'd see to them. I'd always find time for a few minutes of friendly conversation. I worked for the respect of most of my people—the Bradys and the Scarpellis, for instance. They trusted me, and when I gave them a campaign poster for their window, they'd never refuse me. And when I told them our candidates needed their votes, I was rarely disappointed.

"And then I'd always have to be on the alert for new people moving into the precinct. When I started as precinct captain, that wasn't so much of a problem. People stayed put then. Toward the end of my time in the precinct, though, even the ethnics were becoming mobile. The postman helped me out with that problem. I always remembered him with a nice gift at Christmas, and he helped me identify the new residents in the neighborhood. My barber was helpful, too. We used the back room of his shop as a polling place, and there were some incidental benefits for him in the arrangement. After each election, he always picked up several new customers. He also boosted my reputation in the neighborhood. From time to time he'd see my name in the paper, and that gave him the idea I was a man of some importance. Anyway, he told his other customers some nice things about me, and I appreciated it."

The organization liked to promote a good lawyer and precinct captain like Pikarski because it provided a positive model for other captains. Pikarski, though, was not enough of a politician to be considered for a legislative position. Obviously, if he were to move up, he would have to ascend to the bench, and, once he became a judge, his days in the precinct were over. A judge at least had to appear to be outside the reach of politics.

"The way I remember it," Pikarski says, "I got my first hint that the organization might have me in mind for something while I was in Springfield for Democratic Day at the state fair. That's a big occasion, and a lot of important men in the party show up. I just decided to get out of the office and away from the precinct work and go down and rub shoulders with them. Well, I was mingling with the crowd, shaking hands here and there, stopping to chat once in a while, when, suddenly, I felt Mayor Daley watching me. I wasn't sure, of course—it wasn't anything overt; but I had the impression he was appraising me out of the corner of his eye. In any event, it wasn't long after that that I was slated for judge.

"But then, before the election rolled around, the organization suffered a disastrous defeat in a bond issue referendum. The loss was acutely embarrassing for Mayor Daley and the organization because they were strongly committed to the bond proposal. Nevertheless, it failed to carry in almost all of the precincts outside the black community. Obviously, the loss represented a reaction among whites in the electorate to a proposal for more public benefits for blacks. But when I ran into Mayor Daley at city hall a few days later, he stopped me and asked me why I thought the bond issue went down. Well, he wasn't asking me to give him a reading on public opinion. He wanted to know why the precinct captains had failed to get the votes in. So I said to him, 'Mr. Mayor, I just don't understand it.' And I reached into my coat pocket and brought out a copy of my precinct results and showed it to the mayor. 'These are my figures,' I told him, 'and they show that my people went for it by better than a two-to-one margin. I just don't understand what happened in the other places. Maybe it wasn't explained well enough.' The mayor beamed and threw his arms around my shoulders. 'Cass,' he said, 'you certainly deserve to be a judge.'"

Casimar Pikarski won the election and was installed in office. There were even more people present than had attended the first major event of his adult life, his and Stella's Polish wedding. The courtroom was packed. In the jury box sat his wife, Stella; his four sons and their wives; Candace, his teen-age daughter; and his two oldest grandchildren.

Pikarski's prime political sponsor, committeeman Jim O'Malley, served as emcee and acted as though the guests had come to honor him for snaring this prize post for one of his own minions. Some had. But most were there to honor the new judge.

O'Malley gavelled the crowed to order: "We are here for the installation of a great family man and an outstanding lawyer who will make a great judge, the Honorable Casimar Pikarski. First, I want to recognize some of my friends who have honored us with their presence today. I see Judge Otto Kerner. I see some of my other judge friends I would like to introduce . . . " The crowd gasped as Mayor Daley came striding into the room from another installation. He quickly scanned the crowd, waved to them, and then assayed the new judge's family seated in the jury box. He took a seat on the dais.

Committeeman O'Malley called upon Chief Judge Gus Bowe, who then administered the oath of office to Pikarski. Then Mayor Daley spoke. He praised Pikarski as an outstanding attorney who had served the people unusually well in the corporation counsel's office and predicted that Pikarski would serve as a great judge. Daley left the judge's stand, shook a few hands, and hurried out the door to attend another installation.

The next speaker was the Honorable Emmett Healy, judge of the U.S. Court of Appeals. He recalled proudly how Pikarski had supported him in two campaigns for both alderman and ward committeeman. But he was most proud of the fact that he had given Pikarski his start as a precinct captain and as an assistant corporation counsel. He went on to point out that the qualities of compassion and hard work that had helped Pikarski to serve his constituents and perform as an outstanding corporation counsel were the very same qualities that would make him a truly superior judge. He closed by predicting that his protégé would be promoted to even more important judicial positions.

While the official court reporter was duly recording this for posterity, he was not alone. There were also representatives from the Polish *Dziennik* as well as the metropolitan dailies. And, most significantly, the lesson of the day was dramatically conveyed to the many precinct captains from the corporation counsel's office who were in attendance: Perform well in your legal job, excel in your precinct, wait your turn, and you, too, can become a judge. The exchange between Fred Hudak and the newly elected Judge Pikarski after the ceremony underscored this: Hudak offered his congratulations and added, "Cass, you'll make a great judge." Pikarski responded, "Thank you very much. You know, Fred, you have just as much right to be a judge as me, and I'm sure you'll make it soon. Your turn is coming."

Both types of precinct captains, the formally educated Pikarski and the practically schooled Grosnyk, were indispensable to the machine, for they forged the direct links between the machine and the individual voters in Chicago's 3,000 precincts. A subject for discussion, however, is whether the machine-linked precinct captains, ward committeemen, and aldermen were, and are, equally indispensable to the residents of Chicago's wards and precincts. Ward committeeman Art McGloon took pride in citing the visible services his ward provided, but these services seem to have little vote-exchange value in some wards today. Just prior to election day in April 1983, a campaign worker in one of the white liberal wards, who was a supporter of Harold Washington, said, "We don't need ward bosses to make this city work. The streets are kept clean and the garbage is collected in Houston, isn't it?" During the Daley years, most ward leaders identified such services as an important reason for their constituents' continued support of machine candidates. Other reasons have been cited by the ward leaders who have spoken for themselves in the preceding pages: Colonel Kenneth Campbell provided "an equalizer" for his ward's poor blacks who struggled against great odds. Vito Marzullo recounted a similar favor he had performed for a former resident of his ward, and Art McGloon spoke of "getting things done for various groups and departments in the city" when he was a state legislator. Ikey Grosnyk, precinct captain, detailed the good-neighbor activities he engaged in for the benefit of his constituents, and the well-educated Casimar Pikarski, the captain of his middle-class, multi-ethnic precinct, reiterated similar services and favors.

Raymond Wolfinger, writing in 1972, has suggested that the major inducement machine politics has to offer is favoritism:

> 'Helping' citizens deal with government is . . . usually thought to be a matter of advice about where to go, whom to see, and what to say. The poor undeniably need this service more than people whose schooling and experience equip them to cope with bureaucratic institutions and procedures. But in some local political cultures advice to citizens is often accompanied by pressure on officials. The machine politician's goal is to incur the maximum obligation from his constituents, and merely providing information

is not as big a favor as helping bring about the desired outcome. Thus *'help' shades into 'pull.'*

Now there is no reason why the advantages of political influence appeal only to the poor. In places where the political culture supports expectations that official discretion will be exercised in accordance with political considerations, the constituency for machine politics extends across the socio-economic spectrum. People whose interests are affected by governmental decisions can include those who want to sell to the government, as well as those whose economic or social activities may be subject to public regulation.

Favoritism animates machine politics, favoritism not just in filling pick-and-shovel jobs, but in a vast array of public decisions.[8]

The politics of interest would seem to be alive and well. The practice of machine politics, with its varied lures to voters—favoritism, jobs, intercession with formal governmental units such as welfare agencies—is likely to continue, Wolfinger predicts.[9]

Vito Marzullo, who still chairs an inner-city ward, told me not long ago that former residents of his ward still ask him for favors because they cannot get help from the ward organizations in the neighborhoods to which they have moved. The one-on-one relationship Marzullo understands so well apparently is valued equally by present and former constituents alike. Ward leader Ed Vrdolyak pointed out recently that an important part of his work, particularly during times of unemployment, is to secure jobs for his ward's residents. Two-thirds of the jobs to which he has access for his people are not government-related but are in the private sector, he says. Vrdolyak's Tenth Ward, like Marzullo's Twenty-fifth, contains few reformist elements. The ward leaders I knew whose constituents were at the lower end of the scale in terms of job skills ran their ward headquarters as informal employment agencies for the jobless and as information centers for those needing assistance with the bureaucracy, especially after the advent of the welfare state. And at the time I ran my race for nomination to office, these machine ward lords seemed secure in their positions, for the machine's success or failure rested in their hands.

It was for this reason that the Daley organization selected candidates who could stir its ward and precinct emissaries to work extra hard during a campaign. As I made my plans to elicit support from the key political leaders in Cook County, I formulated a major stratagem: to convince them that not only did I fit the prototype of their ideal candidate but that I surpassed the other contenders in my appreciation of and ability to motivate the party's vast army of workers—both the working-class captains and their professionally educated counterparts.

4

Daley

Even in a political system characterized by the emanation of power from several levels in a stratarchy, there is always a central figure to whom the lines of power eventually lead. In the Cook County Democratic machine, Richard J. Daley occupied that position for more than two decades, and from the moment I began to run for state office, he was never far from my thoughts. My realization that, eventually, I would need to confront the Irish tribunal's chief justice himself was accompanied by anxiety, curiosity, pleasant anticipation, fantasies in which I impressed him so immediately and so positively that he insisted upon personally sponsoring me, and finally, some solid thinking about how to convince him that I would make the strongest candidate.

My speculations about Daley's response to me aside, I was not at all sure what I thought of him, for he seemed the most contradictory of politicians. Machine politicos and some members of the fourth estate appeared not to have this problem; they were either for him or against him. Daley accepted, at least outwardly, the system of venality and graft that permeated the Cook County machine and that was practiced by some elements of the downstate party, but he also helped slate reformers like Senator Paul Douglas. He supported blue-ribbon candidates for judgeships but winked at election fraud. He had served as legislative liaison for Governor Adlai Stevenson II, but he was comfortable with (if contemptuous of) hacks like Paddy Bauler, who inserted his name in Chicago's history with "Chicago ain't ready for reform." Daley perpetuated racism in housing, but he mediated a citywide conflict over a segregationist school superintendent and engineered his removal. He personally launched the political career of youthful idealist Adlai Stevenson III, but he used brutal tactics on young protesters at the 1968 Democratic National Convention. Because of these paradoxes, I was unable to accept a simplistic view, one way or the other, of Richard J. Daley. He was, however, as everyone knew, at the very center of power in Illinois politics.

I had observed the mayor close-up on two occasions. The first involved the swearing-in ceremony of my father-in-law, Harry Iseberg, as justice of the Chicago municipal court. Seated in the jury box with the other family members—my wife, her two sisters and their husbands, and my mother-in-law—I noted the mayor's brisk entrance into the courtroom as the ceremony began. He surveyed the entire room quickly but thoroughly, then gave those of us in the jury box a little more attention. His interest in the sort of family the new judge headed was unmistakable.

My second encounter with the mayor occurred during the 1968 Democratic National Convention. As my father-in-law and I were walking down a corridor of the Sherman House Hotel, we met Mayor Daley coming from the opposite direction. My father-in-law introduced me: "Mr. Mayor, this is my son-in-law, Dr. Mel Kahn from Southern Illinois University, who is an expert on practical politics." I winced at this immodest remark to one of the nation's foremost politicians, and under his penetrating probe I felt that nothing about me escaped him. But he simply struck a quick smile, gave me a firm handshake, and rushed away to more important business.

The night after that chance meeting, violence erupted in the city's streets as police battled throngs of young people gathered at the convention hall to protest the Vietnam War. The young people blamed the ensuing bloodshed on the mayor's refusal to let them sleep in Lincoln Park. Daley blamed the riot not on the protesters but on "professional agitators" determined to disrupt the convention. By his lack of restraint in this incident, he antagonized not only the protesters but the millions of Americans who resented both his insensitivity to legitimate protest and the strong-arm tactics of his police. The heated exchange in which Daley allegedly cursed Senator Abraham Ribicoff dramatized Daley's arrogance. Illinois State Treasurer Adlai Stevenson voiced the nationwide outrage by calling Daley "a feudal lord" and the Chicago police "stormtroopers in blue." Hubert Humphrey emerged from the convention as the nominee of a divided party, a handicap that fatally hampered his campaign. Daley, the noted architect of compromise and political stability, clearly had miscalculated. Chaos ruled.

To achieve the nomination, it was imperative that I make contact with Daley. Clyde Choate had said he would schedule a personal interview; but when, after several attempts, I failed to reach Choate in Springfield, I unsuccessfully tried to make the appointment myself. At that point Jackson County chairman Ray Chancey contacted Jim Ronan, the state chairman: "Jim, if you really mean business about involving downstate in the party, I'll give you a chance to prove it. I want you to arrange an interview for Mel Kahn and me with the mayor." A week later, Daley's secretary phoned me; the appointment was all set.

Elated and awe-struck though I was, I also figured that my success with Daley would depend upon my ability to assess accurately his personal characteristics and understand the basis of his political acumen. What were his strengths? How did he function politically? To which of my endorsement efforts would he best respond?

Like every other observer of Illinois politics, I knew about the public Daley and, from talking with mutual acquaintances, had acquired fragmented insights into his personality. In the decade that followed my race for nomination to the state superintendency, these fragments would begin to coalesce as I interviewed those who had known Daley well and as I read the biographies that began to appear in the early seventies. Daley's longtime associates described him as a man of personal warmth, sincere religious conviction, and unswerving loyalty to friends and political party. Others spoke of him as shrewd politician and masterful city administrator. Even his political opponents and his many critics credited him with competence. But it was only a few years ago that I sensed the appropriateness of a well-known sociological concept to Daley's unique ability to function in both his role of party leader and mayor.

This concept seeks to describe metaphorically modern man's struggles between the claims of two contrasting arenas—the *Gemeinschaft*, or folk community, and the *Gesellschaft*, or urban, industrialized society, worlds that might be considered less as nonintersecting spheres than as two polarities on a continuum. My interest in these metaphors (created by Ferdinand Tönnies) lies in their usefulness for identifying the human environments and social structures prevailing in

Cook County and, though less saliently, in downstate Illinois as well. The ethnic make-up of Chicago lends itself to analysis within the *Gemeinschaft-Gesellschaft* frame of reference because this ethnicity produced special political conflicts with which the machine had to contend. Richard Daley proved capable of resolving the tension these contrasting worlds created within his own character and personality and, even more successfully, pointed the way for their political resolution in both Cook County and the state. The concepts of *Gemeinschaft-Gesellschaft* offer a clue to Daley's political philosophy and practices.

Our *Gemeinschaft* sensibilities have their source in our rural past and beckon us to a life based upon familial ties and characterized by informal, personal qualities. Love, trust, a sense of common bonds, reliance upon status relationships, and the primacy of noneconomic institutions (such as church, kinship groups, and community and social networks) are values most of us cherish. In short, we seek membership in an intimate community.

But a second type of world, the competitive one, revolves around economic survival in an impersonal, nonnurturing, technological society. In the *Gesellschaft* environment, we are consumption-oriented, depend upon anonymous producers for the goods we use, and base our relationships upon formal contracts rooted in impersonal law. Greed, distrust, protection from strangers, and the primacy given to making a living are values that thrust us away from the intimacy of community to the cold harshness of industrialized society, where we must focus on economic success and must resign ourselves to living in relative anonymity.

The particular genius of Richard J. Daley was his ability to serve, in multiple ways, as a bridge between the *Gemeinshaft* and the *Gesellschaft*, and in a moment, we will consider how he did this. But, first, let us search sociologist Earl S. Johnson's delineation of these two social dimensions for more specific clues to Daley's make-up. Johnson suggests that as folk culture evolved over time into urban culture, the status of individuals changed:

> Person and *Gemeinschaft* were one; it may be said that individuals did not exist, only community members. Each person enjoyed security of self but without the possession of a unique and distinctive personality. Persons had no moral autonomy. One's conscience was a tribal conscience; one's mind a tribal mind.

Persons had but one allegiance, unchallenged and unambiguous. That allegiance was to the standards of the community. To it one owed his existence as a person and to it each tribal group owed its power and its simple and unchanging character.

But when *Gemeinschafts* met and interacted, when simple social systems became more complex, a problem of great importance arose. Simplicity of standards, ideas, and duties disciplined by the cooperative principle was followed by complexity which was disciplined by the principle of competition. In place of security, one now enjoyed liberty but of an increasingly fragile nature because of the complex and ambiguous nature of the environment (the new *Gesellschaft*). . . .

The passage from *Gemeinschaft* did not occur, at least totally. Although human relations became more fabricated, rational, territorial, and impersonal, those which are their opposites tended to persist: natural, sentimental, kinship, and personal. *Gemeinschaft* has persisted and survived in an unsuspected place—in the modern urban *Gesellschaft*. The modern community has a bimodal structure: local neighborhoods and the market place.[1]

Implicit here are the characteristics of Richard J. Daley that nearly all who knew him have named—his sure sense of identity; his lifelong attachment to his neighborhood (Bridgeport); his participation in the collective consciousness of the American-Irish and in the collective conscience of Catholicism—in short, his tribal ties. Daley's accomplishment was to be able to move back and forth, metaphorically speaking, between his folk community and the urban society that lay outside its gates and to reconcile and coordinate their frequently conflicting interests and demands. He was a constant booster of Chicago's ethnic cultures and of their strong desire to nurture the personalized values of kinship, national heritage, and intimacy. At the same time, he realized that urban men and women cannot live by spiritual bread alone. Nonagricultural peoples must strive in the urban marketplace to sustain self and family and to purchase the modern conveniences that now stake claim as necessities. To these ends, Daley was determined to maintain a political power structure in which his own friends and cohorts, particularly the Irish, attained both status in the eyes of their respective ethnic communities and the financial rewards that provided privilege, position, and security within a larger, infinitely more complex society. Although ever protective of his own group's interest, he also placed his skills as an intermediary at the disposal of other groups who likewise strove to cross over successfully into the larger arenas of power.

Richard Daley recognized the problems of people who struggled between these environments as well as those who attempted to favor one over the other. Some political leaders can appeal effectively to the dwellers of the impersonal world of industrialization. Others can empathize with those who find their greatest security in the clan or neighborhood. Daley's uniqueness lay in his talents as broker between both types of groups—those desiring personal contacts and those satisfied with the impersonal; those accepting another's word as his bond and those relying on contract; those functioning in families and those alone in the crowd. Out of these contrasts, the real stuff of his megalopolis, Daley refined a machine structured upon the familiarity of personal relations, on the one hand, and the impersonality of the concrete jungle, on the other. He further succeeded in resolving conflicts between competing *Gemeinschafts*, as one ethnic group contended with others for political power. Specifically, he functioned as a pragmatic coalition builder, working to maintain the political alliance of Catholic ethnics and blacks while, at the same time, preserving the supportive combination of powerful financial interests and organized labor.

From time to time, Daley altered the respective payoffs to groups in pursuit of the larger, over-arching goal of sustaining the system, continuously making adjustments to maintain and bolster his coalitions. For example, he gave far less attention to meeting the demands of Chicago's black population in the 1950s, when it numbered only about 500,000, than in the 1970s, when it had soared to more than 1 million. He was a pragmatist, and he could count. Obsessed with numbers, he earned a reputation for operating like a human calculator, tallying up group political capital, votes cast, and dollars contributed.

As a power-broker, Daley responded to exhibitions of power by others, but he also knew when to exert power himself through bold, innovative action, especially if the exertion demanded minimal effort and expended minimal political reserves. He could, however, quickly discern the need to table a plan, delay a decision, or dismantle a stratagem. And he possessed a special genius for turning occasional defeats into ultimate victories by embracing or coopting his antagonists. Daley's tolerance for political setbacks may have related to the fact that they occurred so seldom—his foresight, flexibility, and talent for mediating conflict succeeded far more often than they failed, for when he had to strike a deficit in one column, he usually could find a way to balance it in the other.

His adeptness at political brokerage resulted in part from his attention to detail and from a phenomenal memory. A Democratic party leader observed: "Daley keeps abreast of the minutiae pertaining to city government and the party. He is the hardest-working public official I ever saw." Indeed, Daley spared no effort to marshal information and kept his thumb on the public pulse through extensive use of scientifically constructed surveys and public opinion polls. In his daily staff meetings, his monitoring of each department of Chicago's bureaucracy continued to impress those who had worked with him for years. His bookkeeper's eye for detail served him well in a city government as complex as Chicago's, and like good professionals everywhere, he routinely sought up-to-date and accurate information.

Daley's penchant for facts proved useful, too, in his position as leader of his political organization. Following the 1960 "cops and robbers" scandal, after which new police chief Orlando Wilson had received a free hand to clean up crime, Congressman William Dawson, one of Daley's early mentors, requested a meeting with the mayor and confronted him with bitter complaints about the policy-wheel crackdown on Chicago's south side. According to one witness, he asked Daley to "call off the dogs." "You're causing me financial ruin," Dawson moaned. Daley turned, opened a drawer, pulled out a file, and scanned it. After a time, he looked at Dawson and remarked, "I see you did unusually well with your funeral business last year and also with the stock you hold in the dairy. I don't see why you're complaining." My informant claimed that Daley had a similar rundown on the income of every other ward committeeman.

Daley's perception of the value of extensive and accurate information about everything that affected the workings of both his own party and city government earned him the deference of the organization's general membership. It was partly this professionalism that made him superior to others as a power-broker, for the *Gesellschaft* requires, above all, competence.

As Daley's position and power solidified during the decade of the sixties, so, too, did he come under increasing attack from journalists and in magazine and book profiles as well, especially after the 1968 Democratic convention riots. Until the last years of his mayoralty, however, critics could find no sure grounds for venturing against the Daley image of personal integrity. Information that surfaced in 1974 cast that integrity in a new light: Daley had, for seventeen years, owned a holding company with current assets of more than $200,000, a business arrangement that, while not illegal, involved conflict of interest. But at the time of my special and focused interest in the mayor, he was generally considered beyond reproach. His friends and supporters could recite a litany of qualities—the moral values and customs instilled in him by his community support groups of family, kin, and church—that in their eyes made him deserving of power and that, they said, exerted ultimate influence over many of his policy-making decisions. Ikey Grosnyk assessed Daley's personal character-istics in the following way:

"The real secret of Daley is that he's a clean head. I remember the old days from the west side. We would have those big golf days when we would go out on the golf course for a while, and then we'd go inside and really drink it up. In Daley's case, he'd have one beer, and that's all. The other guys would make smart-ass remarks and pinch the waitresses. Not Daley, though—he always conducted himself okay. Now, this doesn't mean that he was any sissy. I remember, when he was young, he used to play on the Cornell Hamburgers' [neighborhood social club] football team. He played tackle, and he was a real mean, rough one, I kid you not.

"The important thing is, the guy has always lived a clean life, and he knows how to conduct himself. He presents a good model for the people in the organization. For example, in the 1954 campaign, the precinct workers were having a meeting one evening, and Daley stopped by to talk to us. 'I don't want to take no chances in this election,' he says. 'Those Republicans are going to be pulling all kinds of tricks—they're going to be wearing big boutonnieres, and they'll probably have little electronic cameras hidden in them. They're going to have hidden microphones. I want you boys to be very careful this next month, until this campaign's over. If anybody tries to give you even a dollar bill, don't take it, because they can fake it up and say it's a twenty-dollar bill. Don't even reach out for a cigar, because they can fake it up and then plant the bill in there and make it look bad for us. I want the cooperation of all of you, because these guys are really gunning for us, and the papers will back them up if they have pictures. So if any of you run short of money during the next month, see Matt Danaher about an advance.'

"This proved Daley was okay, see. He wanted us to play it

straight so the ticket could get elected. But he also knew we might need extra money for our families, and so he arranged to have money loaned to us in advance."

Daley's admonishment to the precinct workers testifies to his familiarity with the habits, as well as the needs, of "the people." His eyes might avert themselves in obeisance to some rascally Irish forebear; his Catholic conscience might leave other men's morality to the judgment of the confession box; but his politician's obssession with winning demanded the absence of discoverable corruption. As of 1972, a powerful ward committeeman could make a judgment similar to Ikey Grosnyk's: "Nobody's been able to challenge Daley's own personal integrity—he's a family man, and he's deeply religious. He's a dedicated person, and when you have a leader like that you look up to him and try to follow his example. That's what all of us in the organization do. Daley loves his city, his family, and his God."

Richard Daley's religious views were basically conservative. He had little tolerance for the new ideas espoused by many modern-day church leaders and clung to the traditional, conformist variety of Catholicism that resisted dramatic changes. Historically, his church had relied upon individual rather than societal efforts to better the human condition. Nothing happened too fast that way; nothing got out of control. Daley's Catholicism, like his political organization, was oriented toward preserving stability above all.

Because he did not believe in rocking the boat, Daley did not emerge overnight as a political phenomenon. He served a lengthy and varied apprenticeship, moving forward through the ranks of party position (precinct captain, secretary of the ward organization, ward committeeman, and then county chairman) while, at the same time, advancing from minor to major political office. His election in 1955 to the mayoralty marked the fruition of thirty years of preparation, training, and experience.

That experience had included working closely with Governor Adlai Stevenson II, who appointed Daley director of state revenue in 1949. John Bartlow Martin says of Stevenson's choice:

> Daley was a Democratic career politician from a ward near the Chicago stockyards. . . . The Director of Revenue was a key man in Springfield, never more so than in this administration, in view of Stevenson's campaign promises to return more state revenue to "starving" local governments. Daley knew the subject, and he knew state and city politics. He served Stevenson well. When he

was appointed, Pete Akers, in the *Sun-Times*, publicly congratulated Stevenson on Daley's appointment: "Daley, still a comparatively young man, has come to exemplify the best in politics. . . . If Adlai Stevenson can induce a few more men of Daley's unique qualifications—ability, political experience and integrity—to associate themselves with him for the next four years he will do much to assure the success of his administration."[2]

As a member of the cabinet, Daley served the politically inexperienced Stevenson as intermediary with other state officials: "No two men," writes Eugene Kennedy, "could have been more opposite in background and yet Stevenson, innocent as a boy who never surrendered his mother's first stories about how the world turns, needed a man with the reputation and ability of Daley. It was not just political reward that prompted the appointment. . . . Stevenson, who had yet to yearn almost painfully for the Presidency, did not act on accepted party principles and allowed many hold-over officials to retain their positions. . . . Daley warned the new governor that these people would betray him, as indeed they did. . . . "[3] Stevenson's continuation of several Republican state appointees in their posts, a generous act of noblesse oblige, caused him difficulties afterwards, and it was Daley who handled the situation for him. Daley, according to Kennedy, "would bear a major responsibility over the next year in helping Stevenson run the state government."[4]

Daley had acted a somewhat similar role eighteen years earlier, when the boisterous Irish Cook County treasurer, Joe McDonough, made him his secretary. McDonough, a high-roller, found that he could squeeze very little office time into his life in the fast lane and left Daley to do the day-to-day work of the treasurer's office. Kennedy observes, "Young Daley was entirely reliable; it mattered little to him that McDonough got the credit for work that he was actually doing. He was, after all, in the counting house itself, mastering the intricacies of finance and budgets, of the funds for the sources of patronage, of the sweetest secrets about the manuevers and processes in the jangling till of power."[5] Daley had played the ant to McDonough's grasshopper. The hard-working Stevenson, however, made sure that Daley got all the credit he deserved for the broker-mediating talents he put to work on Stevenson's behalf.

Daley was most crucially of service to Stevenson as the governor's legislative liaison. Former Governor Sam Shapiro, who had served earlier in his career as a state representative, told me:

"Adlai let me know on several occasions that he regarded Daley as his chief spokesman in the legislature. On the crucial legislation pertaining to the budget, Richard Daley represented the governor. Stevenson had complete trust in Daley's judgment and integrity." Stevenson, who could not relate successfully to the members of the machine, recognized Daley's value. Daley, of course, shared their working-class backgrounds, their vernacular, and their ward-level political experience. As George Dunne once put it, "Daley had a genuine interest in people and could read them—he had an uncanny way of knowing what they were thinking. He was very versatile." This versatility, the ability to get along with those party segments who primarily pursued material gain as well as those more reform-oriented, made him the perfect go-between for the urbane, intellectual, reformist Stevenson and the Cook County organization. Both trusted him.

One assignment Stevenson gave Daley, and it was one that tested Daley's mettle, was the difficult task of gaining confirmation for Walter Schaefer, an intellectual lawyer, to the state supreme court— a political morsel the machine would have preferred awarding to one of its own minions. Daley, as usual, brought this assignment to a successful conclusion. Writing to a friend in 1970, Stevenson's associate Carl McGowan commented that Schaefer's confirmation showed what could be accomplished by the concerted action of a strong governor, supporting a worthy man, and a powerful political organization. Because the machine had this power to act for the public good if guided by an enlightened leader, Stevenson had great respect for the machine politicians and was reluctant to oppose them, McGowan wrote.[6]

Daley's multiple services to the governor earned him a sincere and well-deserved debt of gratitude from the man who, but for Daley, might have been less than a "capable, fairly effective reform governor," as Milton Rakove has described him.[7] Eugene Kennedy has commented: "It will always remain difficult for those who prefer the image of Daley as the political hack, the well-tailored carnivore, to recognize him as the highly conscientious and energetic man who immediately mastered the details of every job. And yet, this was clearly the Daley of the Stevenson years. . . . "[8] What also has gone unrecognized by some is that there was no disjunction between the Daley of the Stevenson years and the Daley of at least the first seventeen years of the mayoralty, since Daley the professional occupied both places in time and setting.

When, in 1954, Richard Daley made his move against incumbent Martin Kennelly for the party's nomination for mayor, Governor Stevenson endorsed Daley. Len O'Connor cites that endorsement as evidence of Stevenson's naïveté, for, only a few weeks earlier, Daley had instructed national committeeman Jacob Arvey to support Pennsylvania's Governor David Lawrence for the Democratic party's national chairmanship instead of Stevenson's choice, Paul Butler of Indiana. O'Connor says:

> It never seemed to register with Stevenson that Daley had stepped on him in order to climb into a position of national influence or that Daley always considered his own good each time an issue presented itself. Thus in 1956 Daley was as enthusiastic as anyone else when Stevenson was again nominated to run against Eisenhower because he knew no one could defeat Eisenhower— even Stevenson himself was aware of how hopeless was his cause—but in 1960 went with Kennedy. . . .
>
> Of course, this was all far in the future in December 1954. And that is the point. Daley always has his eye to the future—even when, as was the case that month, the political action was frantic.[9]

The future was indeed the point. Stevenson may have been self-deluded in hoping to unseat Eisenhower in 1956, but, given that hope, he revealed himself as better-schooled in practical politics than he has been given credit for. Had he backed Kennelly in the primary, and had Kennelly then lost to Daley, Stevenson would have found himself in an awkward position vis-à-vis the Daley-headed Cook County machine when, two years hence, he made a second bid for the presidential nomination. Conversely, if he backed an ultimately victorious Daley, Daley gratefully would harness a now unified county organization behind Stevenson in 1956. Even if Daley lost his primary race, he would not forget Stevenson's efforts on his behalf. Uncomfortably aware of his lack of rapport with the party rank and file, whom better than Daley could Stevenson have chosen as his surrogate to appeal to them in his stead? In terms of self-interest alone, Stevenson's endorsement of Daley for the mayoralty consti-tuted the very essence of political wisdom—it had everything to recommend it and nothing to weigh against it. Moreover, it was an honorable man's discharge of a political debt for Daley's loyal service in the past.

In the 1956 presidential election, Stevenson lost Chicago by more than 40,000 votes "despite," O'Connor concedes, "the best efforts of the Daley machine," for Stevenson "was a candidate the party workers did not like."[10] Unfortunately, not even Daley, in his dual role as party chairman and mayor, had the power to make a president out of a silk purse. And when, in 1960, he activated his influence on behalf of John F. Kennedy's candidacy, Daley numbered only one among many who felt that Stevenson could not beat Nixon in the general election. It was Daley who, four years earlier, had forged the last link in the chain of favors he and Stevenson had created over a period of years. He now owed Stevenson no further political debt, and his pragmatic realism should not be confused with treachery.

Although Stevenson's support for Daley in the 1954 mayoralty primary was symbolically important, Daley was his own best tactician as he exerted his influence within the party to line up support for himself against Martin Kennelly. The machine leadership had decided, collectively, to dump Kennelly because, with uncharacteristic energy, the idealistic Kennelly had tampered with the patronage system, the bread and butter of the machine's better living, by converting patronage jobs to civil service. Kennelly would not be reslated because he had been too active in the "wrong" way. Organized labor, however, felt that Kennelly had done too little, and they had labeled him a "do-nothing" mayor. Labor leader Sam Levin commented, "I used to work with Kennelly. I liked him. One day, I told him about Anton Chekov, who had written a play in which a certain element came into control. They didn't even change the furniture around. I said to him, 'It's the same with you, Martin—you haven't even changed your furniture around.'"

The steel workers union specifically charged Kennelly with failure to reappoint their international representative, John Doherty, to the school board; and the union's parent organization, the CIO, announced that under no circumstances would it support Kennelly. This gave the Democratic politicos a pseudo-reason for not reslating him, and they made that reason public. When the newspapers denounced the "dictatorial action" taken by labor, the machine escaped the brunt of the criticism for a move upon which, for its own survival, it already had decided. Five months before the 1955

Democratic primary, president Bill Lee of the Chicago Federation of Labor called a special meeting, ostensibly to discuss plans regarding the forthcoming Illinois State Federation of Labor convention. A union representative later told me what had transpired:

"After a few minutes were spent on the convention, Lee announced that there was an important mayor's election coming up and then called on Bill McFetridge for some 'wise counsel.' I was surprised, since I had seen McFetridge at only two meetings in the past three years. McFetridge said, 'You ought to know who your friends are, and Dick Daley is our friend. Let's show that we're behind him and pledge some solid support.'

"Many of the delegates enthusiastically supported McFetridge. But one man spoke up and said he didn't have the power to pledge any of his union's funds. I felt the same way, since the election was so far away we hadn't even discussed it—hell, lots of delegates didn't even know who was going to run! A few others spoke up and expressed similar views, and McFetridge wasn't overly enthusiastic about us. But I was astonished at the end results—sixty-five thousand dollars was pledged for the primary. These men certainly were in command when they could promise that kind of money without prior consultation with their unions. I'm certain that the federation ultimately contributed well in excess of one-hundred thousand dollars to Daley's general election race against Merriam in addition to the sixty-five thousand dollars pledged for the primary.

"Later on, I found that that many of the unions have what they call 'fifty-fifty clubs,' which operate on a year-round basis. In this way, they always have money available to give to political candidates of both parties as the need arises."

The unions' mainly Catholic general membership were delighted to give general-election support to a "regular" Irishman like Daley rather than to a "snobbish" Irishman like Kennelly, who "just wasn't one of them." Republican candidate Robert Merriam, though a party maverick, was not only non-Catholic but was a budget-trimmer as well. Smaller budgets meant lower wage scales and fewer jobs for the men whose unions banked on placing many older members in city jobs. Daley, on the other hand, held a union card and had established a good labor record as senate minority leader in Springfield. In short, labor could trust him.

Daley's well-developed talents for brokering between policies and men, talents sharpened in the state legislature and in Governor

Stevenson's cabinet, came into full play when, as mayor, he had to oversee Chicago's complex city government. He put them to work not only for his labor constituency but also for management and for the countless other factions whose fierce standoffs or benumbed stalemates required careful judging, juggling, and readjusting of payoffs for political profit. Mayor Daley occasionally judged it expedient to please "good government" people and disappoint the ward committeemen, when he could talk the latter into going along with him—as, for example, when he refused to rescind a controversial educational reform measure. Traditionally, teaching positions in the public schools had fallen under the patronage system, teachers having received jobs simply by presenting letters from their ward committeemen. This practice had ceased under Daley's predecessor, Martin Kennelly, and Daley resisted ward leaders' pressures to reinstate it. Even though the Daley-appointed school board continued to politicize policy making on other issues, it no longer hired teachers on the basis of ward committeeman sponsorship. It is true that Daley courted the party's reformist elements only when necessary, and his police action during the 1968 Democratic National Convention diminished such tolerance as liberals might have been willing to extend toward him. It strengthened his hand with party conservatives, however, as well as with that large segment of Chicago's citizenry who rallied to the law and order issue.

A recurring task for which Daley consistently earned general credit was his conciliation of labor-management disputes. Besides earning the good will of both these chronic combatants, he also created a reservoir of gratitude from a public that could contrast, with relief, Chicago's smoothly functioning services with those of other major cities often paralyzed by public employee strikes in utilities, transportation, and garbage collection. The late Matt Danaher, formerly Daley's administrative assistant, described Daley's method of negotiating:

"If there is a serious labor dispute that looks like it's not going to be resolved, Daley brings in the parties and takes over the entire offices of the complex. Many a time, I've been thrown out of my own office so that Daley could sit the representative of labor or business in my room. He will put their counterparts in another room, and if representatives of the public are present, they go to still another room.

"He will talk to the mediator, if one has already been on the scene, and ask him for his analysis. Daley will then go to each party and ask them what they see their grievances as being, and they will state them. Daley then writes a summary of these grievances. He has a knack for doing this. He then asks them if he has made a correct summary. Invariably, he has. He then takes the main, boiled-down parts from each party to the other parties, tries to secure an agreement, and comes back with a confirmation; if need be, he will modify.

"I remember one instance where he started at five o'clock one evening and stayed there until three in the morning, when they finally hammered out an agreement. He has an unusual ability to reduce lots of arguments to a few crucial main points. This is extremely beneficial in resolving labor disputes."

The cemetery workers' strike of 1971 revealed additional evidence of Daley's expertise in labor-management negotiations. The *Sun-Times* reported that the mayor, skipping dinner, met with the disputants for six hours, ferrying offers between the two parties, who were kept in separate rooms until the agreement was finalized and announced. Tradition-minded members of the Jewish faith had been especially affected by the strike, having to face the equally painful alternatives of either embalming their recently deceased or finding a means of refrigerating them.[11] In settling this strike, Daley gained political capital in the *Gemeinschaft* world of the most personal concerns and cultural traditions of the Jewish community; and he satisfied as well the *Gesellschaft* world of labor and management, in which relationships depended upon formal contract and significant amounts of money were involved. In so doing, he fortified his public image as the mayor of the city that works.

Keeping the city working meant that Daley had to cultivate businessmen and leaders of industry, most of whom were Republicans, for he believed that as business prospered, so prospered Chicago. He appointed businessmen to important committees, massaged their egos, and in the case of the Republican Chicago *Tribune* went so far as to name a new lakefront convention center McCormick Place, after the late *Tribune* publisher. Daley knew that rapprochement paid dividends. He was able to boast, in a speech made before business leaders in 1971, of an unemployment rate in Chicago only half the national average, a state of affairs that was "a genuine testimonial to the strength of the city's commercial and industrial enterprise."[12]

Daley's popularity with the business community made it almost impossible for Republican candidates to oppose him, because the normally Republican businessmen were beholden to the Daley machine. The machine assessed low tax rates and went out of its way to perform favors for cooperative business people. David Halberstam has described the system accurately:

> As [Daley's] power increased, so did his ability to accommodate people, and his ability to tell them to get on the team or be frozen out. Though Daley was strongly opposed by State Street in his first race, he has since practically destroyed the Republican party as a force within the city. He has given the business leaders what they want, a new downtown area, an expressway, a decent police force, confidence in the city's economic future (and if the school system is deteriorating, their children can always go to private or suburban schools). In return he has had his projects carried out with their support, and has gotten their political backing and campaign funds.[13]

It was not only the affluent heads of large businesses and industries who supported Daley and the machine. In a political milieu dominated by one party, small businessmen also received strong inducements to cooperate. A machine leader emphasized this point:

"Now, there's an incentive for the businessmen to play ball with the organization. Even if they're not in trouble, it's a good idea to engage in what we call 'preventive medicine.' You take care of things, and then if troubles do crop up later on, there's no problem.

"For example, the businessman can be cited with violations of the building code. So that's one reason for staying in good. Or a beauty shop can have some inspector come around and say that it doesn't have the right amount of space inside the cubicles or that some chemical isn't quite according to Hoyle. Now, most of the time these city inspectors mean business, because they're out to protect the health of the people—they're very conscious of that, and so is Daley. But I'm talking about the minor technicalities that can bug people who are legitimate, respectable businessmen. This 'preventive medicine' sort of takes care of things, and it only makes good sense for the Republican businessman to play ball with the organization."

As a result, businessmen either gave Daley outright support or, at least, remained neutral, thus making it an uphill struggle for a Republican mayoralty candidate to galvanize their support. The promachine leanings of the business community often prevented Republicans who opposed Daley in elections from raising funds, for example. According to a Republican official, when conservative Republican banker Timothy Sheehan ran against Daley, he received minimal financial support. One of his banker friends told him, "Tim, if it were anybody else, we would help you like we did when you were a congressman, but we can't against Daley." A few did give funds (in cash) but made Sheehan promise he would never reveal their names.

In this same contest, it came as no suprise when the Marshall Field newspapers, the *Sun-Times* and the *Daily News*, supported Daley. Sheehan, however, had every right to expect the pro-Republican *Tribune* to back him, since it previously had designated him the outstanding conservative congressman in America. But when he solicited the backing of *Tribune* executives, they promised only to treat him fairly. Fair treatment turned out to be an editorial describing both Daley and Sheehan as outstanding and urging all Democrats to support Daley, all Republicans to support Sheehan, and independents to follow their consciences. When the Cook County chairman of the Republican party could not even line up Republican newspapers against his Democratic counterpart, he confirmed his worst fears—his mayoralty campaign was dead in the water.

Although wary of and defensive with reporters throughout his mayoralty, Daley maintained cordial relationships with newspaper publishers, whose informed opinions, along with the results of scientifically conducted polls, provided him the reliable information he needed in his role as professional negotiator. Equally valuable to him were the judgments and preferences of other leaders in the business community and of labor spokesmen, fellow politicians, and cronies. Personal consultation with others was, for Daley, an habitual and dependable *modus operandi*. As a matter of routine, he would ask political leaders what they thought of particular people, ideas, and programs and would query businessmen serving on various boards and commissions about current policies.

One prominent Democratic official described Daley's methods of personal consultation as "very interesting." The mayor, said the official, made inquiries in such a way that one could not precisely put one's finger on his own position. Daley: "What is your opinion on the Senate seat, Bob?" Bob: "I think young Stevenson is the strongest man." Daley: "Bob, I'm glad to hear you say that." What the party official would not know was who else the mayor had sounded out and what Daley himself really thought. For this reason, people often referred to him as Buddha, the inscrutable one. A characterization more appropriate to Daley's national ancestry, and one that could have been tailor-made for him, says: "Self-protection over the years had developed in the Catholic Irish a skill for the evasive and noncommittal answer which bordered on artistry; and the examiner who tried to pin one down to a yes-or-no answer only beat his head against genius."[14] Daley, cards close to chest, kept his own counsel to the last moment in most matters but was especially reticent with respect to slatemaking, the area in which I had a personal interest.

Daley's technique for handling those seeking nomination or promoting particular policies might be described as informal, indirect polling: He would assign others the responsibility for collecting opinions, then weigh and balance them all before arriving at a decision. To a person seeking office, he might respond, "Jim, I think you'd make a good candidate. Why don't you go out and test the water?" A highly placed machine member told me that those unfamiliar with how Daley operated often took this for an endorsement, whereas, in actuality, Daley was trying only to discover how much backing the man could generate and at the same time avoid an advance commitment. In like manner, a group presenting a plan for construction of a new airport or hospital might hear him equivocate, "That sounds like a good idea. Let's see what kind of support you can develop." He would use the same approach with a second group pushing another location. In the end, he normally would fall in with the side evidencing the most strength.[15]

Daley consulted often with his "board of directors," that is, with those party leaders whose judgment and interpretations he had learned to trust over the years. One informant described the relationship between Daley and this inner circle: "All of us have access to the mayor if we need it. We don't hesitate to go and argue with him or occasionally ask him to reverse an action. Sometimes he will change; very often he will not. The major thing, though, is that we get an opportunity to make our points. We also have the opportunity to argue it out with him—we can carry ideas in there."

Former alderman Leon Despres offered a similar analysis: "The organization is more like a board of directors than a one-man affair. I think that is a closer analogy. You could call it an oligarchy, too. Daley is very much like the strong president of a big corporation that is owned by the stockholders. Anyhow, that's my observation of it. He has more to say than anyone else about what the policies of the corporation are—what should be done, who gets the promotions, what goals are pushed for, and which ones are abandoned. But his ideas aren't the works—there's no question about that."

Daley's ideas were not "the works" for the reason that he seldom tried to impose them unilaterally. The habitual working methods described earlier—his gathering of up-to-date information, his careful attention to operating details of the city's governmental units, and his cautious but prolific sounding-out of others' views and wishes—point to what might be called a policy of consensual decision making. But if he misinterpreted his data (or did not have enough of it), miscalculated the balance of opinion, or misjudged a situation, the decision he made could prove embarrassingly temporary.

Just such a misjudgment occurred in 1964. Daley and Tim Sheehan, the Republican county chairman, got together and agreed that instead of each party's slating twelve candidates for the county's twelve open judgeships, they would present the voters with a blue-ribbon, coalition ticket and thereby upgrade the general public's image of politics. Under the terms of this agreement, the Democrats would choose eight lawyers of sterling quality and the Republicans four of the same caliber, all twelve of whom would then run unopposed and be assured of election in the fall. Two days later, however, Daley phoned Sheehan: "Tim, I'm sorry, the deal has to be called off." As Sheehan later discovered, when Daley had announced this innovative plan (which would have guaranteed the Democrats eight judgeships) to his board of directors, they had waxed indignant: The moderate Republicans were in disarray, they argued, and could not decide among Rockefeller, Romney, or Scranton. Furthermore, if Goldwater received the nomination, he would become one of the best "Democratic" campaigners in history, and the Democrats would make a sweep of all twelve judgeships. So why give up four judgeships to undeserving Republicans? Daley stood corrected.

Daley decided to run Stanley Kusper for the city treasurer's office. Kusper, a bright young man from Vito Marzullo's Twenty-fifth Ward, was head of the Chicago election board at the time, in which position he could absorb a good many of Marzullo's low-skilled patronage-seekers. He put them to work in election headquarters keeping the election binders and answering phones and hired them as runners to work in the election morgue and to transport and set up the voting machines. The availability of all these jobs helped Marzullo keep the people in his ward happy. When he protested to Daley, "I'd much rather keep those jobs in my ward, Mr. Mayor," Daley did a quick turnaround. He could find another promising candidate for the city treasurer's spot, but it would be hard to deal with a disgruntled Vito. Marzullo's ward organization was one of the most powerful in the city.

Seymour Simon, president of the Cook County board of commissioners, made it known that he wanted to be reslated in 1966, and Daley concurred, for Simon was competent and had a good image. In a public appearance at Evanston's Orrington Hotel, Daley commended Simon on his job as president of the board and announced his continuation in that position for the next four years. However, Daley had ignored some rather widespread grumbling about Simon among the machine's leadership. Chief complainant was powerful Thirty-first Ward committeeman Tom Keane, who was more than a little upset over Simon's refusal to help re-zone an area in Techny, Illinois, for one of Keane's legal clients who wanted to open up a garbage dump there. Keane rounded up other anti-Simon committeemen and informed Daley that they did not want Simon reslated and had the votes to override Daley if he did not cooperate. Daley might have lined up enough slatemakers to renominate Simon had he been willing to pay the price—bloodletting within the political family. Apparently deciding that the price was too high, he gave in to the pressure and reneged on his public support for Simon.

An informant told me that Daley afterwards had exclaimed in astonishment, "Not a single Jew stood up to defend Simon!" Such a defense, my informant said, might have made the difference in Daley's decision. Seymour Simon himself told me that he had upbraided fellow-Jew Marshal Korshak, "If you had objected that you would not *stand* for their dumping a Jew, they wouldn't have done it!"

On matters affecting the city, however, Mayor Daley sometimes challenged other party leaders and made it stick, as when a chance for civic benefits conflicted with relatively unimportant issues of intra-party politics or with a member's special deals. On these occasions, Daley applied his influence. One ward committeeman, for example, had been cut in on a deal by a group wanting to develop a commercial area in the vicinity of O'Hare Airport before it opened. Through his contacts in city hall, the committeeman had successfully steered the development through all zoning and legal obstacles. After a time, when the property had appreciated considerably, he received a call from the mayor. The city, Daley said, needed some of that land, and he would count it a personal favor if the city could purchase it not at its increased value but at its original, per-acre cost. When the ward committeeman, acting as spokesman for the group, balked, Daley went on. Since the city's cooperation had earned the investors a substantial profit, they now were obligated to return the favor, and the committeeman must convince his partners to sell at the low rate to save the city eminent domain litigation. If the landowners cooperated, said Daley, he would continue to help them in the future. Message understood. The committeeman persuaded his partners to sacrifice their personal interests for the greater good of the city's welfare.

Daley the mayor felt justified in asserting himself with respect to this committeeman's fringe-benefit operation. But Daley the party chairman, his primacy in the organization notwithstanding, seldom intruded on the political prerogatives of the elected ward committeeman, whom the unspoken rules made almost unchallengeable sovereigns on matters pertaining to their own wards. His deference to their autonomy is illustrated in a case involving a machine attorney I had worked with in the 1954 Barratt O'Hara congressional campaign:

Daley summoned the lawyer to his office and declared, "I want you to be a judge. You have an outstanding record, and you deserve a judgeship. But your ward committeeman didn't sponsor you last time. So, as much as I want you to be a judge, there's no way I can help you unless he sponsors you in the first place. It's up to you to see to it that he backs you."

The lawyer, worried about his ability to secure his committeeman's endorsement, talked it over with a shrewd bailiff whose tactical skills he respected. The lawyer should ask his clergyman to influence the committeeman, advised the bailiff, since the committeeman had won his party's most recent primary by only a narrow margin. After all, the church's several hundred members comprised a large and significant minority in the ward.

Taking his friend's advice, the lawyer explained the problem to his clergyman, with whom he was very close. His clergyman sent a letter to the committeeman thanking him for his ongoing assistance to the church and indicating a desire for his reelection in the next primary. Church members, he wrote, would be very pleased to hear that the committeeman intended to sponsor the attorney for a judgeship, since the latter was highly respected in the church and would be a credit to the bench. The ward committeeman, not stupid, at the next slating session warmly endorsed the man he previously had overlooked, and Daley winked at the now properly sponsored attorney, acknowledging his ability to play the game. Failure to secure his committeeman's endorsement would have cost the lawyer his judgeship.

Stratarchy was a fact of machine life. The machine could function efficiently and could perpetuate itself only so long as it maintained its stratarchical deference structure. As Matt Danaher remarked, "The mayor doesn't like to go over the heads of ward committeemen, because they are elected in their individual wards and because they represent the voters in that area." This comment underscores the basic philosophy of the organization: Everyone is a kingpin in his own territory unless he proves a gross embarrassment to the machine or unless he fails to produce.

Daley had to produce, too. Leon Despres: "Daley has his authority only as long as he keeps delivering. If he stopped delivering, the men who put him in would be ruthless in putting him out, just ruthless. And what the committeemen like about Daley is that he's the best they've had. He didn't build the organization from formlessness the way Cermak—or even Kelly—did, against odds. He found the organization ready-made, and he greatly strengthened the lines of power to the central group."

And a ward committeeman commented, "Daley listens to the objections of people and fellow politicians; then, he either sets them straight or changes his own position—he has the courage to tell people they are wrong when they are wrong. And he himself has the courage to change, if need be. But regardless of what he does, he makes smart decisions. We expect him to produce, and as long as he produces, we respect him and trust his judgment. If he should fail to produce, then he'd be out on his fanny. You can't argue with success, and Daley has been very successful—he produces time and time again. You can't argue with that kind of track record."

Daley's working relationship with the Cook County organization contingent in the state legislature followed much the same pattern as that with the committeemen (and the two categories often overlapped). He kept abreast of the legislature regarding both the content of legislative bills and the individual performances of the Chicago delegation. A former Illinois house leader told me, "I always made a report to Daley on the members of the legislature so that he could review them and make judgments for the future. In it, I discussed things like attitude, attendance, carousing, chasing women, and legislative performance in general. If I rated a member low on any of these, he could forget about us backing him for something bigger in the city." The high priority Daley placed on legislative performance as the basis for future advancement in office was confirmed by another legislator: "Daley believed in a very important principle: 'As West Point is to the United States Army officer corps, so Springfield and the legislature are to the city of Chicago.'"

This perception of the state legislature as training ground went hand in hand with another idea, that Chicago (not Springfield or Washington) constituted the most desirable locus of political life. One ward committeeman, who was an admirer of Congressman Dan Rostenkowski, said to me (in the late 1970s): "You know, it's a damned shame—Danny's such a nice guy, and if he just wasn't so lazy he wouldn't have to stay in Washington. He could become somebody big in Chicago—maybe even mayor!" Congressman Rostenkowski can feel assured that he has had the good will and political support of this ward leader, whose well-intentioned remark might be interpreted less as naïveté or mere provincial near-sightedness than as a case of *Gemeinschaft* relativity. That is to say, relative to its ethnic neighborhoods, megalopolitan Chicago as a whole might seem to constitute a *Gesellschaft*, the great world beyond the boundaries of Home. But from a different perspective, Chicago could be seen as a *Gemeinschaft*: It was the known, comfortable, accessible locus of unofficial government when compared with Springfield and Washington, which, as seats of official government, represented alien *Gesellschaft* milieus.

Given that perspective, then, the state legislature could best be penetrated, and some measure of control established there, via "letters from home," that is, instructions, reprimands, and the like, from Daley and other machine leaders, in response to "report cards" issued by the "head boys." The state legislature was like a school, where machine delegates learned and practiced the professional skills that essentially *Gemeinschaft*-oriented folk must possess in their dealings with the complex, unreliable, and indifferent (even hostile)

Gesellschaft dimension of modern American culture. The machine contingent in the legislature were, in effect, the Cook County tribe's ambassadors to the government arena where many *Gemeinschafts* met.

Daley respected the rights of the Democratic legislative chieftains to lead their own members in Springfield, which, as were the wards to the committeemen, was the legislators' turf. As long as they performed successfully, they enjoyed much latitude. Successful performance, in this case, meant seeing to it that the legislature allotted sufficient amounts of revenue to Cook County; the greater the amount, the better the city could provide public services and, of course, keep its own tax levy in line. Daley maintained contact with party leaders in the capitol (his phone calls were relayed to the appropriate machine delegate under the code words "Chicago is on the line"). And he engaged them in discussions in which they felt free to speak their minds openly. A former legislative leader defined Daley's role in these discussions: "We would always meet with him when we came back from the legislature and before we went down again. He never came out and told us specifically what to do—he would talk around things and explore things with us but never said, 'I want you to do it this way, or else!' "

This analysis was confirmed by another legislator's description of the relationship between Daley and the machine's two leading spokesmen in the legislature, John Touhy and Art McGloon: "Daley engaged in free and open exchange with Touhy and McGloon. Daley's role focused on Chicago's interests, and he would talk in terms of the realities of the legislature itself and the politics of winning support from respective legislators for policies the machine favored. McGloon focused on how the media would react to various legislative positions, and this frequently led to serious disagreements with Daley. Touhy had the ability to take tough issues such as birth control and look at possible long-range impacts should the party decide to take a stand. At no time did either Touhy or McGloon have to restrict themselves with the mayor, even when they disagreed with him. And the arguments were sometimes *very* heated."

One notable contretemps between Daley and a united front of Touhy and McGloon occurred in 1969. Daley had climbed out on a very weak limb by privately contriving an agreement with Republican Governor Richard Ogilvie on a tax package for the state. The state was badly in need of money, but provisions of the outdated Illinois constitution made it difficult to figure out how to assess corporations and individuals respectively in a way that would be equitable but, at the same time, constitutional. In an interview for *Illinois Issues*, former Governor Ogilvie tells the story:

> We came up with what we thought was a constitutional foolproof way of doing it—a flat 4 percent. . . .
>
> . . . I ran into the situation where [downstate Democrat] Clyde Choate . . . didn't feel that individuals should pay the same as corporations, sort of a classic Democrat position. And Daley, while he was very powerful, was limited on what he could do and he could just not deliver enough downstate senators to pass that revenue program. And I had, of course, a serious problem in my own party.
>
> I had a number of votes I could count on, but it had to be a bipartisan effort and we finally had a compromise. After I talked to Daley, he said, "I just can't get those guys. It's going to have to be a 4 and 2½ split."[16]

Daley could not line up Choate and other downstate Democrats because he also could not "get" two of his own Chicago "guys"— Touhy and McGloon. Art McGloon filled me in on the details of how he and John Touhy foiled the mayor:

"Ogilvie originally wanted a four-percent corporation tax and a four-percent income tax, and Daley was acting fairly noncommittal when Touhy and I talked with him about it. I had the hunch that he and Ogilvie had worked out something where Daley would get a chunk of the action for the city, but he didn't want to talk about it yet. Later on, Arrington [Russ Arrington, the leading Republican in the state legislature] was acting pretty confident that he had the votes to pass Ogilvie's tax package.

"Well, Touhy flailed his arms around and did some cussing and said that this just wasn't going to happen. Then he suggested that neither one of us accept any phone calls from Daley. So when Daley phoned the next day, I told the secretary that I was involved in roll call and couldn't take the call. A second call came fifteen minutes later, and I told the secretary the same thing. The third time, she showed up on the floor in person, and she was almost in tears, and she said, 'Chicago's on the line—you've *got* to take it!' And I refused to. That's how Touhy and I were able to cut out the tax pressure from Daley.

"Then Touhy and I went down to Ogilvie's office. Ogilvie insisted that he couldn't go for only a two-and-a-half-percent income tax because he had made a commitment to the business lobbyists that corporations and individuals would pay the same. We told him that he didn't have the votes and that we did. Furthermore, he would have to kill his bills that would have curtailed our political power in Chicago, we told him. He didn't want to do that, he said—he had campaigned on that issue. We insisted, and he shook hands on it. I said, 'Governor, your word is always good. But if you have a massive heart attack as soon as we walk out of this office, nobody will ever honor the agreement. Please get Smith down here.' [Ralph Smith was the Republican speaker of the Illinois house.]

"Smith came into Ogilvie's office, and the governor threw his hands up in the air and said, 'Ralph, they've got the votes, and we have to kill the four-percent income tax and the election reform.' Smith was shocked. Then Touhy said, 'Ralph, baby, let's go up and kill the bills before anyone changes their mind.'

"And that's how we got the income tax rate reduced and sidetracked the election bills. And when Touhy and I saw Daley that weekend, he said nothing about the phone calls we refused to accept. In fact, he complimented us on making a good deal with Ogilvie."

Although Daley sometimes had a good notion and, in pursuit of it, tried to overstep the limits of his authority, his political success as party leader was attributable largely to his recognition and acceptance of those limits. He understood that delegation of authority and distribution of power throughout key positions in the organization were the most pragmatic and effective ways to preserve stability and to achieve the machine's goal of a better living for its members. Daley would have dismissed the term "stratarchy" as professorial jargon, but he perceived that, operationally, it was this reciprocal deference structure that made the best use of people. Stratarchy worked pragmatically in that it produced concrete results for the machine; but it also functioned symbolically by satisfying people's needs for a sense of responsibility and some measure of autonomy. It was tacitly understood that those to whom authority was delegated would be held accountable to Daley and to other party leaders. But the obverse also obtained: The leader would be continued in his position only so long as he abided by the unspoken rules of the group and facilitated the organization's achievement of its goals. This philosophy of the uses of power and of the powerholders' obligations was part of Daley's Irish political heritage, and it might be said that he not only embodied it but refined it.

Because the preservation of the machine formed the first priority of all its members, any intraparty dissension that threatened to get out of hand had to be dealt with firmly but subtly, to avoid sundering the party. This demanded infinite flexibility on the part of Richard Daley. Daley's flexibility, the handmaiden to his pragmatism, was most sorely tried when he and the inner circle had to deal with truly obstreperous and, from Daley's point of view, unreasonable party elements. Daley would handle these situations by standing firm on his decision but, at the same time, manipulating his antagonist so that the dissident remained within the party but did so *sans* fangs and claws.

The case of attorney John Stamos is illustrative. Stamos, a capable interim state's attorney whom the party refused to slate for a full term of his own, angrily refused the nomination for state attorney general. He considered the offer a sop and stated his displeasure in no uncertain terms. To a Daley emissary who brought Daley's proposal, Stamos said, "I know who sent you over here, and you can tell him to take the attorney general spot and shove it up his ashcan!" The party later slated Stamos for a prestigious appellate judgeship, a move that mollified him and his *Gemeinschaft* group, the Greek community; but it also kicked him upstairs to a position where he was, in effect, out of elective politics.

The case of Seymour Simon has been mentioned earlier. When the machine did not reslate him to the position of president of the county board, Simon, a ward committeeman and alderman, continued to stew over his dumping, irritating Daley and the board of directors so sharply that they appointed him judge of the appellate court and thereby plucked this thorn exactly as they had delivered themselves of Stamos. While Daley could fight rough, subtlety served more purposes. On the many occasions when those who criticized or tangled with him were taken back into the fold, the "fold" frequently turned out to be, in one sense or another, out to pasture. That some of those pastures proved undeniably green with respect to status and economic rewards (a judgeship, for example) did not change the fact that in terms of political power the dissident party member had been effectively neutralized. The pragmatic and flexible Daley and his fellows might "reward" where they could not punish (if punishment might alienate powerful interest groups), but either reward or punishment would serve the same end—self-preservation.

Mayor Daley's handling of social issues reflected his pragmatic approach to resolving conflicts that threatened to endanger the machine. The controversy over the public dispersal of birth control information was one such issue. Daley, a non-ideologue but a strong Catholic, had originally opposed making birth control information available through the county health department. But because of the budgetary pressures generated through the Aid to Dependent Children program, he shifted his stance. With respect to this issue, Daley the *Gesellschaft* man triumphed over Daley the *Gemeinschaft* man, the dictates of financial exigencies in the public sector overcoming the internalized pressure of his religious community's moral values.

One of the most serious and longest lasting controversies the mayor faced in the sixties was the highly emotional dispute over the reappointment of Dr. Benjamin C. Willis, the controversial superintendent of Chicago's public schools. In many ways, it was a battle between competing *Gemeinschafts*, the major antagonists being the blacks and the eastern European ethnics. Most blacks and liberals, viewing Willis as an arrogant racist determined to maintain segregated school patterns, strongly opposed his reappointment in the summer of 1965. Most white ethnics, however, perceiving him as a folk hero committed to preserving the sanctity of the neighborhood school, wanted him retained. Regardless of the ultimate decision, Daley and the machine risked considerable numbers of party defections by essential ethnic groups over this emotionally charged issue.

As Willis's four-year term ran out, Daley's appointed eleven-member school board, containing representatives from most of Chicago's major groups, stood sharply divided on the matter. Three of the appointees functioned as "swing" members because they often demonstrated great flexibility. Amidst the furor over reappointment, the "swing" members met with Mayor Daley and then emerged with a plan barely acceptable to the faction-riven board. They reappointed the controversial superintendent for a period of nineteen months, until his sixty-fifth birthday, at which time he would retire on a generous pension. While this did not really satisfy either the blacks and liberals demanding termination or the white ethnics insisting on a new four-year term, Daley, the master of compromise, nevertheless preserved balance among key segments of the Democratic party by giving something to each side. Had the decision provided either no reappointment or a new four-year term, vital segments of the machine might have defected in the next election.

Daley, at times, appeared to be more than simply politically cautious and protective of the machine; at times he appeared to be antiblack. In 1968, he issued orders to the police department to "shoot to kill" looters and, the *Sun-Times* reported, instructed an investigating committee to look into the part the schools may have played in civil violence.[17] He angrily characterized civil rights demonstrators (some of whom marched through Bridgeport) as troublemakers rather than as concerned American citizens attempting to bring about legitimate social change. Without so much publicity, he once stated, maybe they would get on the bus and go back home, implying that the demonstrators were from out of town, that Chicagoans themselves had nothing to protest about. Dissidents were unwelcome emissaries of the hostile *Gesellschaft* that lay outside Cook County, and Daley, who had enacted a gun-control law, would brook no disorder in his city.[18]

Yet, he was capable of supporting black aspirations on both an individual and a group basis. Cook County Commissioner John Stroger, Jr., a black, told me about the time he was tied up in court and arrived late for the dedication ceremony of the William Dawson Center. He noticed Mayor Daley's eyes looking around until they came to rest on him, from which Stroger understood that the mayor wished to speak to him. After the ceremony, Stroger approached the mayor, who greeted him cordially and, taking him aside, said earnestly, "John, it's very important to realize that in politics you have to keep your priorities straight. William Dawson was the outstanding leader of your people. You are a young leader of your people. You should have been here at the very start and not have come in late. I hope you will always realize how important it is to keep your priorities straight." I did not ask, and Stroger did not say, whether any prominent antimachine blacks were in attendance at this dedication to Dawson. The mayor, of course, would have noticed. After the mayor's death, a prominent liberal lawyer would comment, "I think that Daley, in his own way, was very concerned and interested in blacks pulling themselves up and improving their lot in life. He was not interested in radical changes, though."

Increasingly, he leaned toward blacks in his later years, when the growth of the black population in Chicago and the emergence of black civil rights leaders vastly increased their political bargaining power. Perhaps the most important instance of Daley's belated recognition of blacks was the 1966 open-housing agreement worked out with Martin Luther King, Jr., after weeks of civil rights marches into white neighborhoods. David Halberstam has described the meeting of the two men as "an almost classic conflict of two great forces: Daley with a tightly organized American political base—layer supporting layer of organization structure, votes tangible, deliverable—pitted against a man whose power base was vague by traditional American terms, and was more moral than practical."[19] Eugene Kennedy fleshes out the encounter: "Daley read from a forty-page memorandum, prepared by Earl Bush, which outlined the programs which the city had developed to deal with the problems of discrimination and blight. Dr. King sat uncomfortably with a group of his associates as the mayor read off the list of ordinances, plans, merit-review hiring policies, and other specifics, pausing regularly to raise his head and say, 'We've got this. Now why don't you help us in it!' . . . King would turn to an aide of Daley's at the conclusion of the meeting and say, 'It isn't enough that he's doing these things. He's got to let us do them.' "[20]

It is understandable that Dr. King and other black leaders needed to engage in which might be called "nonrecognition politics," at this time and in this place, to give Chicago's blacks (and blacks across the nation) a symbolic victory. To have recognized Daley's proposals and programs would have felt like moral cooptation, retreat to paternalism, and resignation to plantation politics. The open-housing ordinance was not readily enforced, and Dr. King must have had little hope at the time it was created that the victory would be anything more than symbolic. There was in the Chicago of the mid-sixties no black/reformist power base or countermachine in Chicago strong enough to force the machine to deal with it. That would not come about for several years.

Daley, in the sixties and early seventies, gave blacks as much as his primary power base—the white ethnics—would allow. That was the political reality he faced. But there was another reality as well, a problem facing all major cities across the nation in the post-World War II years: the accelerating influx of blacks (and Hispanics and the poor whites from the near-South) into metropolitan areas and the resulting inability of local governments to take care of their needs. In a 1983 interview in *Chicago* magazine, Cook County Commissioner John H. Stroger, Jr. commented:

People have attempted to criticize Mayor Daley on race, but racism existed in this city and this country way before Daley was born. Under Mayor Daley's leadership, blacks got a chance to participate more actively in city and county government than ever before. When I first came to this city there were no black judges and now there are almost 30 on the Circuit Court. Daley even used his influence to get a black named to the U.S. District Court. He first had the idea that a black hold elected office in city government, and that was Joseph Bertrand as city treasurer.

The social ills that plague big cities—reduction of the tax base, the shift to the suburbs, crime—go back more than 25 years, go back before Mayor Daley. The problems of the cities—Charles Dickens and Victor Hugo wrote about them, and they weren't talking about racism.[21]

David Halberstam, writing in 1968, said of Mayor Daley: "He has managed to keep the machine viable, to bring cost accounting to the city government, to keep up with many reforms in the New Deal tradition, and, in the words of one political scientist, 'to make the machine a limited instrument for social progress.' "[22] And: "It was one of the ironies of Daley's rule of Chicago that because he had succeeded so much in other areas his failures on race relations seemed so marked. Unlike other mayors, one sensed that he had the power to do something."[23]

But did Richard Daley in fact have the power to accomplish large-scale, wholesale social reform? Or, to put it another way, how much influence could he exert in the direction of civil rights and still hold on to the positions (mayor, party chairman) that would allow him to exert any influence at all? These questions, while not easily answered, are nevertheless not idle ones. The extent of Daley's influence can perhaps be assessed by considering some of the thinking of those who have studied the concept of leadership.

In a recent conversation with political scientist Kenneth Janda, I suggested that Daley seemed to me not to have been the unchallenged ruler portrayed by Mike Royko and other members of the media. The media, Janda commented, tend to exaggerate the power of political leaders, partly, he thought, because it is far easier to dramatize a salient individual than an entire group. Referring to the social science literature on the concept of leadership, Janda pointed out that the symphony conductor is commonly used as the model of the omnipotent, authoritarian leader. The conductor need not negotiate with the trumpet players or with the clarinet section. His word is absolute and final. "In contrast with the symphony conductor," said Janda, "you can see that the political leader has all sorts of limitations and must engage in a great deal of bargaining."[24]

Sidney Verba has suggested that the most influential member of a group, that is, its leader, may also be the most susceptible to influence by the other members. "The group's demand for conformity to its norms and the special need of the leader for acceptance by the group combine to place stronger demands for conformity upon the leader than upon any other group member"; and, "Political leaders are expected to conform to group norms and yet to respond to demands for innovation. This leads to special tensions when attempts are made to change group attitudes or behavior in some significant way. Can the leader be at the same time a group leader and a follower of group norms? Can he be at once innovator and conformist?"[25] The fact that Richard J. Daley was able to retain the leadership position in his party (and thus in the city) for more than twenty years lends weight, as do instances presented here, to the supposition that he was under considerable constraint and pressure to conform to his group's norms. He was, further, cross-pressured by demands placed upon him by forces external to the organization he led. It might be said that he was, at one and the same time, the most influential but the most influenced member of the machine.

Edward C. Banfield, in his classic 1961 study, *Political Influence*, wrote:

> When one speaks of the influence of a person, the reference is usually not to what he is doing or has done but rather to what he could do if he tried. A governor, for example, is not without influence merely because he does not choose to exercise any. The pertinent question, usually, is not how the governor *does* change the situation but how he *could* change it. It is seldom enough, however, to know that a person could (or could not) achieve a certain result by exerting all of his influence. Usually there are circumstances that prevent him from exercising more than a part of it. A man with a very modest property may, strictly speaking, have the ability to take a luxury cruise around the world, but he is not likely to take one because he has a family to feed, clothe, and shelter. Similarly, a governor may have ample influence to secure the passage of a certain bill but may fail to exercise it because he must save his influence for other uses.

Thus there are really two separate questions: What is *A*'s ability to achieve the intended result? And, what is his ability to achieve it without incurring disadvantages ("costs") which he regards as equal to or greater than the advantage of the result?[26]

Mayor Daley, as head of Chicago's informal, as well as formal, government, had to "pay" for the powers and influence he had at his disposal. That is, his authority "cost" him. To retain his leadership, he had to trade his influence for the votes that would keep him in his dual position as mayor and party chairman. With respect, specifically, to the racial issue, so long as Chicago's white ethnics outnumbered the blacks in voting power, Daley, to stay in business, had to "sell" his influence to the former.

Banfield says further: "[I]t must be counted a disadvantage of informal control that its operation is, generally, highly uncertain. Here again the question is often one of 'profitability.' If the political head pays a high enough price, he may be able to buy the certainty of being obeyed. But there seems to be a principle of increasing costs at work: beyond a point, each increase in the probability of being obeyed costs more than the one before it, and the total cost becomes prohibitively high long before certainty is reached."[27] If Mayor Daley had managed to enforce the open-housing agreement reached with Dr. King or to institute other large-scale social and economic reform measures in Chicago against the wishes of the white ethnics, he ran the risk of having to pay for this particular exertion of his powers by being turned out of office. This cost would have been, for him, "prohibitively high."

Later on, the costs would decrease. In 1975, we can catch a glimpse of Chicago's political head, Richard Daley, as he expended some influence on behalf of blacks and white ethnics equally. Jeremiah Joyce had just won election as alderman of the Nineteenth Ward and, according to Sanford Ungar, writing in the *Atlantic* in 1977, "immediately became one of Daley's favorites." Ungar continues:

No sooner did Joyce take office than he became convinced that the middle-class communities he represented, Beverly Hills and Morgan Park, were capable of being successfully integrated. "We could live with a 25 percent black population," according to Joyce's estimate, but already the one public high school in the area was 64 percent black; some of the whites who objected to that trend but could not afford to send their children to parochial or private schools were already moving away. The new alderman sought an audience with the mayor, to explain the potential value of "an official fifty-fifty quota system" for the high school in stabilizing the communities. Although Daley was repeatedly on the record denouncing quotas as "un-American," he helped behind the scenes to arrange meetings for Joyce and his allies with members of the Board of Education, and to apply pressure for adoption of Joyce's plan. Today the high school is half white and half black, an arrangement that is enforced through a grammar school lottery. It apparently pleased both racial groups.[28]

The mayor felt able to forward a policy that promoted racial harmony and desirable social change because both the elected alderman of the Nineteenth Ward and his middle-class, racially mixed constituency initiated the policy. Further, and more importantly, it was a policy that required little expenditure of political capital on the part of the mayor but one that profited him in several ways—good government (responsiveness to the constituency), good will (which, potentially, would translate into votes), and social progress (justice to the ward's residents and easing of racial tensions).

In the last year of his life, Richard J. Daley probably would have reasserted a self-assessment levied in 1968: "If I've made mistakes, I've asked for forgiveness, just as I have forgiven others."[29] The statement is sentimental and humble. Yet, its simple acceptance of the facts of a human life, Daley's own, suggests the opposite of its explicit meaning, as if to say, "There really is nothing to apologize for." Revealed is the satisfaction of a broker of men and policies who, successfully balancing coalitions and standing up to the pressures of others' personal ambitions, managed through the years to maintain both his own position and the effective operation of his group, the Chicago machine, and the relatively smooth functioning of the city to which he devoted his life.

This, then, was the man to whom, if I could manage it, I must present a positive image. Failing that, I must at least take care not to threaten what I did know to be Daley's central purpose—to sustain the organization by providing a better living for its members. To this purpose, Daley had to assess accurately the relative power of various claims within the city and pay special attention to maintaining ethnic balance. He had to bargain carefully. He was reluctant to expend political capital needlessly, and as the case of the blacks indicates, he gave only in proportion to what he received, readjusting relative payoffs to ethnic groups when changes in the size of their vote required it.

Above all, the success and maintenance of the machine depended upon its candidates winning office. As a result, Daley was conscious of the need to slate strong contenders and at the same time to forge a ticket appealing not only to regular Democrats but also to independents and liberals, who often could make the difference in a countywide or state election. In order to make a place for myself on that ticket, I had to convince Daley that, of all possible candidates for the post I sought, it was I who could best help the party win the patronage-rich lower offices so vital to the Cook County organization. But, first, I had to demonstrate not only strength within the county but considerable downstate backing as well. In short, my aim was to persuade him that I, too, could bridge the gap between Cook County's complex structure of ethnic-based social and political units (which were dependent upon business and industry for economic survival) and the small, agricultural communities downstate.

It was relative to Daley's role as political leader that Chancey and I went to see him about my bid for the party's endorsement. On the designated day, Chancey and I emerged from the elevator on the fifth floor at eleven o'clock, thirty minutes before our appointment, and encountered the police guard outside Daley's office. The policeman phoned the inner office, received approval for us, and then escorted us into a large reception area. Forty-five minutes later, we were still sitting. Soon, however, we learned that the mayor was engaged in a press conference, convened because of two crises of the previous day. First, a gun battle on Chicago's south side had killed two policemen and, second, the federal government had released a devastating report accusing Chicago of exceeding safe pollution levels within the city. Now newsmen were grilling the mayor of the "city that works."

Daley emerged from this conference red-faced, but for another hour and twenty minutes we were kept waiting, during which time we noticed a number of young men in Ivy League suits carrying, one after another, file folders in and out of the mayor's office. These were the "whiz kids," whose expertise and image Daley found useful. Finally, nearly two hours after our scheduled appointment, Daley appeared at the door, made a circular motion with his thumb, like that of a beckoning umpire, and yelled out, "Chancey!" We entered the sanctum sanctorum.

The norms by which Daley operated became apparent at once. His original recognition had been directed toward my political sponsor, Chancey—for here was county chairman speaking to county chairman, political leader to political leader. And now it was Chancey, by previous agreement between us, who opened the conversation. He could advocate without appearing presumptuous, as I could not, and as my sponsor, it was his role to speak first.

"Mr. Mayor, Mel has gone through the appropriate procedure. The first thing he did was to see me and clear it with me. I decided he would be a strong candidate. He helped us a lot during Governor Shapiro's campaign, and I give him plenty of credit for our carrying Jackson County for Shapiro, while we lost most of the other downstate counties. He has consistently shown that he is a winner. The second point is that we followed the right procedure by going to the state central committeeman, Clyde Choate. Clyde arranged for us to talk to Paul Powell."

At that, the mayor grinned, approving our observance of protocol, and then he turned to me: "What is your financial backing?"

"Well, Mr. Mayor, John Alesia of the steelworkers authorized me to say that I'll receive financial backing from his union as well as from other unions. And I've been assured by the Jewish community that I'll receive the same kind of support that any other candidate of my ethnic background would receive. [Governor Shapiro had told me to use this phrase.] So, organized labor and the Jewish community are my two main sources of financial support."

"What's your background?"

"I've worked politically within the party for . . . "

"No, no, I mean education background—do you have a Ph.D.?"

"Yes."

"Good."

I had the distinct impression that had I said, "no," he quickly would have eliminated me as a possible candidate.

Next question: "Do you have a family?"

"Yes, Mr. Mayor, I'm married to a wonderful Chicago girl. We have three fine children, and my wife comes from a solidly Democratic family. In fact, her father has worked very hard for the organization." I was hoping Daley would ask my father-in-law's name, but he did not.

We talked a bit longer, and after only four-and-a-half minutes had elapsed (I timed it), the mayor arose, shook our hands, and began to usher us out. Feeling heady with what I took to be our success, I attempted what I thought could be a master stroke—one, however, that requires some explanation.

A friend of my father-in-law, long experienced in the ways of Chicago politics, had advised me that I should tell the mayor I wanted him to be my top consultant and to handle my patronage for me. To this I had replied, "Nothing doing. If I can't handle my own office, then I don't want the job. I'm not going to have it run by the mayor of Chicago. There are just too many professional slots in this area that he wouldn't be acquainted with. Furthermore, I'm in a better position than Daley to assert academic expertise—he's spent his entire adult life in nonacademic jobs."

"Of *course* the mayor doesn't expect to do that! Tell him you want him to handle your nonprofessional patronage."

"No. I've already committed myself to my county chairman on that, and I can't go back on my word."

"Look, Mel, at least ask Daley for his advice. It will be music to the old pro's ears."

Soon after this conversation took place, I discussed it with Chancey, telling him that I had responded negatively to the suggestion. Chancey said, "No—if that's what it takes to get the nomination, let's do it. It means that I'll be second in command on nonprofessional patronage, and that's okay. It won't bother me a bit. And, besides, Daley might say 'no.'"

So, now, as Daley began to show us out of his office, I turned to him and said, "Mr. Mayor, I'm not just an educator—I'm politically oriented, too. If I become the nominee, I'd like to consult with you on campaign strategy as well as on nonprofessional patronage."

At that, his face reddened, and he retorted sharply, "No, no, we have too many politicians around. I'm looking for an educator, not a politician. That office has already turned into an embarrassment to the other party. I want to avoid that kind of stuff. I want a professional education man in that office who isn't worried about pleasing me on patronage. The only thing I ask is that you do a good job if you get it, not embarrass the party, and give us something we can point to with pride. I want a well-educated man for that slot."

Daley's reprimand made me feel like a kid caught with his hand in the cookie jar—I had presented myself in the role of politician, and he had found it necessary to set me straight for not focusing on my role as educator. An astute politician later explained to me, "Daley probably wasn't against your being aware of patronage, but he didn't want to place himself in the position of letting an outsider claim that he had talked patronage with Mayor Daley."

The second half of my remark to Daley—that if I received the nomination I would like to consult him on campaign strategy—had not been a mistake but was not a novel suggestion, since Daley did make himself available for such consultation. One politician told me, "During the times that I was on the state ticket, we would meet with the mayor three or four times as a group. Sometimes he would meet with us individually."

A candidate session with Daley, one informant said, was like a lightning-fast game of pitch and catch between professional baseball players. The candidates would "burn in" really tough questions, and the level of toughness would accelerate through the session. Daley could shoot out the answers as quickly as the questions came, and his specific, detailed answers would leave the group marvelling at his grasp of the intricate facets of individual issues, particularly the difficult ones.

Going to "school" under Professor Daley was something I would enjoy immensely, but I knew, and the experienced Daley knew, that in the end the candidate had to campaign for himelf. Reminiscing about the mayor one time, Art McGloon recalled: "Daley always used to say, 'You can put a guy on the dance floor, but he's gotta do the dancing himself.' "

As Chancey and I were about to leave the mayor's office that afternoon, Daley looked me straight in the eye and said, "Mel, there's a lot of talk at times about things being wrapped up. Let me give you my word that this endorsement isn't locked up. It's still open. I've seen people come into the slatemaking session, do the best job, and walk off with the endorsement. Your work is cut out for you. Continue what you are doing in trying to show your endorsement by many backers, but when you come before the slatemakers, make it the best presentation of your life. Good luck."

The Walter Mitty fantasies in which I had bowled the mayor over with my savvy and winnability had not survived the reality test in our face-to-face meeting. But I did find out later that Mike Bakalis and I were the only aspirants with whom Daley had seen, a discovery that helped assuage my embarrassment at the memory of how he had slapped my hands for talking patronage. And, after all, he had given his word that the nomination would remain open until, a few weeks hence, the candidates faced the slatemakers, the final act in the drama of seeking office.

Having played my scene with the leading character, Mayor Daley, my interpretation of my script called for me to seek out a very important supporting actor—Paul Powell, who was to downstate Illinois what Daley was to Cook County. My next scene would be set in Springfield in the office of the man known as The Gray Fox of Vienna.

5

Paul Powell:
The Gray Fox of Vienna

In 1969, Paul Powell, after almost forty years in Illinois politics, had achieved the leadership of downstate Democrats. The term "downstate" was used to refer loosely to all areas of Illinois outside of Cook County itself, and the party bond between the Cook County Democratic machine and the state organization was an intricate one. In his book, *Don't Make No Waves, Don't Back No Losers*, Milton Rakove analyzes this bond:

> The history of the relationship of the Chicago Democratic machine to the Democratic party in the state of Illinois is a record of subordinating statewide Democratic interests to the interests of the Chicago machine. The major thrust of the Chicago machine's policies toward downstate Democrats has been to try to make sure that no powerful statewide organization is created as a counter-vailing power center to the Chicago organization. In pursuit of that primary goal, the Chicago organization has always been prepared to deal with downstate Democrats and Republicans on a *quid pro quo* basis of dividing up the political spoils so that politicians in both parts of the state can remain secure in their power bases and benefit from state policies which would protect those bases.[1]

This gentlemen's agreement was broken only once, Rakove says, when Democratic maverick Dan Walker defeated machine-slated Lieutenant Governor Paul Simon in the 1972 gubernatorial primary race.[2] Rakove is correct insofar as the office of governor is concerned. But twenty-three years before Walker successfully challenged the

Daley machine, Paul Powell flung down the gauntlet in the 1959 contest for the speakership of the Illinois House of Representatives. Even though Powell had served as speaker in 1949, the 1959 contest was more significant because it pitted him against Mayor Daley and the Chicago machine. Most importantly, this contest enhanced significantly the leadership role of Powell as a power-broker in the state Democratic party. How Powell managed this feat will be recounted later in some detail.

But as my own campaign progressed, I was about to have a meeting with this colorful, near-legendary figure. I already had heard a wealth of anecdotes about Powell and had gleaned perspectives on the man both from those who knew him well and those who did not. If Richard J. Daley remained something of a complex study even to his friends and longtime associates, Paul Powell apparently presented a simpler face to the world. This is not to say that opinion of him was not divided: at the extremes, he was viewed either as an admirable legislative leader whose self-identification with the little guy was complete, or as the personification of government venality who never missed an opportunity to sell out his populist constituency to the moneyed interests. There is much evidence to support both claims. But when I asked people to tell me about Powell, I got the clear impression that many of those who viewed him in the second way liked him in spite of themselves.

Anecdotes about Powell were many and choice. He emerged in these stories as engaging raconteur and rousing stump orator; as shrewd political wheeler-dealer in the legislature and gaudy campaign showman who was his own best act; as financially generous to others yet neurotically parsimonious in his private lifestyle. He was known to be a *bon vivant* numbering hundreds of acquaintances, but, according to one of his friends Powell was an intensely lonely man, despite the gregarious surface.

As my impending meeting with him grew closer, a wave of concern swept over me. I was looking forward to the encounter because of Powell's reputation as a highly stimulating personality, but I was also aware that foremost among his party foes was my friend and mentor, Jackson County chairman Ray Chancey. Wisely, Chancey had taken this mutual dislike into account by arranging for one of Powell's friends, Harry Kilby, to accompany me into the interview (Chancey would join us only toward the end). So, on a crisp morning in early September 1969, Ray, Harry, and I set out for

Springfield for this all-important meeting. As we left the outskirts of Carbondale, I was glad for the leisurely drive ahead, which would contrast sharply with my hectic schedule of the past few weeks. But I found myself musing uneasily on the reasons for Chancey's and Powell's disaffection.

Because he was a successful realtor, Chancey, unlike most downstate county chairmen, did not choose to hold a patronage job from Powell and therefore was not subject to Powell's political pressure. There were other sore spots in the history of their relationship. For instance, Chancey had objected swiftly and strenuously when Powell hired an outsider for the Jackson County driver's license office. In fact, Chancey's stringent protest had compelled state central committeeman Clyde Choate—himself a protégé of Powell—to influence Powell to transfer the interloper out of the license bureau.

A more intense friction had developed concerning a dinner honoring C. L. McCormick, a Republican state representative hailing from Powell's home town of Vienna. Although billed as a nonpartisan event to "honor an outstanding public servant," its purpose, from Chancey's point of view, was to raise money and provide free publicity for McCormick's reelection effort. Since Chancey wanted to elect a Democratic representative from his own county, he took umbrage at Powell's role as master of ceremonies for a Republican incumbent's fund-raiser. Chancey protested so vehemently that the influential *Southern Illinoisan* featured his criticism on its front page, and even Clyde Choate found it opportune to announce that a previous engagement would prevent his attendance at the dinner.

These two occurrences had intensified the preexisting friction between Powell and Chancey, and I found myself in a quandary: Chancey was my sponsor, but, realistically, I could not acquire a statewide nomination without support from Powell, the second-most powerful Democrat in Illinois and the man who represented the key to downstate slating power. During most of his thirty years in the state legislature, Powell had towered above all other downstate party leaders and, moreover, had become secretary of state, the most prominent Democrat state official in Illinois. This office controlled great numbers of patronage jos and thus permitted continuation of Powell's legislative influence.

Powell enjoyed many friendships with county chairmen, and, in addition to these personal bonds, his patronage often provided the lifeblood for their political organizations. He was even able to collect political due bills from the Daley machine. Since the vast secretary of state operation included many political appointments in Cook County, it could hire out-of-work Cook County Democrats whenever Republicans captured such patronage-rich offices as president of the Cook County board and state's attorney. In short, the machine had to pay deference to Powell because he wielded great power in the state legislature and could take care of Cook County machine loyalists with his patronage.

Paul Powell was truly a son of the southern Illinois small-community culture. Informality, emphasis upon friendship, early poverty, and a firm view that the political process should benefit one's friends—all these qualities characterized Powell. His down-to-earth style expressed itself in unrefined mannerisms, an indifferent taste in clothes, and speech patterns that included a fondness for aphorisms couched in the universal language of food: "My daddy always said, 'If you can't get a full dinner, then settle for a sandwich' "; "I smell the meat a-cookin' "; "My friends always eat at the first table"; "The horses that do the pullin' in the field will be the first ones the hay is thrown to."

Powell related to his constituents in the personal and direct manner that the small-community environments of downstate Illinois made possible. Better even than the captains of Chicago's precincts, he had a gift for making people feel important and demonstrating his concern for them. A southern Illinois political worker testified to this concern: "My husband died at about three-thirty on a Friday afternoon. On Sunday evening at the funeral home, something happened that a person just doesn't forget. It was in February, and the weather was very, very bad. At nine-thirty that night, Paul Powell came rolling up in his limousine—he had traveled eighty-five miles on dangerous, icy roads to pay his respects. He never forgot to help his friends in time of need, and I won't forget what Paul did till my dying day."

Powell returned to Vienna each Memorial Day to place flowers on graves, and at Christmas time he distributed dozens of poinsettia plants to friends and acquaintances. During his sojourns in his hometown, it was his habit to walk its familiar streets and stop to talk to and shake hands with people who were down on their luck.

Helping friends in difficulty was an important part of Powell's make-up, but it was one that sometimes brought him under attack.

When Republican State Auditor Orville Hodge was the toast of Springfield, he lived in the penthouse of the St. Nicholas Hotel, where Powell occupied far more modest quarters. Hodge would give his old, monogrammed shirts to the thrifty Powell, who would wear them monogram and all. Some years later, Hodge went to prison for embezzlement, and most Illinois politicians developed instant amnesia at the mention of his name. Powell, on the other hand, visited him regularly and attempted to secure his early release, standing by his friend when others turned away. When it came to spending his money in the course of daily life, Powell was a skinflint (he often left only ten-cent tips in restaurants), but he generously came to the rescue of friends or employees with burdensome health problems. In one instance, he wrote out two checks totalling more than $16,000 for a friend whose wife had to undergo cobalt treatment at the Mayo Clinic.

Powell seemed possessed by a compulsive need to surround himself with an ever-expanding circle of others. This included a reaching-out to clergymen of all faiths, and, although a Protestant, he nonetheless numbered among his many good acquaintances both priests and rabbis. Early in his career, his close friend Tony Cassolary arranged for him to meet for some charitable purpose with a large group of priests. Powell at first felt uncomfortable with the idea, because he himself was a Mason. In the end, he borrowed a Knights of Columbus pin from one of his aides, met with the clergymen, and captivated them all. He struck up a special friendship with Father Calhoun and, impressed with his new friend's speaking prowess and great devotion to the Democratic party, often used him for benedictions at downstate Democratic rallies. Father Calhoun's favorite prayer on such occasions took the following form: "Dear God in Heaven, we know that you are a Democrat. And you know that we are all Democrats. Please bestow your blessings on this important Democratic rally so that we will have the strength and the ability to win the election. Amen." Father Calhoun's assumptions about the Deity's political preference no doubt amused Powell, who loved a good joke—and the more obvious the joke the better.

With respect to personality, the differences between Powell and Daley could not have been greater. Daley could be charming when he chose to be, and those close to him have attested to his ability to relax among friends. But others have commented on the reserve and wariness that seldom permitted them to feel easy in his presence.

ell you a story that gives the lowdown on them
re was this boy who was chasin' a rabbit, and the
hollow log. The boy went in there after 'im and got
and wiggled, tryin' to get out, but he just couldn't
sheer desperation, the boy got to thinkin' about
nd his Republican Depression. This made 'im sink
t crawled right on outa there! [Laughter.]
mphrey's Republican opponent has made a lifelong
the special interests—the fat cats. And when John
m in 1960—and that's what Hubert Humphrey's
8 [applause]—he got himself a job on Wall Street,
comfortable. After all, he took care of them people
nd the least they could do was pay 'im back—fat-cat

his campaign, you and me better keep tabs on this
. For instance, he's goin 'round tellin' people not to
 to a candidate's party. Well, I can't say as I really
elonged to the sorry Republican party—that opposed
that favors the rich, that's opposed ever' single piece
hat's ever been proposed for helpin' the average
d be ashamed to admit it, too. [Laughter.] And that's
 long-standin' offer—an offer that no Republican ain't
 to take me up on: Show me *one important* thing the
er done for the average person, and I'll eat the biggest
ou can find. Believe me, it's a safe offer! [Wild

e of us that love America, our country can't afford a
esident. We *need* Hubert Humphrey—and we need 'im
to work, work, *work* for this great man. As people with
se, you owe it to yourselves. As good Americans, you
r country. If we carry the message to the American
core the biggest upset since Harry Truman did the job in
applause.]
we carry Illinois, we'll carry the nation for Hubert
the most important office in the world—president of the
 of America!" [Applause, whistles, cheers.]
 rousing address and the winding-down ceremonies that
ade my way through the crowd, shook Powell's hand,
ulated him on his speech and on his loyalty to

Powell, on the other hand, endeared himself to numbers of his constituents and fellow politicians by his great capacity for fun, even if sometimes at the expense of others. As a prankster, he was both inventive and opportune. In the 1968 general election campaign, he often subsidized financially strapped candidates by inviting them to travel with his party, all expenses paid. One candidate accepting Powell's offer was Fannie Jones, who sought the post of clerk of the Illinois Supreme Court. One day, as they prepared to fly back to Springfield from Chicago in a four-seater plane, Powell instructed the pilot to stand behind a pillar where no one could see him. Powell then escorted Fannie Jones and Jim White, his purchasing director, to the plane. He helped Jones into one of the back seats and buckled her in. Then he climbed into the pilot's seat next to White.

Powell turned around and said, "Fannie, there's nothing to worry about. I got my license last week, so I know all the latest stuff." To White, he mumbled: "Jim, this panel isn't like what we saw in the book. What's this button?"

At that point, Jones, wrenching at her seat belt, yelled, "I'm getting out! I'm not going to fly in this plane!"

This sort of practical joke lent credence to a description of Powell, by one of his friends, as "a kid who never grew up," as does the story about the time someone sent Powell (then Illinois secretary of state) a box of decorated yo-yo's that glowed in the dark. For weeks thereafter, he practiced yo-yoing in his office, darkening the room so that any visitors could see how well the yo-yos shined. The kid in Powell was evident, and audible, every time he drove his Cadillac to athletic events, which he entered with sirens screaming. Some of the more adult varieties of play in which he indulged included cruises on luxury yachts provided by friends and occasional jaunts to Las Vegas. At the race track, he always bet on the gray horse if one were running—purportedly a good-luck gesture because of his own nickname, "The Gray Fox."

The child in Powell manifested itself in darker ways, however, ways that took the form of compulsions and obsessive fears. His fear of personal poverty led him, for example, to engage in hoarding. Even after he became secretary of state, he continued to occupy the same dingy room at the St. Nicholas Hotel where he had lived during his years in the legislature. The view from his window was a depressing one, looking out as it did on the parking lot of the railroad station across the street. But after his death in 1970, nearly $800,000 was discovered in shoe boxes in a closet of his room. One of Powell's sources of funds consisted of the small bills people would thrust into his hands or pockets when he traveled throughout the state meeting constituents. No one, it was said, ever saw Powell spend these rolled-up, crinkled bills; so, in all probability, they went directly into his hoard. People also gave him gifts of food, which he stashed in his freezer, and a friend reported that some of it stayed there for more than fifteen years and had long become spoiled. One story told of the time Powell instructed his chauffeur, Emil Saccaro, to take a ham home to the missus. Saccaro picked up the ham, but it was so rancid he had to throw away the clothes he had on.

Personal eccentricities aside, Paul Powell was the craftiest political leader in downstate Illinois. A man who never lost an election race in his life, he had earned the respect of top state leaders of both parties for his political acumen. The high mark of Powell's political campaigning occurred in 1960, when, wearing the largest Masonic pin he could find, he stumped downstate for John F. Kennedy—an act that demonstrated much political courage, since downstate sentiment ran heavily anti-Catholic. At the end of every speech, Powell would state dramatically:

> When John F. Kennedy was out in them icy waters savin' his men,
> he didn't ask what their religion was. Our only question should be:
> Is he a true American, and will he make a great American
> president? The answer is "yes" on both counts.

As Powell traveled around Illinois, newsmen often tagged along to cover his activities, and, though he sustained running feuds with their publishers, most of the newsmen joined him for meals and banter. One evening at supper, a reporter complained teasingly, "Mr. Powell, isn't that story about John Kennedy out there in the Pacific getting a little old? Can't you do something to change it?"

Powell replied, "Yeah, that's a good idea. Tonight when I've got 'im out in them icy waters, I'm gonna throw about eight sharks in there—with plenty of blood flowin'."

Powell was an awesome political campaigner, and Senator Paul Douglas dubbed him "the best stump speaker in America." Because his presence provided a sure-fire draw for large crowds, candidates and county chairmen avidly sought him to speak at their rallies, whose partisan Democratic audiences loved his style and boisterously

cheered him on when
shared patronage an
enjoyed excoriating th

I gained firsthand
his campaign for reele
Taylor, a reporter for t
really wanted to see the
Vienna for the Gray Fo
how many dozens of r
Paul Powell performan

The Vienna High
bunting and gigantic A
five bands playing patri
thousand. (Vienna itself
The stage was packed w
governor, Sam Shapiro,
early October, and the D
the state ticket. Hubert H
of the 1968 Chicago Den
no signs of political resu
liability to the party's slate
forces had grimly set up se
effort to lighten the load o

The popular Powell,
introduced the candidates,
singled out for special prai
served in the Illinois legisl
speech:

"Fellow Americans:

"The men you've met h
they seek. They're good m
personal friends of mine, and

"But there's one office th
because it affects each and ev
that's the office of president o

"Hubert Humphrey has
to be president. He has stood
factory worker. He has stood
crystal clear, and he's always
people like you and me.

"Now, I'll t
Republicans. The
rabbit ran into a
stuck. He wiggle
move. Finally, i
Herbert Hoover
so low that he ju

"Hubert Hu
career of servin'
Kennedy beat
gonna do in 196
where he felt *re*
for many years,
style.

"Now, in t
tricky candidate
pay no attention
blame 'im. If I
social security,
of legislation t
person—then I'
why I repeat m
never been abl
Republicans ev
bale of hay
applause.]

"For thos
Republican pr
bad. I ask you
good horse se
owe it to you
people, we'll s
1948! [Loud

"And if
Humphrey fo
United State

After thi
followed, I
and congrat
Humphrey.

"Young man," he replied solemnly, "it ain't much of a man that won't stand up for his friends when they need help."

Powell expected his friends to repay the favor when he needed their political support, and one of the methods he used to make paying the piper easier for them was the bread-and-circuses approach. An adept showman, Powell has been described as a carny at heart who reveled in the spectacular rallies and galas that made up his campaigning stock in trade. The state politicians who begged his attendance at affairs in their home areas scrambled likewise to include themselves in any political entertainments he staged. During his first race for Illinois secretary of state in 1964, Powell the impresario exceeded his own personal best when he brought in former President Harry Truman to add a touch of national prestige to his parade and rally. Powell got a notion to use only Ford convertibles and let his aides know that he favored Lincoln Continentals, if they were available. As a result, franchisers throughout the country supplied these luxury-model cars for the big event. Powell passed out campaign buttons containing fifty-cent pieces, an heretofore unheard of gimmick, and distributed specially designed shopping bags, sun visors, and balloons by the thousands. Inviting seventy-five high school bands to perform in the parade, he paid their motel bills, dinner and breakfast included, at a cost of more than $23,000. But the biggest parade attention-getters were the aerial bombs—Powell arranged to have one set off every three minutes. "I want *ever'body* to know I'm in town," he declared.

Although campaigning for himself and others constituted a pleasurable necessity for Powell, the "meat and potatoes" of his political career lay in the state legislature, an arena ideally suited to his rural way of being in the world. An assessment of Powell's position in the stratarchy of Illinois power politics was given me not long after I moved to Carbondale to take up my teaching duties at SIU. In response to my question, "Who is the most powerful downstate leader?" a high-ranking state party official responded, "The man who delivers the most downstate votes is Mayor Al Fields of East St. Louis—he operates his own machine. But Paul Powell, even without a strong organization of his own, is the most powerful downstate Democrat because of his unrivaled influence in the state legislature."

Powell understood well the clubhouse nature of the Illinois legislature. While all American legislative bodies possess varying degrees of camaraderie, in Powell's Illinois the legislative bond was singularly pronounced because the lengthy tenure of those elected produced a high degree of membership élan. The relative lack of legislative turnover stemmed largely from the state's unique system of cumulative voting. Under this procedure, each of the multi-member legislative districts elected three legislators in the lower house. A voter could cast a total of three votes and divide them any way he or she wished—three votes for one candidate, one-and-a-half votes for each of two candidates, or one vote for each of three candidates.[3] As a result, minority representation was virtually guaranteed—if a majority party put up three candidates, that party's voters would split votes, whereas the minority party candidate would receive all three votes from his party's voters.

Regardless of party affiliation, all legislators were considered to belong to "the club," with Powell leading the way in promoting the concept of a club membership that cut across party lines. Two incidents are illustrative. When Democrat Sam Shapiro of Kankakee first decided to run for the state legislature, he paid a visit to Democratic leader Powell seeking counsel on campaign strategy. Powell told him that as a matter of tradition he always supported the incumbent, irrespective of party, and therefore could not give Shaprio campaign assistance. "But," he added, "if you win—if you're elected to the legislature—then you'll be a member of the club, too. And I'll give you all the help you need any time you run for the legislature." Another time, a veteran state representative came under heavy fire from the media when they discovered that vouchers for travel between Springfield and his home in downstate Illinois included a detour to southern California. Powell pointed out to the legislators that their errant colleague had been a member of the club for many years, and, since his wife was giving him a hard time, he was entitled to take a little side-trip. Powell's "one of our own" appeal persuaded the legislators not to punish the itinerant.

Despite his much-publicized chicanery in business ventures, Powell was known to keep his word to fellow legislators, a quality essential for building mutual respect within the club and for facilitating productivity among its membership. He repeatedly stressed the superiority of the legislature as a training ground for any other political office: "There oughta be a law that the boys have to have legislative experience before they can become members of the executive branch. Then they'll have some idea of what government's all about." Legislators, to a person, agreed with Powell and appreciated his articulation of the idea as well as his more specific follow-up: "You can't flip a guy into the governor's chair. He's gotta have some real legislative background and experience, or he'll never understand what it's all about."

Powell habitually lent money to both active and former members of the legislature—for two reasons: First, he genuinely held legislators in high esteem, and it pleased him to render them a personal service (though he always had his aide, Bob Walsh, check into these loan requests to confirm their legitimacy). Second, Powell's loans obligated other politicians, whose chits he later could collect in a showdown on the floor of the legislature. One classic story concerns a legislator who, when Powell agreed to lend him $10,000, asked for the note to sign. Powell responded, "What the hell, ain't your word good enough?" Evidently, to Powell, the *Gemeinschaft* principle of mutual club membership sufficed—a formal note was a *Gesellschaft* phenomenon and had no place here.

As leader of the legislative club, Powell could shepherd bills through the law-making process with remarkable success. On behalf of his own constituency, he helped Southern Illinois University transform itself from a small normal school to a megaversity. People throughout southern Illinois acclaimed him the patron saint of the booming school that bolstered agricultural and economic development in the region, spawned many doctoral programs, lured several distinguished emeriti faculty to its campus, and possessed a fleet of seven airplanes. In addition, Powell pushed for the completion of Highway I–57 through southern Illinois before most main roads had been built in the northern part of the state. He looked after his people.

But he also took care of others with whom he had made alliances. Club members knew that Powell's presence in their corner would likely ensure their bills' passage. Public officials throughout Illinois, especially those in small towns, felt they could rely on Powell to resolve their political difficulties with the state irrespective of party affiliation. In reciprocation, Democratic and Republican leaders alike gave him patronage, which he skillfully purveyed into jobs for his constituents.

Powell reached a milestone in his legislative career when the Illinois house elected him speaker in 1949. Notwithstanding differences with Governor Stevenson in both style and legislative substance,

Powell performed loyally as legislative leader and competently discharged his responsibilities to his party's patrician governor. One of Stevenson's major campaign planks had been creation of a fair employment practices commission (FEPC). Even though Powell's own southern Illinois region fervently opposed FEPC, he led the fight for its passage and saw it squeak by with the narrow margin of four votes. Another time, Powell, allegedly on the take from the truckers' lobby, nevertheless lived up to his speakership vows when he pushed through a bill limiting the weight of trucks on the highways. An appreciative Stevenson called him in and thanked him for his help. Powell replied, "Governor, I'm sure glad you're givin' me your thanks, 'cause that bill cost me the fifty-thousand bucks I woulda got from them boys."

Stevenson could count on Powell to do his job; but he could not count on him to hold his tongue. Powell was capable of waxing bluntly critical of Stevenson and once told him: "Governor, you've got only one problem, but it's a big one. You don't understand the people. You were born on the wrong side of the tracks with a gold spoon in your mouth. You're gonna have to get over that and start thinkin' like real people do." Whatever Stevenson might have felt about this unsolicited opinion, his high regard for Powell's legislative acumen was borne out in a note he sent Powell in October 1949: "Dear Paul, . . . I think there is no doubt from all I have heard that you established a new level of performance, tempered by humility and humor—two virtues that have become all too rare in our public life. The Governor is proud and fortunate to be on the Speaker's side of the aisle!"[4]

Others agreed with Stevenson's recognition of Powell's legislative craftsmanship. John Bartlow Martin, in his biography of Stevenson, observed: "[U]sually by the time a bill reaches final passage a close watcher can predict the outcome. In those days [the late 1940s] only a few legislators—Paul Powell was one—possessed the power to actually change votes during debate."[5] This comment points both to Powell's political savvy and his extraordinary oratorical prowess. In the words of a senior legislator, "We would often close the doors of the chamber so that no staff would enter while Powell was in a debate. We wanted no distractions while listening to him." Another legislative veteran remarked, "There were many things that I found interesting about my service in the Illinois legislature. But nothing could ever come close to the experience of watching and listening to Paul Powell on the floor of the house."

While Powell remained faithful to Stevenson in the policy area, this did not prevent him from going about the business of helping himself and like-minded legislators consummate special money-making deals. The most widely publicized such deal took place in the wake of the 1949 session, wherein the legislature unanimously passed a bill legalizing harness racing at Sportsman's Park. Powell did not formally sponsor the measure, but he was known to be the guiding force behind it. Subsequent to its passage, twelve people—Powell, a handful of fellow politicians and their wives, and some state employees—got in on the ground floor when Sportsman's Park interests offered them large blocks of stock at the ludicrous price of ten cents per share. Former state Senator Paul Simon, referring only to "a shrewd, folksy downstate Representative," described the deal:

> He bought nearly 17,000 shares in his wife's name and was allowed more than a year to pay. Meanwhile, he received $16,900 in "dividends," enabling him to "buy" the stock without any capital outlay whatever.
>
> The Chicago *Sun-Times* . . . reported that his return on this investment amounted to $23,000 in 1963. When a reporter queried him about the transaction . . . he replied, "The only mistake I made was that I didn't get more."[6]

While Powell had done nothing technically illegal (he had purchased the stock after the measure had passed) many legislators considered the low purchase price as good as a payoff for the bill's passage. Powell, of course, saw it merely as a chance to steer some available benefits toward his friends and himself. He particularly disturbed Governor Stevenson by cutting Jim Mulroy in on the deal. Mulroy, the governor's executive secretary, gave $100 for 1,000 shares of stock and received a quick return of $1,750, no mean profit by any standard. When the newspaper stories broke, Mulroy protested his innocence—he had acted, he said, fully within the law. Stevenson, much to his disgust but mindful of the taint on the administration, had to ask him to resign. Though the governor valued Powell's stalwart support of substantive policies, he deplored Powell's political ethics.[7]

In one instance, some of the Cook County delegation found Powell's deals a nuisance. George Dunne, president of the Cook County board and former state legislator, told me the following story:

"I remember when the legislature passed a bill increasing the state sales tax to bring in some much-needed revenue. And Abner Mikva was sponsoring a bill that would increase the tax on racing as well. But Powell had proposed a tax bill that would protect the racing interests.

"I went to talk to Paul about the situation, and I pointed out that the legislature couldn't be in the position of sticking an additional sales tax on the people while letting the race tracks off—that it wouldn't be fair to the little guy. But Powell wouldn't back down.

"Well, when Mikva's bill came to the floor, I voted for it, several others from Chicago did, too, and Powell's bill went under."

In the battle of the race track tax, some members of Cook County's delegation gave substance to Mayor Daley's perennial proposition that "good politics is good government, and good government is good politics." The machine normally treated Mikva, a renegade Democrat, with suspicion. But its alliance with him on this issue paid off both in good government, in the form of economic fairness to the people of the state, and in good politics, the preventive pragmatism of not arousing the ire of the voters who kept the machine in power. Powell, who proclaimed himself the friend of the average man, obviously did not always play that role. The race track fight and the Sportsman's Park affair were but two examples of Powell's penchant for the politics of rascalilty, in which his friends and those he hoped to make his friends reaped some profits. The consequences of this anything-goes style became clear when Powell battled Mayor Daley in the dramatic contest for speaker of the Illinois house.[8]

The 1959 contest betwen Paul Powell and Mayor Daley's choice, Joseph De La Cour, for speaker of the house highlights the antagonism between downstate and Cook County. The 1958 general election had given the Democrats a ninety-one to eight-six advantage in the house. Since fifty-four of the Democrats came from Cook County, the will of the machine would prevail in the Democratic caucus, and, in accordance with established custom, the entire delegation would vote for the caucus choice. Should any Cook Countians be foolhardy enough to deviate, there remained, as always, some machine-obligated Republicans to deliver whatever further votes were needed to elect De La Cour. To an observer of the presession scene, the Daley organization would, as a matter of course, control the potent speaker's position and firmly run the 1959 Illinois house.

Paul Powell and the downstate Democrats harbored other notions, however. To their ancient grievance against Cook County's domination of the state party had been added bitter anger when reapportionment gave the Daley forces increased legislative strength. Moreover, the speaker of the house held so much power that were a Cook County Democrat to occupy that post Chicago arrogantly would abandon the give-and-take bargaining that traditionally obtained between the two centers of power. In sum, a Cook County Democrat as speaker would tighten the grip the machine already held on the state party. This could not be allowed to happen.

Powell and Governor Stratton's top aide organized several downstaters to set up a high-stakes bet on the speaker's race with a group of Chicagoans having direct access to the Daley machine. This Powell-flavored gimmick would accomplish three purposes: First, it would serve notice on those legislators as yet uncommitted that the downstaters were confident of winning the contest. Second, it would spur the Powell workers toward an all-out effort to swing over the laggards and to keep the already committed legislators in line. Finally, it would offer smart bettors the prospect of a little extra jingle in their pockets.

With the 1959 Illinois house session about to begin, the Cook County Democrats caucused in Chicago and, Mayor Daley in attendance, invoked the unit rule, which required everyone to bind himself to the majority decision. As expected, they slated Joseph De La Cour for speaker and William Clark for majority leader.

In Springfield, both parties held their caucuses the day before the opening of the session. Fifty-four of the Democratic solons present at the regular caucus for all the state Democratic legislators echoed Chicago's decision to endorse De La Cour and Clark. But Powell and twenty-two other Democrats skipped the caucus and went to the Lake Club for thick steaks, whiskey, and cigars. There, they unanimously endorsed Powell.

The Republican caucus produced acrimony and dissension, for Powell, like a fox in a henhouse, had been busily at work among them. Cook County Republicans, threatening to walk out if the party decided to cast all their votes for Powell on the first ballot, forced an agreement that only after the first ballot would individual Republicans be released to support Powell. Republican floor leader William Pollack of Chicago announced the system they would use. As the roll call progressed, he would assess the situation and give a "thumbs-up" sign if a given Republican should vote for Powell. "Thumbs-down" would mean a vote for Republican Warren Wood.

When the house met on the following day, Powell set a milestone in his political career: With the help of downstate Democrats, Republicans, and the Republican governor, Powell was elected.

Mayor Daley reacted bitterly to the Powell victory:

> By the vote of the people of the state in the last election, the Illinois house has a majority of Democratic members, with the largest contingent of this majority from Cook County. I have always believed in the principle of rule by a majority.
>
> This principle has now been defeated by a combination of Republican and downstate Democratic members contrary to the express will of the people who expected an election by the House of a speaker selected by the majority of Democratic members of that body.[9]

The Chicago *Sun-Times*, Powell's longtime critic, attacked him editorially:

> Mayor Daley let himself be outsmarted by a bunch of country slickers. The election demonstrates a lack of party responsibility, especially by the Republicans. Sharing culpability with the Republicans are the downstate Democrats who supported Powell—a spoilsman of enormous ambitions and appetite, who has long allied with the worst elements of his party. One question that will be asked again and again is, did Powell promise that there would be no further legislative investigation of leads uncovered in the Hodge scandal? Was the price to Stratton that there will be no legislative probes to unearth any skeletons whatever in the administration's closet?[10]

Mayor Daley then took temporary leave of his political senses. Hoping to capitalize on a combination of Cook County Democrats, anti-Powell independents, and many Republicans, he talked Clark into introducing a resolution that would strip the speaker of his traditional power to appoint committee chairmen. As expected, prospective chairmen lobbied hard against this resolution, and the motion lost by an astounding margin of 127 to 36. To make matters worse, thirteen Cook County Democrats voted against it, a previously unimaginable response to a Daley-sponsored stratagem. Left with nothing but bravado, Daley announced that Clark would be the legislative leader of the Chicago Democrats regardless of what Powell wanted.

Powell countered by letting it be known "discreetly" that he would appoint a six-member policy committee, with three antiorganization young Turks comprising Cook County's representatives, if the machine did not make peace.[11] He then added injury to insult by offering the position of house majority leader to De La Cour, Powell's Cook County-designated opponent for the speakership. De La Cour declined it. Only then did Powell offer the position to Clark. Clark denied Powell's authority to make the appointment, but added that he nevertheless had every intention of serving in the position, because the Democratic caucus had nominated him. (Clark also had a practical reason for not accepting the appointment from Powell: If Powell could appoint, Powell could discharge, could later remove Clark from the post at will. Clark was not about to set a precedent.)

Powell kept up the pressure—it was up to the speaker to select a majority leader, and if Clark wanted the job he would have to accept it from Powell. According to one prominent Democrat, "They went 'round and 'round on that particular issue." Six times Powell summoned Clark and reiterated his proposition; six times Clark rejected it.

This stand-off continued for two weeks, seriously delaying the organization of the house. In a seventh meeting, Powell offered Clark one last chance, and if Clark again rejected it, Powell would make Clyde Choate majority leader. Furthermore, Powell had the key to room 440, the majority leader's office, and would neither give it to Clark nor allow the phone service to continue. Clark stood his ground: The Democratic majority had elected him; it was not Powell's appointment to make.

The next day, Powell called him in and purred, "Bill, how about me appointin' you majority leader *because* you was elected by the Democratic caucus?" The weary Clark gave in. Powell, using the wording agreed upon, made the announcement at a hastily called press conference, and everyone saved face.

But in the aftermath of the dispute, Powell acted out his most cherished maxim, "My friends always eat at the first table." Those who had signed on and had stuck by him in the speakership fight received committee chairmanships.

Daley retaliated. During the state party's 1959 slatemaking session, the Cook County-dominated state committee refused to nominate those who had supported Powell, a group that included both Clyde Choate and Alan Dixon.

It was Powell's turn. In the 1960 primary, he broke ranks and supported maverick Joe Lohman for governor against Judge Otto Kerner, the party's slated nominee. Kerner won easily. But when, that same year, the Chicago police scandals erupted, Powell found himself sitting in the catbird's seat. Republican Governor Stratton, in a specially convened session of the legislature, introduced a bill to establish state control over the Chicago police department. Powell had the power to push the bill through and thus inflict deep wounds on the machine. On a number of measures opposed by Daley, in fact, Powell had already given crucial support to Stratton as repayment for Stratton's ordering Republican reinforcements into the speakership fight. The old Gray Fox, the Daley organization at his mercy, chose instead to call a truce. Chicago, Powell announced, could handle its own police problems without state control. Furthermore, although he had supported party dissident Joe Lohman in return for past favors, he now would stand solidly behind Judge Kerner for governor.[12] In light of these concessions, the view from Chicago revealed a Paul Powell transformed from enemy to ally. Having defeated the Daley forces in the Battle of Springfield, he had wrested from them a new respect, and, one imagines, it must have been with a collective sigh of relief that they welcomed him to their legislative team.

In the 1960 general election, the Republicans recaptured control of the house by one vote and fully expected not only to organize it but, particularly, to name the speaker. The Republican candidate, William Pollock, announced that "any Republican defecting to the Democrats will be read out of the party." Paul Powell's new ally went to work. Daley invited Powell to Chicago, and there the two of them agreed that Powell would seek the speakership once more, Daley pledging full Cook County Democratic support. With downstate votes already locked up, Powell would have all eighty-eight Democrats plus a gift from Daley—the deciding vote would be cast by a Cook County Republican beholden to Daley through patronage. The scheme went according to plan, and Powell became speaker for the third time.

In 1964, Powell won election as Illinois secretary of state, the post that crowned his political career. One not negligible benefit of his position was that he no longer need scramble for patronage by cultivating others; he now had at his disposal more than 5,000 jobs of his own. These he distributed to deserving county chairmen, both Democrats and Republicans. His largesse paid off in two ways: He enjoyed great success in passing legislation to benefit the secretary of state's office, and as the Democrat who from 1964–68 possessed state patronage second only to the Democratic governor, his voice carried much weight in the decision-making process of the state Democratic central committee. As the highest-ranking Democratic state officeholder after Republican Richard Ogilvie won the governorship in 1968, Powell's status in the Democratic party escalated. Moreover, he continued to wield considerable influence over downstate legislators.

Because of Powell's stature, custom dictated that those seeking the party's nomination must check in with him along the way. The nature of these meetings varied according to the type of aspirant who presented himself for Powell's inspection. Reformists would receive a brief reception, with Powell inquiring perfunctorily about the candidate's qualifications and background and then giving such general advice as, "When you're up there in front of the slatemakers, make sure you don't talk too long." Powell allotted favored prospects lengthier interviews, however, and he considered any topic fair game for the ensuing, freewheeling session.

On the day I sat in his office facing him, I found him friendly and entertaining. I had worried needlessly. At first, he spent some time reminiscing with Harry Kilby, the stellar precinct captain from Murphysboro who had accompanied me. Then Powell talked at great length about newspaper bias, particularly that of the Chicago papers, claiming that they delighted in headlining the problems of Congressman Adam Clayton Powell but that they used his last name only so as to imply that *Paul* was in trouble. After one such story hit the headlines, he said, he found his wife in tears: "POWELL'S WIFE ON PAYROLL," the headline emblazoned. "Honey," she had cried, "how can they say that? You know I've never been on your payroll in my whole life!" Powell insisted that this last-name-only style was intentional and concluded that the Chicago papers did perform a valuable function—"They make fine wrappers for garbage!"

He looked over my resume for a few moments and, noticing that I was from Southern Illinois University's department of government, remarked, "If Orville Alexander hired you, you can't be too bad." (Alexander, chairman of the SIU department for twenty-nine years, had been one of Powell's boyhood friends.)

"Mr. Powell," I said, "I share an office with Chuck Goodsell, who chairs the Daisy Powell Memorial Scholarship Fund. Under his leadership, the awards are going to truly deserving young people of the highest character."

"I'm sure glad to hear you say that, Mel. I've also set up four other scholarships besides the SIU ones, 'cause I think education is real important."

I went on: "The people of southern Illinois and the university itself know only too well that you, more than any other individual, have brought us from a third-rate normal school to a quality university. We'll never forget what you did for us when you were the top Democrat in the legislature."

I was expressing my true feelings, and they obviously struck home. Powell stopped speaking mostly to Kilby and started conversing more with me. We talked politics for a while, and he spoke fondly of Alben Barkley and Harry Truman, whose life-sized portraits hung on his walls. I asked, "The story about your bringing President Truman to Illinois in 1948 over the objections of the Cook County leaders—is that story accurate?"

His face lit up. "Accurate? Hell, yes! And it's true, too! Why, I went in to see them Chicago guys, and they looked like the Last Supper with the original cast. Can you imagine, them same guys would complain about me cooperatin' with the Republicans in the legislature, but they wouldn't even stand by their own Democratic president. Well, *I* showed 'em. I went out and arranged for the whistle-stop train myself, and Truman came rip-snortin' through Illinois and won the state and the election, too. The president used to tell me, 'Paul, I'll never forget what you done for me.'"

Powell then offered me "an important piece of advice," which he led up to by saying: "Never insult the people, Mel. Paul Simon made a big to-do about tradin' in his lieutenant governor's Cadillac for a Ford when he took office. Some newspapers and do-gooders liked that, but the people didn't. The people expect their public servants to travel first-class." Then the advice: "If you get to be superintendent, don't never let me hear of you turnin' in your Cadillac—unless you want a Lincoln Continental!"

Finally, he got down to business.

"Now, here's the thing—because of my position and my involvement in battles over other races, I ain't takin' a formal stand on your contest. Al Penman, from my own office, is goin' after the superintendent nomination, and I'm keepin' hands off. I'll give you a suggestion, though: Daley likes a person who can get support; so when you line up your endorsements, make 'em count. If anybody says he's endorsin' you, ask 'im to write a letter to Mayor Daley and to send you a carbon copy. Get 'em Xeroxed, bind 'em nice, and then give 'em to Mayor Daley and all the people on the slatemaking committee. Then they'll be able to see your actual endorsements."

As I was leaving, Powell gave me a cordial handshake and put his left arm on my shoulder. "You're a fine young man, Mel, and I like the way you handle yourself. This is your first time runnin' for office, you started late, and the odds are against you. If you don't get the nod, don't feel too bad about it, 'cause there's many other years ahead. But go after them endorsements. And get 'em on paper."

Powell's assessment of my chances provided a certain sense of realism, and I believed he knew what he was talking about. If he felt the odds were unfavorable, then undoubtedly that was the case. But he had given me a good tip—I should ask for endorsements in writing.

It was generally known that Powell's primary purpose in the upcoming November slatemaking meeting was to block Adlai Stevenson III's bid for the U.S. Senate seat. If Powell prevailed, if instead the slatemakers nominated a downstater (Alan Dixon, for example), the Chicago boys would never allow a second downstater an important slot on the ticket. So Powell's support of my candidacy was a long shot, and I knew it. But I also knew that my session with him, which had lasted fifty minutes instead of the scheduled thirty, had gone unusually well. Chancey, who had joined the meeting late, remarked afterwards, "The two of you really hit it off." And Kilby had added, "I've seen Paul around a lot of people, and I can tell what he thinks about them. He really likes you. And I can tell he respects your politics background. The two of you slung it back and forth real good."

In the tense days before the slatemakers were to gather, conflicting reports concerning Powell's reaction to our meeting were passed on to me. Dan Mitchell of the Young Democrats had heard from a county chairman close to Powell that Powell had observed, "Kahn's a fine young man with plenty of horse sense." But a different tale, emanating from Powell's aide, Bob Walsh, had Powell sneering, "That Kahn and Choate would sure love to get their hands on that thousand jobs in the superintendent's office. Wouldn't they just *love* to carve up that juicy meat! I can just see 'em lickin' their chops." The fact that Choate was "Powell's boy" would not have prevented Powell from coveting the superintendent's patronage control. A thousand jobs were very juicy meat indeed, and Powell must have longed to do the carving himself.

Jealousy among politicians was a fact of political life, and whatever Powell's real attitude toward me was, I now had to turn my thoughts to the slatemakers, who would make the decision. As Powell had suggested, endorsement letters could make a decisive difference. But I could almost hear the Gray Fox telling me that, to get them, I would have to do some mighty hard "pullin' in the field."

6

The Rugged Opposition

Fourteen men sought the Democratic nomination for state superintendent of public instruction, and many were already well into their campaigns when I belatedly decided to toss my hat into the ring. So I made a list of these "availables" and attempted to evaluate them in terms of the overall threat they posed to my own candidacy: How well known were they throughout the state? What education and experience would each bring to the superintendent post? What political backing could each count on from prominent party members? Where were they from (the geographical factor)? What financial support could each one claim—how much and from what sources? I did not possess enough information to answer all these questions with respect to each prospective candidate, but with the facts at my disposal it appeared evident to me that my two main competitors were Brandt Crocker and Michael Bakalis. If they were as serious as I, the task of transmitting signals to the slatemakers would be arduous and grueling for all of us.

Brandt Crocker, the early front runner, looked formidable at first. An assistant county superintendent of schools in Adams County, he held a doctorate in education from the University of Missouri, had been active in Democratic party politics, and possessed strong downstate political backing. Because the superintendent office was primarily public school-, rather than university-oriented, Crocker, with his extensive administrative experience at the public school level, appeared by far the most qualified of all the contestants. He had been named the Outstanding Young Man of Quincy for 1959 and had received an Optimist International Youth Service Award and the Distinguished Service Award from the Junior Chamber of Commerce. He was a member of the National Education Association, the Illinois Education Association, Phi Delta Kappa (the educational honor fraternity), the American Association of School Administrators, and Kiwanis International.

Crocker lived in Quincy, which was in the Twentieth Congressional District. The Democrats had never had a statewide candidate from this area of downstate, though Republican incumbent Ray Page was from Springfield, also in the twentieth Congressional District. In his mid-forties, Crocker projected the image of maturity that most people expect in a school administrator but did not carry the university stigma that attached to many of the aspirants because of the violence occurring on college campuses. Like Page, Crocker was an ex-athlete (football), a status that carried a certain attraction for some voters. Moreover, he could count on the support of state Senator Elmo McLain (also from Quincy), whom his fellow legislators liked and respected. McLain introduced Crocker to some influential people and lobbied conscientiously on his behalf with other state senators and representatives.

Crocker clearly appeared to have the edge. But he became vulnerable and lost his favored status with many Cook County officials when he told state chairman Jim Ronan of Chicago that if he ran for office the state central committee would have to supply him with funds to support his family. Even though he later told Ronan that his hometown friends in Quincy had pledged $50,000 and that he did not, after all, need party money, the damage already had been done. The state committee was seeking a candidate who presented a more positive financial base, and Crocker could not fully erase the earlier image of himself as crying for financial aid.

Dr. Michael Bakalis of DeKalb started behind Crocker, but he proved an astute and much more active competitor. Even as a youth growing up in Chicago, Bakalis had launched himself into politics, taking pride in his status as an organization Democrat and assisting his stellar precinct captain, John Noonan, in Chicago's west-side Thirty-seventh Ward. And although many young people worked against Richard Daley when the idealistic Robert Merriam opposed him in 1953, Bakalis had campaigned for Daley.

After receiving his Ph.D. in history, Bakalis joined the Northern Illinois University history faculty. He attempted to become involved in the DeKalb County Democratic party but discovered that the local party existed more in name than in fact. Moreover, it was unresponsive to potential members from the university, as Bakalis found out when he contacted the party chairman to let him know he was available to work. He received no answer. The chairman, a bartender, felt indifferent about building the party, despite the great change taking place in the DeKalb population. Bakalis later commented, "Northern Illinois University had experienced a tremendous influx of Democratic faculty members, and there was a great opportunity to really build." Bakalis became a master builder, the moving force in creating a Democratic Club in DeKalb County consisting of university people as well as others who were policy-oriented. He later served as president. The club held regular meetings that focused not on patronage but on significant issues.

Some of Bakalis's background I learned from newspaper coverage of his activities, but the inception and strategy of his campaign I found out from him personally after the campaign was over. He had begun to eye the superintendent position in late 1967, he said. Realizing, though, that he needed a springboard for launching his campaign, he wrote to prominent state Senator Paul Simon inviting him to speak on the Northern Illinois University campus. Simon, a political maverick, responded positively because he himself aspired to statewide office and was already accepting invitations to speak around the state. In their meeting after Simon's speech, the two men established good rapport: "I found him the kind of guy I could respect," Bakalis recalled. "In fact, I became one of his coordinators when he ran for lieutenant governor in 1968; I was in charge of both DeKalb and Boone Counties." Simon won the election and phoned Bakalis to say, "You're the type of person we want to get involved in the party." The wife of a prominent Chicago attorney worked in the same campaign and told me that Bakalis had impressed her greatly with both his willingness to work and his effectiveness.

In the meantime, Bakalis had become friends with Dave Carey, a part-time graduate student who worked as legislative assistant to John Touhy, the Democratic minority leader in the Illinois house. Bakalis and Carey frequently met for coffee in the university lounge, where they discussed the prospect of Bakalis's running for office. But which office he should seek was something the two of them had to consider carefully. The state representative post, they agreed, would be almost impossible for a Democrat to win, a conclusion they reached also with respect to the state senate and the U.S. Congress. As they ticked off each office in DeKalb County's Republican constituency, Carey told me, it became evident that no Democrat had a realistic chance of winning any of them. For this reason, they decided to take a look at statewide offices, their review of which reaffirmed Bakalis's original thinking that he should run for state superintendent of public instruction. This might be an opportune moment to try for it, Carey thought, because it could well be the last time the superintendent's office would be an elective one. Many reform groups were advocating that it become appointive.

Bakalis put the question of seeking the nomination to Paul Simon, who, though noncommittal, indicated that Bakalis would make a good candidate for the office. Simon suggested people to see and objectively analyzed the pros and cons of a Bakalis candidacy. As Bakalis told me:

"Some of these I was already aware of, but Simon placed everything in clear focus:

"Pro: I did have the credentials. There was my teaching experience at the elementary, secondary, and college levels. I had a doctor's degree and the proper formal training. I was a fairly decent speaker, and I was a decent-appearing person.

"Con: I was still only thirty years old. The stereotype of a school administrator is of a person who is older, much older than I was, and this had to be considered a negative factor.

"My name was another factor. The strong foreign aspect of the name Bakalis certainly was not the same as having a name like Clark or Page in regard to statewide Illinois politics.

"A third negative factor was my university connection. Student protests in the sixties had placed the universities in disrepute with many people, and this position was regarded primarily as a public-school type of job.

"Four, there was a question of my finances. Simon told me it had cost one hundred and eighty thousand dollars to run his campaign for lieutenant governor, and this was not nearly as much as he needed. We figured that it would take at least two hundred thousand dollars, and this was a lot of money to raise.

"Fifth, I had no real clout. I had no super advocate. I had never met Michael Howlett, the state auditor; or Bill Clark, the state attorney general; or Richard Daley, the mayor of Chicago; or Paul Powell, the very influential secretary of state. I had never seen Alan

Dixon. So the handicaps were very great because I did not have the strong political sponsorship needed at that stage."

Both Simon and Bakalis recognized that political influence was not confined to Mayor Daley, that it was dispersed throughout the party layers, and that others exerted influence in the slatemaking process. It would be necessary to win most of them over.

Bakalis and Carey started planning their moves. They divided the campaign into four main phases: first, contact with party leaders; second, statewide name recognition; third, financial backing; and fourth, grassroots support from the teaching profession. This was a nomination, not an election contest, and, rather than talking with every single county chairman, their most efficient strategy, they decided, would be to contact only the most influential party leaders. Because of the heavy responsibilites attaching to Bakalis's dual positions of assistant dean and professor, it was imperative that he make his time count.

One of the first people Bakalis spoke to was Illinois national committeewoman Dorothy O'Brien of DeKalb. Without committing herself, she nevertheless was very encouraging and offered Bakalis whatever help she could give him. Bakalis soon found out that even though party leaders might privately favor his seeking the nomination, and thus render significant assistance, most were unwilling to make a formal endorsement that could conflict with the slatemakers' final decision. This was a problem I would also encounter.

Bakalis wrote a personal letter to Paul Powell requesting a meeting, and it was granted. Although the meeting took place some six months before I got to Powell, Bakalis came no closer than I to gaining the man's definite support. Friendly but noncommittal, Powell pointed out the many difficulties in running for office; so by no stretch of the imagination could Bakalis feel that Powell provided any encouragement. Bakalis's friend and colleague, DeKalb County chairman Martin Dubin, then arranged for him to meet Adlai Stevenson III. Although an interesting meeting, Bakalis said, Stevenson, too, remained noncommittal and in fact made it quite obvious that he hoped Donald Prince would run again. Prince, a highly regarded administrator, had sought the office unsuccessfully in 1966.

Next, Bakalis invited State Auditor Michael Howlett to give a speech in DeKalb. As he drove Howlett to his motel, they talked about Bakalis's prospects, Howlett offering encouragement and seeming to take a personal interest in someone who, like himself, had come from Chicago's west side. The powerful leader apparently liked the idea of launching a young man's political career.

Bakalis met with state senate minority leader Art McGloon, the contact having been made through John Noonan, Bakalis's parents' precinct captain. Bakalis recalled:

"John Noonan had been precinct captain in our area for more years than I can remember. In fact, as a youngster, I often helped him in election activities. I saw McGloon in his ward committee office on Lake Street one Saturday afternoon.

"We talked at great length, and he was quite encouraging. However, at no time did he or, for that matter, any of the other people come out and boldly announce that they were for me. One of the things I continued to realize was that the men in the organization liked to keep their options open, and they did not lock them up in advance. I could see, however, that McGloon was very receptive. In fact, he seemed to have an element of pride in the fact that someone from his very own ward might be slated for a state office. He also seemed to like the idea that I had an administrative post as dean and that I had the educational background. This was a very encouraging sign.

"McGloon also served as committeeman of the Thirty-seventh Ward of Chicago. Therefore, I had more than a state legislative leader on my side; more importantly, I had one of the powerful Daley lieutenants actively working on my behalf."

The gregarious and highly respected McGloon went all out for Bakalis, communicating to several other leaders (among them, Clyde Choate) that he had an outstanding administrator who was also a strong Democrat. Dave Carey meanwhile talked constantly of Bakalis to his boss, the influential John Touhy, state house of representatives minority leader and Daley confidant. Touhy agreed to meet with Bakalis, did so, came away with a very positive impression, and subsequently became a strong booster. When I began my own campaign for the superintendent slot and jotted down an evaluation of each of my competitors, I noted that Bakalis's home turf was McGloon's Thirty-seventh Ward and that Bakalis's campaign manager, Dave Carey, worked as Touhy's assistant. These two facts indicated to me that Bakalis would be a potent political adversary.

Bakalis's efforts to meet, talk with, and stay in touch with the important state Democratic party leaders cannot be overemphasized in their significance. Just as an important piece of legislation frequently comes to be known by the name of the legislator who sponsors it, one can also speak of the "pride of sponsorship" wherein a politician takes credit for backing a young, aspiring candidate. This relationship developed between Bakalis and those important party men whose advice and backing he sought. Each of them—Touhy, McGloon, Simon, and Howlett—came to feel that he was primary sponsor and advisor, and Bakalis not only eagerly accepted their counsel but gave them the impression that their respective advice was crucial to his strategy. The importance of McGloon's and Touhy's receptiveness to Bakalis hinged on their roles as legislative leaders who enjoyed constant contact with Mayor Daley. A strong impact on them made it likely that they would pass on their impressions to the mayor, who, while not the sole decision maker, had much to do with the ultimate choice.

Proof of Bakalis's serious candidacy came when Mayor Daley granted him a meeting. State Auditor Michael Howlett accompanied him to the session, which Bakalis later described:

"Altogether, the interview lasted about a minute-and-a-half or two minutes. Howlett did not speak for me; I spoke for myself. The mayor asked about my background and specifically asked if I were a family man. I told him I was. I also talked about my personal background and told him what I was teaching and about my connections with the Democratic party.

"I knew that he had already heard of me, but he seemed very unresponsive. I would say that I was somewhat nervous in this regard, because I realized that here was a man whom presidents and would-be presidents went to see, and it was quite an experience. I did not come out of the meeting with Daley feeling particularly confident."

Months before this meeting with the mayor, however, Bakalis had written every member of the state central committee a letter outlining his qualifications and asking for a personal conference. He received very few replies; and, of those, some said it was too early to have such a meeting, meaning that, again, they did not want to risk backing the wrong person. Nearly all of them suggested that Bakalis write also to the key county chairmen.

Bakalis did pick up support from his own committeeman and from the state central committeewoman from Rockford. He also met with Jim Ronan, who, though noncommittal, made Bakalis acutely aware of some of the realities involved. For example, Ronan said, one of the most negative aspects of Bakalis's candidacy was that the superintendent post was commonly considered a downstate position. In the parlance of Illinois politicians, anything outside of Cook County and its "collar" counties ordinarily fell into the category of "downstate"; but because of DeKalb's proximity to Chicago, it could not quite so clearly be assigned the downstate label.

Dave Carey, in his conversation with me, echoed Jim Ronan's observation:

"I operated on the premise that this was primarily a downstate post and that, while whatever we got from Cook County could be a real bonus, nevertheless it was very important that we receive adequate downstate backing. As a result, I capitalized on the downstate representatives whom I had worked with in my capacity as a staff assistant to minority leader Touhy and was thus able to line up several of them to write letters. These letters went to Daley, Powell, Stevenson, and Simon. The main thing was to show that Mike had very strong downstate grassroots political support."

Carey arranged for Bakalis to meet with six legislators in Springfield, with the idea of continuing to expand the network of contacts. Bakalis, making a special effort, also talked with state representative Sam Maragos and Jim Kirie, the latter particularly important inasmuch as he served on the Cook County slatemaking committee. Carey took Bakalis to Jim Kirie's restaurant one evening, and the three of them sat talking from eight until midnight. Kirie, like others before him, enumerated the obstacles in Bakalis's path to the nomination but finally came around and agreed to back him. Altogether, Bakalis met about fifteen legislators from the downstate area.

Before long, the extensive contacts began to pay off. Bakalis later commented: "Every so often I would see Ronan, and he would mention, 'I see that you are getting around.' What I did was let them know I was available, that I was not just going to sit around and twiddle my thumbs. I wanted to convey the impression that I was willing to go out and work for the nomination." In the meantime, Carey continued to push Bakalis's candidacy with legislators and with others who called regarding their own concerns. Rather than make an obvious, overt pitch, Carey would introduce the subject casually whenever he found an opening, saying something like, "By the way, there's a terrific guy named Mike Bakalis running for state superintendent. He strikes me as a winner. You might look him over." The usual response would be, "I will. I've heard about him."

Carey also called all the state representatives who would be sitting on the slatemaking committee, asserting that he knew Mike firsthand, that Mike was uniquely well qualified, and that Carey would personally appreciate their supporting Bakalis. Carey's employment on the staff of the Illinois house minority leader advanced his case. The objective was that when Bakalis went before the slatemakers, he already would have met every single one of them personally. Minority leader Touhy commented on this first phase of the Bakalis effort:

"Dave Carey, my assistant, had told me that there was a bright young man he would like me to meet who was interested in the superintendent post. I said that I would like to meet him. Mike came to see me and said, 'I would like to run. How do I go about it?'

"I gave him a list. I urged him to see everybody on it, to make his contacts. 'Let them know about your interest in running,' I said. 'Get around to the different parts of the state and see how it goes.' I also told him that if he received the nomination, he would have times in the middle of the campaign when he would regret it all and would want to give up in despair. I warned him about what he would face.

"Well, Mike worked a whole year; he worked very hard. He got around the state, and I kept getting reports that people had met Mike and that he was making a very good impression. I want you to understand, though, that I would have told the same thing to any man seeking my advice whom I thought would be qualified—that he should go out and work hard."

The second phase of the Bakalis campaign aimed at increasing name recognition throughout the state. Bakalis recalled:

"I decided to generate as much name recognition as possible, and so I moved around and got myself booked to meet people as well as to give speeches. I took every opportunity that came my way. I billed myself as a person who could speak on campus unrest, which seemed to be a very important topic as far as a lot of program chairmen were concerned.

"An even bigger factor, as far as they were concerned, was the fact that I did not charge any fee. The result was that I was able to generate quite a few speaking engagements for myself, which, in many instances, were covered by the news media, replete with stories and pictures. I assembled this material to present to Jim Ronan, the state chairman, so that he could see that Bakalis was getting known.

"I realized that campus unrest was an important consideration to a lot of people, and I sent out letters to many civic groups, both in Chicago and around the DeKalb area, indicating that I was available to speak on this topic. One advantage I had as an administrator and a dean was that I supposedly had some expertise in this area."

In his speeches on campus unrest, Bakalis pointed to four major causes of the turmoil: population growth, shifting academic emphasis, involvement of the university in society's problems, and attitudes of students and faculty themselves.[2] The accelerating growth of American universities placed new pressures on students, who had been oversold on a college education as the only road to success and happiness and as a right rather than a privilege. Consequently, many radical students from an affluent society were making trouble, Bakalis said. Dean Bakalis triumphed over Professor Bakalis, as the young campaigner sought to build a bond of consensual concern with his audiences rather than engage in the complex effort that goes under the professorial rubric of pursuit of truth.

Faculty, according to Bakalis, were now required to devote a significant amount of time to writing and research in order to compete for promotion, a pressure that rendered them less able to concentrate on excellence in teaching or to support school and student activities. Students reacted adversely to this neglect and associated impersonal, bureaucratic universities with that which they considered bad in society. But to ignore the demands of groups such as Students for a Democratic Society and black militant organizations would be a grave error, Bakalis pointed out. These groups must be allowed to participate meaningfully in the important areas of university life.

Within the confines of what he did say about the issue of campus unrest, Bakalis's tone was that of judicious concern. But of greater significance was what he did not say. None of the newspaper articles he supplied to me indicated that he ever specifically addressed the controversial U.S. involvement in Vietnam. In asking his audiences not to ignore groups opposed to the war (for example, SDS), Bakalis could indirectly show his sympathy for antiwar dissenters without, however, directly alienating those who supported the war. His political adroitness can be noted also in the fact that his public utterances on campus turmoil followed in the grand tradition of campaign speeches by offering a little something for everyone. Middle- and upper-class audiences could derive some comfort from the idea that their children were perhaps not to blame for the atmosphere of confusion and rebellion existing in the colleges they attended. Bakalis had pointed, after all, to impersonal (and possibly inevitable) villains—change and growth. On the other hand, blue-collar people could accept readily his suggestion that the radicals and troublemakers were products of an affluent society, young people who had not experienced hardship and privation and who therefore might expect to be handed their degrees without having to earn them. Those members of Bakalis's audiences who were reform-minded and idealistic could applaud his perception that administrators must allow campus radicals and reformers a voice in important university decision-making bodies.

Bakalis pointed out that, as an institution of society, the university was being asked to involve itself in the problems of society as a whole, problems that young people felt they had not created and that they perceived as necessitating major changes. But the university's role—how it could actively help bring about these changes—remained uncertain, and an easy and speedy solution to the problems besetting the nation's colleges could not be hoped for. In his remarks to the Ottawa Women's Club, Bakalis concluded: "We are in the midst of an education revolution, and there is no clear picture of where it will go." Bakalis thus did not actually reject the notion that universities should involve themselves in society's problems; he observed only that their role was not yet clear.

Bakalis succeeded in establishing himself as qualified to speak on the subject of campus unrest but, at the same time, as detached and objective in his analysis. He avoided identifying himself as part of the problem but did not attempt to present easy solutions in a bid for votes. His speeches reflected the astuteness apparent in his overall campaign strategy.

When Bakalis could see that his speaking engagements around the state were beginning to bear fruit—his name was becoming known—he made sure he kept in close touch with the regular party Democrats. He stepped up his attendance at Democratic functions, consulting with the rank and file as well as with party leaders. But, as in the past, little political activity transpired during the summer. He did attend the Democratic Day event in Springfield and also went to the state fair, where, though invited to sit on the platform, he was not asked to speak, for he held no position in the party. To sit on the platform and meet the party leaders, however, represented a political bonanza.

Dave Carey, as active during the name-recognition phase as

during the political-contact stage, personally lined up several speaking engagements for Bakalis. Carey found this easy to do, because he had been assigned to handle five disputed legislative election contests, a task that involved traveling into counties such as Montgomery, McComb, and Saline to conduct meetings and carry on investigations. These party assignments provided an excellent opportunity to become acquainted with top party leaders as well as with newsmen. Carey later observed, "I made it a point everywhere I went to meet with the press and to talk up Mike Bakalis. In most places I was able to secure favorable stories in the newspapers, and in some instances I wrote the story myself."

Jerry Owens gave a full-column spread to Bakalis in the *Illinois State Register* in July 1969, just three months before the slatemaking session. Owens designated Bakalis as one of the three leading contenders for the superintendent's post; and, after giving the facts of Bakalis's personal history, Owens went on to say:

A former teacher at Evanston High School in Evanston, where he set up team teaching and low-ability-teaching programs, Bakalis has been at NIU since 1965. His first job at Northern was to serve as liaison between the history department and Illinois's secondary schools, enabling him to travel across the state for three years studying the public school system.

Active in a variety of educational organizations and projects, Bakalis has written articles for professional journals and now is writing a book titled, *The Strategy of Excellence: Illinois Education in the Nineteen Seventies....*

... Bakalis will have several factors in his favor when Democratic slatemakers meet to endorse a candidate, including his youthful verve.

His college post could be either a plus or a minus. It helps provide a contrast to Page, who never held a prestigious university teaching post and had little public school administrative experience. On the other hand, some party veterans feel that campus turmoil of recent months has tainted the image of college faculty members and that it might be better to slate an administrator from the public school ranks.[2]

In addition to Owens's article, John Madgezazy, who wrote a weekly column for the Waukegan paper, devoted a column to Bakalis. These write-ups helped to publicize Bakalis's name throughout the state.

The crucial third phase of the Bakalis strategy involved securing financial backing. Early in the campaign, he sought funding from his own ethnic group, the Greek community—which meant Chicago, there being very few Greeks downstate. In a letter to Greek-American Chris Vlahopoulos, a former aide to Governor Otto Kerner, Bakalis revealed his interest in the position of state superintendent and asked for an opportunity to sit down with Vlahopoulos and talk. Vlahopoulos responded that even though he was out of politics he felt flattered to receive the letter. When he later became a staff member for the state central committee, he invited Bakalis to Springfield for lunch, at which time he thanked Bakalis for contacting him and said it was the right thing to do by way of touching bases with everybody. He felt an affinity for Bakalis, he conceded, because they were both Greek; but, as a member of the committee staff, he had to remain unbiased—had, in fact, to bend over backwards to avoid showing favoritism and to give all contenders a fair opportunity.

Like others, Vlahopoulos emphasized the obstacles facing Bakalis. First, the ethnic factor—state political leaders liked names that people could pronounce easily, he said, and the prevailing bias against foreign-sounding names would be to Bakalis's disadvantage. Second, Bakalis's connection with a university—if the campus were to explode during the campaign, Bakalis, or any other professor, would be vulnerable on the law and order and campus-dissent issues. A third factor was that Bakalis was young. Not only was he young, he looked even younger, a definite handicap as far as party leaders were concerned. Fourth, geography—even though Bakalis lived in DeKalb, he was actually "a Chicago boy," raised in a Chicago ward and educated in the Chicago area, which might work against him because the superintendent position traditionally went to a downstater.

In spite of these disadvantages, some positive considerations obtained, the most important of which was "Greek money." Rumor had it that at least $150,000 would be forthcoming from the Greek community. Even if the party itself had money, the slatemakers and politicians did not like to spend it on the state superintendent post. A man with "Greek money" behind him would greatly impress them, and party officials believed Bakalis to be such a man.

Bakalis and Vlahopoulos, as well as party leaders, did have reason to believe the rumor of financial backing by the Greek community. To begin with, Bakalis would be the first Greek ever to run for a state office, and so ethnic pride was involved. Also, many

Greeks felt angry because John Stamos, the interim Cook County state's attorney, had not been slated for a new, full term. Another factor augering well for financial backing by the Greeks was that a substantial part of the Chicago Greek community lay in the Thirty-seventh Ward of the very influential state senate leader and Chicago ward committeeman Art McGloon. As a result, McGloon would have a double incentive: Not only would he be helping a young man from his own ward, but he would be developing political capital with his Greek constituents. These positive factors apparently outweighed the negative ones, for the rumor that Bakalis would have "Greek money" behind him achieved wide currency. Although I had no way of ascertaining its truth, in the interests of caution I could not afford to ignore it.

Dave Carey knew that the financial factor predominated in the minds of the slatemakers because Donald Prince had raised only a paltry $83,000 when he ran for state superintendent in 1966. Both Carey and Bakalis, knowing that it would take more than $200,000 to run a successful statewide campaign, focused strongly on the fact that, early on, $50,000 of the expected $150,000 in "Greek money" already had been pledged. Carey later told me:

"We used the term 'Greek money' over and over again so that it would make an imprint upon the slatemakers. As a result, many of them, as well as pros around the statehouse, started to talk about the 'Greek money.' In fact, it even started cropping up in the press. This was to the good as far as we were concerned, because we wanted to hammer that point home—we knew that it was a very, very crucial factor.

"Eventually, the figure grew from fifty thousand dollars to one hundred thousand, then to one hundred and fifty thousand dollars and two hundred thousand dollars in the minds of many people. One person even wrote an article stating that there was five hundred thousand dollars pledged to Mike Bakalis. Later on, I got into a very strong argument with somebody who accused me of using the five-hundred-thousand-dollar figure. I had to point out to him that I myself had not used the figure—that it was used by other people.

"The important thing is that the image of Mike having a sufficient supply of 'Greek money' began to gain credibility with many people in high places."

Bakalis agreed that the financial factor figured significantly in his nomination strategy:

"As I moved around, it became apparent that a key consideration in determining the final outcome would be the ability of a candidate to support himself. Carey is a very enthusiastic salesman, and he began to plant the seed that Mike Bakalis could be counted on to raise finances. He talked about 'Greek money' being available from Chicago.

"Well, what happens is that sometimes things get exaggerated. That is what occurred in this particular instance. The word began to spread that there was this Greek from the northern part of the state who had access to all kinds of big money in the Chicago area, and that he would easily have fifty or sixty thousand dollars to start his campaign before even going to the regular sources of financial aid.

"As time went on, we became more and more convinced that this could be a key element to our benefit. The word kept spreading that Bakalis had the money. We did nothing to squelch this."

Two months prior to the slatemaking session, Bakalis set the fourth phase of his campaign strategy in motion: he began to go after grassroots support from the teaching profession, speaking to teachers' groups at every opportunity. In addition, he had friends in the teaching profession arrange gatherings in their homes where he could meet their colleagues. For instance, he was invited to meet with thirty teachers in a York High School teacher's suburban Cook County home. Bakalis and Carey had prepared a list of influential people in the Democratic party—Daley, Ronan, Simon, Powell, Howlett, McGloon, Clark, and Dixon—and Bakalis asked each of the thirty teachers to write them letters. He did not provide a preprepared letter form but asked for originals, the idea being to impress Daley and others with Mike Bakalis's broad base of support.

Daley and Ronan sent acknowledgments to all the letter writers, and, in many instances, other officials also responded, obviously aware of sentiment for Bakalis. Carey told me, "We kept up this steady stream so they would not forget." One unique aspect of the letter campaign was that a number of letters came from southern Illinois, which was not Bakalis's home constituency. Carey gathered much of this mail through personal friendships with people in that area. Many letters were written by residents of Randolph and DuPage Counties, and about a hundred letters came from residents of Carmi, near the Indiana border. Because he thought the political leaders would discard them, Carey again did not prescribe form letters but, rather, asked people to compose their own, to imply a genuine outpouring of grassroots support.

In a speech to teachers in the Elgin area, Carey's hometown,

Bakalis explained what he thought the office of superintendent ought to be in contrast to what incumbent Ray Page had made of it. Page, Bakalis said, had made the office "excessively political," had misused public funds and public trust as well, with the result that children were the victims. Bakalis called for "educational leadership, not administration following the dictates of the state." He pledged that were he to win the superintendent race, he would not seek reelection, for he felt that dependence upon political campaigning to retain the office was detrimental to performance. In his view, Illinois ought to have a state board of education (it was one of only two states without one), and an ideal state board would be made up of teachers, laymen, and students, with teachers having the major say-so with regard to professional standards. In the week following this speech, representatives in the state legislature received 800 letters and telegrams on Bakalis's behalf from the Elgin area.

Dave Carey learned of an impending appointment for vice-chairman of the Commission on Urban Education and deemed it a good opportunity for Bakalis to receive additional newspaper coverage and at the same time hold a responsible state administrative post. The potential benefits were twofold—statewide publicity and plausible experience as an educational leader. Carey approached state Senator McGloon, who was to make the appointment and, upon discovering that McGloon already had designated someone else, pointed out the valuable exposure the appointment would give the candidate. Bakalis concurred. McGloon thereupon arranged matters so that Bakalis was named to this symbolically important post.

Bakalis's attributes as a campaigner were formidable, but he also profited greatly from Carey's active assistance. A state leader commented, "Both Carey and Bakalis masterminded the campaign for the entire year prior to the slatemaking session, and they had a lot of cooperation. Particularly helpful were the people who had worked with Carey as staff assistants and interns in the state legislature. They did a tremendous amount of work." Chairman Jim Ronan later summed up Bakalis's campaign achievements: "I was hearing all kinds of good things about this young, bright boy who had solid financial backing and was touching educational bases. He was also touching political bases. He was making good impressions wherever he went."

Mike Bakalis had established himself as the hardest working of all the campaigners. He had made many important contacts among party leaders and legislators and had generated strong support from many teachers. One disadvantage he could do nothing about was that he aspired to a downstate position but had an ethnic base in Cook County; overall, though, he had made himself a leading contender by being clever, industrious, and active. More importantly, unlike Crocker, he had, from the outset, given the impression of strong financial backing. Bakalis loomed as my foremost opponent, and I felt sure that if Cook County were the sole arena for the contest, Bakalis would win. I had a lot of catching up to do.

7

The Odyssey

I knew that Crocker and Bakalis were ahead of me in the race. I heard Bakalis's name mentioned often, and both he and Crocker were known as administrators, whereas I was not. But, in the absence of preprimary polls, reputation was all I had to go on, a situation somewhat analogous to what Jimmy Breslin would later (after Watergate) describe as the "blue smoke" or "illusion" theory of power. "All political power is primarily an illusion. If people think you have power, then you have power."[1] Or, Breslin points out, as Thomas Hobbes put it, "The reputation of power is power." I felt like a marathon runner who possessed the necessary staying power but could not gauge (just as my supporters could not gauge) the distance between myself and the front runners because of all the smoke they were generating. I knew only that they were there.

Though this worried me, I told myself that I nevertheless held a trump card—Daley had told me pointedly that the man who gave the best presentation might well walk off with the nomination. As an experienced political orator, I felt sure I could match, or even surpass, Crocker and Bakalis in our crucial appearance before the slatemakers, the final act preceding the endorsement decision. But I knew also that professional politicians are wary of the man who travels strictly on his tongue; so I had to close the gap substantially. If I could not catch the two front runners prior to the slatemaking session, I must at least demonstrate that I was relatively close to them and was well ahead of the other twelve contenders.

Obviously, all of us were competing for preslatemaking support from two key groups—political leaders and education interests. In my case, however, the urgent need to play catch-up demanded that I cultivate other major party elements as well. Realizing that the Democratic party is a collection of many interests, I settled on the following strategy: I would go after organized labor, ethnic groups, and a population segment that had become alienated as a result of the Vietnam conflict and the 1968 Democratic convention debacle in Chicago—young people.

In the wake of the 1968 Democratic National Convention, the machine lost the general election contests for president, governor, and U.S. senator and also lost control of both houses of the Illinois legislature. To invigorate the limping party, the machine decided to court actively the alienated young, and rumors persisted that Mayor Daley wanted his critic, Adlai Stevenson III (then thirty-eight years old) to head the 1970 ticket as the senatorial candidate. Though I had six years on Mike Bakalis, I was no older than Stevenson; like Bakalis, my teaching kept me in daily contact with young adults. So I saw in the Democratic party's wooing-of-the-young movement a chance to make my mark. I would attempt to present myself to party leaders as the prospective nominee who could best bridge the generation gap.

Shortly after receiving the go-ahead from my principal sponsors, Ray Chancey and Clyde Choate, I sought the help of Dan Mitchell, the Young Democrats' southeastern regional director, whose jurisdiction encompassed twenty-nine counties in south-central Illinois. Mitchell not only agreed enthusiastically to give his support but invited me to launch my campaign as "champion of the young" by attending a statewide Young Democrats meeting in Marengo. He felt this group would be fertile ground for generating some very active support. At first I hesitated; at thirty-eight I might be considered a graybeard by the college crowd. Mitchell reassured me, "It's all right; some of the people in the organization are even older than you."

He had spoken truly. When, on the afternoon of the rally, we walked from his car toward the clusters of people standing around the parklike expanse just outside the town of Marengo, I noticed several middle-aged people. And, from snatches of conversation I overheard as we waited for the meeting to get underway, I concluded that a considerable number of those in attendance belonged to Mayor Daley's Cook County organization. Apparently, my assumption was correct in that the mayor, whom young people had criticized severely as a result of the 1968 convention, wanted to use the Young Democrats to reestablish the party's image with younger party members and voters.

Mitchell introduced me to the state president, Herman Franks, and asked if I might speak to the gathering. Gladly, Franks said, but I would have to confine my remarks to two or three minutes, since both State Auditor Michael Howlett and State Treasurer Adlai Stevenson III were the featured speakers. As it turned out, neither Stevenson nor Howlett showed up—a big break for me, because Franks then asked me to give the main speech. The scenario duplicated the hackneyed show biz plot in which, at the last minute, the understudy has to go on for the star—I had advanced from a walk-on part to the lead. So with a scant five minutes' notice, I ducked into the washroom, locked the door, and jotted down some notes.

In the time-honored tradition of political rally picnics, the crowd guzzled beer. Luckily, I had a booming voice, and it proved a definite asset that afternoon because there was no microphone. Even so, the situation could have been better; gusts of wind tossed my words to and fro. In general, though, the audience listened attentively, and I soon blocked out those who made trips to the beer cooler to moisten their parched throats on this scorching September day.

I delivered a rousing partisan speech, punctuated on several occasions by applause. Feeling the heady wine of success and very much aware that two reporters were present, I announced my candidacy for nomination. Later, I would find out that I had committed one of the cardinal sins of Illinois Democratic party politics. Now, however, I innocently enjoyed the congratulations people showered on me, especially when several offered to speak to their county chairmen on my behalf.

I returned to Chicago that evening and, the next day, visited Alderman Kenneth Campbell. Campbell and I had already established good rapport during the afternoon I had spent at his ward headquarters in the ghetto some years earlier. Now, as we sat together again in his office, I briefly sketched for him my recent campaign activities. He listened with friendly interest and then made a comment that startled me because of its uncanny relevance to my experience of the day before:

"Mel, nobody should ever declare himself a candidate. If you say you're a candidate, you're affronting Mayor Daley and the rest of us—we decide who the candidates are. What you do is say that you are 'available' and that if you don't get the nomination, you'll support with all your ability the man who does get it.

"Now, if you have a name—say, Adlai Stevenson—and have finances of your own, you might play the game of bucking the organization. However, this is not appreciated. But if you're Joe Nobody, you need the organization more than the organization needs you. And so you are 'available.'"

"I'm afraid it's too late," I admitted. "I already made that mistake yesterday at a Young Democrats meeting in Marengo. I announced that I was a candidate for the office, and there were reporters present."

"Well, just act as though you never made such an announcement. Chances are the downstate paper won't be read around here anyway. But, from now on, you're not a candidate—you're *available* for the nomination."

I left Campbell's office feeling a bit better about my *faux pas* of the day before and hoped he was right, that the downstate paper's report of it would go unnoticed in Chicago.

Later that day, I contacted Alderman Ralph Metcalfe, the most powerful black in the machine.[2] Metcalfe was extremely busy because of his selection, by Daley, to negotiate a solution to the impasse between dissident blacks and the building trades unions. During the twenty minutes I spent with him, the phone rang seven times; and, since I did not get the chance to present my case, the interview was unsatisfactory. It was obvious from Metcalfe's questions that his mind was on something else. In contrast to the exuberance I had felt when Alderman Campbell had said, "I'm for you; I'll help you with the right people," I received no indication of support from Metcalfe. He was the highest-ranking black in the machine, and his indifference worried me. His parting words were, "Well, you'll be invited to appear before the slatemaking committee, and at that time we'll look you over. Do a good job in presenting your case." I could not count Metcalfe on my side; he had merely filled me in on the proper procedures.

The next person I called on was ex-Governor Sam Shapiro. In spite of a solidly booked calendar, he had invited me to join him for a fifteen-minute late lunch in his LaSalle Street law office. He greeted me warmly, offered me a comfortable chair next to his desk, and buzzed his secretary to take our lunch orders. She returned soon with the best kosher corned beef sandwiches I had ever tasted.

"Governor Sam" opened the conversation: "Mel, I think you

have very good qualifications for the superintendent post, and you've got my support."

"Thank you, Governor, that's very good to hear. But I have a real problem. Mike Bakalis started much earlier than I and is ahead of me in the race. Also, he has the Greek community solidly behind him. Is there any chance of lining up the Jewish community behind me?"

"If you lived in Chicago, that wouldn't be difficult, but your being a downstater presents problems. As I said, your qualifications for the office are excellent, and I'll present you to the Jewish community as a highly acceptable choice. I personally am very appreciative of what you and the Jackson County organization did in winning your area for me in '68, and I'll help you in every way I possibly can. Of course, I'm not a party leader and am now politically inactive. But I know certain people who have something to do with slatemaking, and I'll see to it that your resume gets into the right hands."

A week later, I visited vice-chairman Earl Kumpel of the powerful Sangamon County (Springfield) organization, whom I had met through his daughter, Karen Zink, a secretary in the Southern Illinois University government department. Kumpel, a forthright, outspoken man, worked diligently at politics and was particularly proud of his role in converting his formerly Republican precinct into a Democratic stronghold in Sangamon County. He also took pride in scouting out young people whom he then developed as party workers and groomed as candidates for public office.

The outgoing Kumpel took me on a tour of the state capitol to meet some prominent officials. I was amused by his winsome manner with secretaries and impressed by his ready access to key state Democrats. As the day progressed, Kumpel voiced a mounting interest in my "availability," commenting at one point, "Mel, you're certainly qualified for the job, and for a nonpolitician you understand patronage quite well." Patronage mattered vitally to his Sangamon County organization, whose locus in the state capitol necessitated providing jobs for a high proportion of its nonresident members. Failure to do so meant that these workers left Springfield. So Kumpel's county organization placed a premium on slating patronage-oriented candidates. I had told Kumpel, "As superintendent, I would give competence top priority with respect to the professional positions, and I would handle these personally. As for the nonprofessional positions, applicants would, first, have to have good job qualifications, after which party loyalty would, of course, be a factor in my selections. Under no circumstances would I appoint anyone who hadn't received approval from his county chairman."

Foremost among those to whom Kumpel introduced me was Tom Owens, chairman of the Sangamon County organization and a man whose position as supervisor of buildings and grounds for the state capitol placed enormous patronage at his disposal. Owens, with a degree in landscape architecture, was one party stalwart (among many) giving the lie to those who accused the machine of choosing only hacks. In his job, he, as much as any individual, symbolized the patronage concept of competence and loyalty. In his role as county chairman, Owens, a political protége of Paul Powell, had demonstrated the ability to mold a formerly weak Democratic organization into a worthy competitor of the county's Republican party. Our friendly, fifteen-minute chat focused on my views regarding patronage, views that he evidently liked. He said he wanted to see more of me.

After we left Owens's office, Kumpel waxed enthusiastic about my chances. A political savant, he knew I could not call myself a candidate and agreed with the Chicago people (and with Clyde Choate) that my "availability" for the nomination restrained me from openly conducting press conferences or courting newspaper people. But Kumpel realized also that if an organization invited me to speak and the press "just happened" to be present this would constitute legitimate coverage. He would try to arrange a media event through Tom Owens, he said, and, true to his word, called me a week later to report that Owens wanted to get together with my county chairman and me.

Soon thereafter, Ray Chancey and I traveled the 140 miles to Springfield, where the two county chairmen established a good working relationship. Owens would invite me to speak to his organization, he told us, with television, radio, and newspaper people present. He would extend the formal invitation as soon as he received word from my major political sponsor, Clyde Choate. Since Choate was my state central committeeman, not to request his blessing would be out of order, Owens explained. Choate was not an easy man to get hold of, but Chancey undertook to track him down and inform him that I would be well received in Springfield. When, three weeks later, Choate gave Owens the nod, the county chairman formally invited me to speak to his county organization.

Before leaving for Springfield, I worked out a press release with the help of a political science colleague, Earl Hanson, for distribution to the downstate media as well as to the Associated Press and the United Press International. Clyde Choate had told me earlier that Sam Hancock, the UPI reporter in Marion, could be relied on to place political news on the wire, a nugget of information that allowed me to generate wide media coverage on this and several subsequent occasions. The press release for my Sangamon County speech read:

> Pledging to do something about the fact that one-third of the students in Illinois cannot adequately read their textbooks, Dr. Melvin A. Kahn of SIU announced his availability for the Democratic nomination for State Superintendent of Public Instruction. Dr. Kahn also came out strongly for teacher representation on all educational boards and commissions. He stated, "It is high time we recognize the teacher in the classroom as the cornerstone of our educational system."

On the evening of October 22, I walked into the headquarters of the Sangamon County Democratic organization, where Tom Owens waited to introduce me around. The other leaders of this county machine were, like Owens, people of unusually high caliber. Al Lucas, a well-known corporation lawyer, had served prominently as a member of the state legislature; and Jim White, a black leader, headed the purchasing department for Paul Powell's vast secretary of state operation. Sy Friedman had been legal counsel to the previous Democratic superintendent of public instruction and now held the same position with the Illinois Association of School Boards. These men possessed exceptional capability for directing a first-rate organization, and I would feel fortunate indeed to win their support.

The political headquarters of the Sangamon County Democratic organization was unique. It occupied a large, modern building that formerly had been a supermarket. Upon entering, I noticed a sign that read: THIS IS NOT AN EMPLOYMENT AGENCY. WHAT HAVE YOU DONE TO DESERVE A POLITICAL JOB? In addition to a nicely furnished reception area, a special workroom included an addressograph, a mimeograph machine, and extensive files that were organized and labeled for targeting various subgroupings of the voting population by age, sex, occupation, and education level. A major accomplishment of the organization was that its headquarters served as a focal point for community activities. Not only did this perform a public service, but the spin-off provided a fund of good will and a favorable image for the Democratic party. Always conscious of that image, the Sangamon County organization had designated a special room for media interviews. Tonight, a lavish buffet and expensive liquor had been offered to reporters an hour before my talk was to begin. I wanted to impress them at this early point in my campaign particularly, because I needed good media coverage to establish name recognition throughout the state.

At seven o'clock, after a short introduction by Owens, I began my brief speech, in which I attempted to establish four main points. First, I would be a winner—a forceful and effective campaigner who would help the party. Second, I was a loyal Democrat who belonged to the political mainstream. Third, my credentials were suitable for the job. And, fourth, I offered a constructive program for bettering the school system, specifically, I would upgrade the vital area of reading, the core of all public school learning. Though my development of these four points was not spelled out by the newspaper accounts that appeared the following day, I did receive especially full and favorable coverage by the *Illinois State Register*:

A 38-year-old Southern Illinois University professor of political science appeared before top Sangamon County Democrats Wednesday night to announce his availability for the party nomination for state superintendent of public instruction....

... During his 15-minute speech the articulate educator said he feels the most crucial problem in education is "that one-third of our Illinois students cannot adequately read the textbooks assigned in their classes. Since reading is basic to other school work, the poor readers have great difficulty with their other subjects."

Kahn said if he is nominated and elected state superintendent he would press for establishment of "regional reading centers" in order to keep the state abreast of the latest developments in reading research.

He said he publicly announced his candidacy in Springfield and made his initial appearance before the Sangamon Democrats because this is "the nerve center" of state government and politics in Illinois. Twenty or more of the vice chairmen were present.

... [Kahn] hesitated to attack Page, saying that he wants to accentuate the positive at the present time, but he did volunteer that he thinks Page pays disproportionately high salaries to nonprofessional personnel in his office at the expense of trained educators.

"Page has considerable political ability," Kahn said, "but it has not been used sufficiently enough on behalf of school teachers, school children and taxpayers in this state."

Familiar with student problems at the university level, Kahn said campus turmoil and demonstrations in recent years have been caused by 'a hardcore, small minority" who want to disrupt everything but have no legitimate complaints.[3] He labeled this type of student "phony" but said the majority of college youths are good, decent students like two he had at SIU—former Rep. Allen Lucas' son and precinct committeeman Earl Kumpel's daughter. He called them "good, clean kids." . . .

. . . "The pressing problems of Illinois education pose a strong challenge [Kahn said]. I welcome the opportunity to meet this challenge by offering my background of 12 years of teaching experience at the elementary, high school and college levels. . . . "[4]

Later, I found out that the newsman who wrote this account, Jerry Owens, had close ties with the Sangamon County Democratic party and that he was trying to build me up as a statewide candidate. The *Illinois State Register* ranked highly among Illinois dailies— almost everyone in Springfield read it, residents as well as politicians from all over the state. And because the legislature was in session at the time, the name of Mel Kahn was brought to the attention of legislators from every part of Illinois. I felt rather good when I received a note from my friend and colleague Jack Van Der Slik, who was serving a faculty internship with the Legislative Reference Bureau in Springfield. He wrote, "Dear Mel, I don't know who's handling your publicity, but you're sure getting great exposure in the state capitol!" I owed a sizable debt of gratitude to Jerry Owens.

The financial problems of running for office hovered over my campaign from the beginning. Professional political leaders had told me I would need between $200,000 and $250,000 to run a satisfactory race for a state office, and the party was acutely aware of the financial aspect. The spectre of Donald Prince, the strapped Democratic candidate of 1966's election, haunted me, just as (I later discovered) he haunted Mike Bakalis. It was generally agreed that the shortage of campaign funds played a crucial role in Prince's defeat in the superintendent's race; and in 1969 the party wanted a candidate who could raise enough money, independent of party coffers, to win this office, with its approximately 1,000 patronage jobs.

Another serious problem I faced in the nomination struggle was the slatemakers' overriding need to balance the slate geographically. In this respect, downstate Lieutenant Governor Paul Simon's announced availability for the senatorial nomination jeopardized my chances for a place on the ticket. Immediately following Senator Everett Dirksen's death, Simon held a series of meetings with the leaders of the various southern Illinois counties. In fact, one of his phone calls had been taken by Clyde Choate while Chancey and I were sitting in Choate's living room in Anna. Choate had simply told Simon, "Yes, Paul, I agree. The Senate nomination should go to downstate," a politically shrewd statement that gave Choate the flexibility to support any downstater whomsoever. Choate soon joined Powell in backing Alan Dixon, shifting to Simon only when Dixon appeared to have little chance of success.

As part of his series of meetings, Simon arranged a luncheon with the leaders of the Jackson County executive committee, including, of course, Ray Chancey, who used the occasion to affirm that he would fully support Simon for governor or senator, but not until two years hence. He urged Simon not to resign from the lieutenant governorship now, in the middle of his term, and thus allow his Republican replacement to succeed to the governor's chair should the office become vacant. Chancey's strongest reason for wanting Simon to hold off was that Simon came from our general geographical area; his nomination would automatically exclude me from the ticket. Later, as Dixon's prospects waned, Clyde Choate endorsed the popular Simon, and did so (depressingly for me) immediately preceding the meeting of the state central committee in Springfield. Chancey, on the other hand, contacted Simon and firmly reiterated his opposition to Simon's nomination, warning him to stay in the lieutenant governorship. Simon paid no heed.

The "Stevenson problem" also arose during the campaign. Chairman Chancey had perceived Adlai Stevenson as the strongest man to lead the ticket in Jackson County. Unlike many political leaders from downstate Illinois who were against Stevenson, Chancey was well attuned to the Southern Illinois University community where Stevenson had wide support. Jackson County had changed from a strong Republican county to a Democratic one largely through Chancey's ability to involve new faculty, a strong majority of whom were Democrats. They had proved themselves diligent workers whom the party needed to keep Jackson County voting Democratic.

Chancey wanted Stevenson slotted for the U.S. Senate. His stance contrasted with the plans of the two top southern Illinois Democrats, Paul Powell and Clyde Choate, who were boosting native son Alan Dixon of Belleville for the senatorial nomination. Powell and Choate called a press conference and announced that all the county chairmen of the Twentieth and Twenty-first Congressional Districts had endorsed Dixon. Chancey fretted because the Powell-Choate duo had not consulted him, but said little, realizing that my chances for nomination to my office depended less upon him than upon their backing. Chancey knew that both these men could veto me.

The conflict came to a head at a Chancey-sponsored luncheon for Adlai Stevenson. One of my university colleagues, Matthew Kelly, raised the question of whether Jackson County would support Stevenson.

Chancey replied, "You bet we're going to be for Stevenson. He has it wrapped up, and at the appropriate time we'll come out for him."

"Stevenson needs your help now," Kelly responded. "Powell and Choate are trying to head him off, but a strong statement from Jackson County, right in the heartland of Dixon's strength, would stop him and guarantee Stevenson the nomination."

Chancey answered firmly: "We're not going to torpedo Kahn, our own man. We can have Stevenson regardless of how we handle it. But if we have him your way, we are going to antagonize Choate and Powell, and then we can forget about Kahn's nomination. This county has never in its entire history had a statewide candidate, and now that we have a strong chance we're not going to blow it by coming out for Stevenson at the wrong time." Chancey then turned to Stevenson and asked, "Do you agree, Adlai?"

"I never involve myself in the internal affairs of other county organizations," Stevenson replied.

Chairman Chancey next turned to Kelly: "Are you for Kahn?"

"Yes," Kelly responded, and his move to secure endorsement for Stevenson at the luncheon came to an end.

Both the Simon and Stevenson situations illustrate the strong interrelationship between the various state offices at the slatemaking stage. If a higher office, such as U.S. senator, were to go to a southern

Illinoisan, it was highly improbable that another southern Illinoisan could win a place on a ticket that must be balanced geographically.

Though these two major problems of finances and geographical balance persistently plagued me, in mid-September my thoughts turned to cultivating support from organized labor. And I felt quite confident as I remembered back to an evening several months earlier, when I had stood up to address a crowd packed into the court room that served as the meeting room for the Carbondale city council. I had looked directly at Mayor Dave Keene, whose vote on the personnel ordinance presently before the council could tip the scales either way:

> This proposal violates the basic concepts of fair play: To substitute the opinion of an administrator for an impartial review board is blatantly wrong, because it does not give a fair shake to our city employees. To say that a man who works for the city must forfeit his right to be active in city politics is to saddle him with second-class citizenship. Our city employees work very hard to protect our health and safety, and we should treat them with the same respect we desire for ourselves.
>
> Members of the city council, I ask you to reject this biased and unfair proposal and assign it to the city incinerator, where it so rightly belongs.

The room had vibrated with applause from the sixty-five members of the plumbers' union who comprised a majority of the audience. Mine was the only nonunion voice that had spoken against the proposed ordinance. Bill Held, the union's business agent, had come over then and had shaken my hand. "This is a great surprise. I didn't know we had any professor friends at the university. You did a tremendous job!" The council's subsequent three-to-two vote against the proposal had marked the beginning of a good friendship between Held and me.

As my first step toward wooing labor support, I now got in touch with Bill Held again. One of my major strategies was to send positive signals to the slatemakers that Mel Kahn had acquired concrete, definite support groups, and I figured that labor backing would give me a significant advantage over my opponents. Not surprisingly, Held came through. He assured me that he would muster the support of the powerful plumbers' union in Chicago as well as that of the entire building trades unions in southern Illinois. He also hinted strongly that if I received the nomination, my proven commitment to labor would guarantee me considerable financial support from the unions.

Charlie Mileur of Murphysboro, the former president of his carpenter's local, provided additional strength. His son Jerry had been a graduate student in the SIU government department, and I had interviewed the older Mileur two years previously. He proceeded to line up support from various union business agents.[5]

John McDermott, director of the Southern Illinois Labor Institute, had been a friend since my arrival on campus, and his Labor Institute had published a version of my doctoral dissertation. Having also worked together for Hubert Humphrey's nomination and candidacy in 1968, we had much in common politically. McDermott, a former business agent who enjoyed extensive labor contacts, volunteered to gather widespread labor backing for my candidacy. Most significantly, he arranged for me to appear before a monthly meeting of the Southern Illinois Business Agents Association.

McDermott's introduction demonstrated his support:

"Mel Kahn is a genuine friend of labor. He looked me up when he first came to campus, and we've worked together ever since. He comes from a union family. And when Bill Held and the plumbers really needed help against an antilabor personnel code, Mel was the only one from the entire community who stood up for labor. I'm very pleased to present a real friend."

I stood, acknowledged the applause, and began:

"John, thank you very much for that fine introduction. In fact, I consider it the second best introduction I've ever had in all my years of public speaking. You may be interested to know that the nicest one occurred when I gave a talk before a women's club, and the program chairman didn't show up. So I did the introducing myself.

"Now, I have high hopes that this is one group that isn't going to hold it against me that I'm prolabor and that I come from a union family. My dad is a life member of Local 365 in Miami, Florida, and he used to see to it that, as kids, my brother and I marched in the front of the Labor Day parade. All my life I've been catching hell because of my prolabor stand. So, as I said, I hope this is one group where it will pay off for me to stand up and be counted.

"There are some very real reasons why I believe labor ought to be interested in the office of superintendent of public instruction. First of all, the superintendent has a lot of say-so on which books are approved and which ones are excluded. One of the things that concerns me as the son of a union man is the antilabor bias that appears again and again in various books used in the public schools. I say to you that if we're ever going to correct the distorted, unfair image that many people have of organized labor, then we have to use those books which are fair and objective in chronicling the vital role that labor has played in building our great country.

"As superintendent of public instruction, I will do everything possible to see to it that unionized teachers are treated fairly. While I would prefer that strikes not occur, I will insist that where there are no fair, impartial procedures for mediation and arbitration, the right to strike, which is so basic to the freedom of all Americans, is guaranteed for teachers.

"There is a third factor I would like to share with you. I believe a school superintendent has a moral responsibility to see to it that all construction of educational facilities is structurally sound and safe. The surest way I know to guarantee safety in construction is to demand that all workers on the job have completed a legitimate apprenticeship and have met the highest standards of workmanship. The best way to accomplish this is to insist that work be performed by union members rather than by scabs. This is vital not only to the labor movement but to each and every school child.

"Beyond these, there are other significant reasons why labor should be interested in education. First of all, organized labor has always been by far the most enlightened interest group in bettering both its own lot and that of all people. It is labor which has been in the forefront of pushing medical care for all Americans. It is labor that helped explode the idea that education belongs only to the children of the wealthy. And so organized labor, which is responsible for the American system of free public education, has a responsiblility to continue its interest in education on behalf of all Illinois children.

"I promise that I will do everything humanly possible to guarantee that the kids of this state receive quality education, improve their reading skills, and get a fair, impartial version of labor's contributions. And I give you one solemn pledge: I will continue to say in public what I have said here today about what labor means to the American way of life. I will stand up and be counted. I am proud that I have worked with people of the caliber of Bill Held, Charlie Mileur, and John McDermott. I hope that all of us will work together so that we can not only improve education in this state but also develop an awareness on the part of people everywhere that organized labor is a positive force in mankind's quest for progress.

"Thank you very much for the opportunity to visit with you today."

I had no sooner finished my talk than Charlie Mileur made a motion to endorse me, someone seconded it, the gavel sounded, and the chair announced that I was officially endorsed. Feeling elated, I then made the near-fatal mistake of sitting around and savoring the heady wine of success. One man turned to me and asked, "How do you stand on government's forcing blacks into unions?" I felt that the eyes of the union were upon me as those gathered there awaited my answer, but I bought a little time by responding "Well, that's an easy question. How about a hard one?" Their laughter broke the tension a bit. Then I plunged in:

"In terms of safety, unions ought to approve only competent people as master mechanics and craftsmen. But any American citizen who has fought for his country and pays taxes is entitled to the same opportunity as the rest of us. And, quite candidly, I think labor can do a better job than it has done in admitting more people from minority groups to training programs. At the end of the training program, evaluators ought to apply fair standards and certify only those able to do passing work. But the judgment should be reasonable and impartial; and, most importantly, everyone should have the initial chance to compete for entrance into what, in the past, have been closed programs."

Though my remarks apparently satisfied these union representatives, I had had to relearn an old lesson—get out while you're ahead. I had just won a critically important endorsement and had damned near lost it; a "wrong" answer, wrong as far as these people were concerned, might well have proved my undoing.

The endorsement produced an immediate, beneficial result: Charlie Mileur, on behalf of the Council of Building Trades Representatives, sent to Mayor Daley himself a letter announcing my official buildings trades union stamp of approval, mentioning my role in getting a nonunion provision removed from the Carbondale city personnel code, and reminding Daley that the building trades unions were very active politically throughout southern Illinois.

With downstate labor backing solidly locked up, I now turned to

Chicago, fixing on John Alesia, political action director of the powerful steelworkers union, as my first target. Although I had met him fifteen years earlier during my student days at the University of Chicago when I worked with labor groups in the 1954 Barratt O'Hara congressional campaign, I did not know him well enough to seek his personal sponsorship directly. I decided on a more circuitous route. I had worked closely with the steelworkers union in Indiana while a doctoral candidate at Indiana University, and I now phoned Harry Doherty, the district leader of that union in central and southern Indiana. I told him my plans, and he heartily endorsed my nomination bid, saying, further, that he would see Alesia at the AFL-CIO convention in Atlantic City the followng week, play golf with him, and attempt to put him firmly in my corner.

After the AFL-CIO convention, I phoned Alesia. "Doherty made a strong pitch on your behalf," he told me, "says you're one helluva guy. You bet we'd like to see you get elected!" He added, however, that the steelworkers traditionally did not back candidates prior to the official slating by the Democratic organization since it would be embarrassing if the party then endorsed someone else. But he suggested I tell the mayor that the steelworkers would give me financial backing should I win the nomination.

Disappointed though I was, I had at any rate acquired the next-best thing to an outright commitment—the assurance that the steelworkers union found me acceptable and that I could count on campaign money from them. Since none of the other candidates could claim this type of support, I felt I had achieved a real coup.

A labor leader even more important than Alesia was Bill Lee, longtime friend of Mayor Daley who held the influential position of president of the Chicago Federation of Labor.

Lee greeted me in his office and listened attentively to what I had to say, but, as I had now come to expect, explained that his organization could not make any kind of endorsement before the slatemakers met. He let me know, however, that I came highly recommended by Stanley Johnson, vice-president of the Illinois State AFL-CIO, whom I had met while doing research for a book on labor politics. Lee went on to say that I was the kind of person to whom labor could give strong support were I slated to run. When I asked if he would tell that to Daley, he answered that, because it would amount to an informal endorsement, he could not. I understood, of course. But, though somewhat inured to the hedged-bets routine by now, I could hardly hide my frustration at Lee's withholding a commitment I badly needed.

I had not fared as well with Lee as I had hoped. Nevertheless, I could still present myself to the slatemakers as an aspirant with labor backing, for the Council of Building Trades of Southeastern Illinois actively supported me, and the steelworkers had provided financial support. To my knowledge none of my competitors had acquired labor support, so I had the edge there.

During the time I sought backing from labor leaders and others, I occasionally diverted myself with campaign excursions of a lighter nature. The annual Randolph County bingo night offered a respite from the frenetic pace of more serious campaigning. Although the boredom of playing bingo soon got to me, as long as I bought cards and gave them to other players I was regarded as a nice guy, and that way I could engage in banter with those party leaders in attendance. I had the most fun at a fish fry in rural Half Creek. Wending my way through fifteen miles of dusty back roads turned out to be well worth the effort. Camaraderie prevailed, the fish were delectable, and the accomplished fiddler encouraged everyone to get involved in a foot-stomping hoedown. All this, combined with free beer, made for a rousing evening.

Another diversion I allowed myself was a long talk with Dean Hammack, a former legislator from Pickneyville, who prided himself on being a "Paul Powell Democrat." His conversation sounded one theme—"Don't trust appointed bureaucrats. The only good people in government are those the people elect."

But these detours from the main campaign trail occurred rarely. As soon as I had established my labor contacts, I made my next move. Important though labor backing might prove, I needed, even more, to win backing from the educational community, the natural constituency for a school superintendent. So I began making the rounds of what I hoped would become my second major support group.

My first contact in the field of education was Elmer Clark, dean of the college of education at Southern Illinois University, whom I had known originally as graduate dean at Indiana State University. Dean Clark was not only an interested listener but also gave me several suggestions, one of which was that I contact Wayne Stoneking, the executive secretary of the Illinois Education Association (IEA). While Stoneking could not endorse me officially, Clark said he might nevertheless end up doing me some good.

I arranged to meet Stoneking during his participation in a conference on the SIU campus. As Clark had predicted, Stoneking emphasized that his organization could not endorse anyone. But he approved of my proposal to upgrade professional standards and especially liked my plan to appoint representatives of the IEA, as well as rank-and-file teachers, to the main boards and committees governing public education in Illinois. Because of the neutral status of his organization, I believed it inopportune to ask for a letter to Mayor Daley. I would have to remain satisfied with achieving name recognition among professional educational leaders such as Stoneking; if the machine did consult with them, hopefully they would give me a favorable nod.

I also needed backing from educators in Chicago, and my first contact there was Bob Adams, like myself a graduate of the divisional master's program in social science at the University of Chicago. An intelligent, articulate man who worked within the domain of voluntary organizations, he had at one time served as executive secretary of the Chicago Teachers Union.

Adams was astute regarding Cook County politics and cautioned that to receive open support from either the Chicago Teachers Union or its rival, Illinois Education Association, could hurt me with the other group. He suggested I informally cultivate people in both organizations and try to get their leaders privately to pass word to Daley of my acceptability. He also described John Desmond, the head of the Chicago Teachers Union, as a highly influential person and advised me to approach him with deference. Another person Adams urged me to see was Dr. Harold Gempleman, a reputable scholar in the area of drug prevention.

My visit with Dr. Gempleman revealed a man deeply concerned about drug addiction in the schools. He did not care whether politicians were Democrats or Republicans, he said; he cared only about the development of antidrug programs. He indicated that, because teachers lacked training in identifying addiction in its early stages, students were not provided with intelligent arguments about drug abuse. Moreover, the minimal education presently offered amounted to little more than tactics the kids did not find plausible. A program of two-day workshops for teachers could provide some badly needed training in this area, Gempleman felt. Should I become superintendent, he would recommend a young person in preventive medicine as a consultant; if none were available, then he himself would serve. Gempleman pointed out that drug addiction in the schools would make a good campaign issue and offered his expertise on the subject, but with the qualification that should the Page people demonstrate a willingness to confront the problem of drug abuse, he would support them. As a nonpartisan, he did not particularly care who held the superintendent post but simply wanted to see Illinois start an effective program. Clearly, I had met a man with both knowledge and dedicated concern about a serious problem affecting our children. That concern struck a responsive chord in me personally. If I could communicate to others even half as effectively as Dr. Gempleman had communicated to me the burgeoning need for drug education in schools, I would have accomplished something eminently worthwhile, whether I won the nomination or lost it.

In making contact with John Desmond, the powerful president of the Chicago Teachers Union, I decided to ask a union leader friend of mine to act as intermediary. My friend cooperated and set up the interview with Desmond, a man close to Mayor Daley.

I arrived ten minutes late for my appointment because of a traffic snarl, and, although it was now his lunch hour, Desmond was quite nice about it. He put me through my paces and apparently liked my form, my prolabor responses in general and my particular assurance that I would support the right of teachers to organize with unions. Desmond stated that although his organization could not endorse anyone prior to the slatemakers' action, it would give me full support if I received the nomination. Since the incumbent, Ray Page, seemed extremely vulnerable, I pointed out that my major struggle would be not the election but the nomination contest. I had received similar statements of approval from several other sources, I told Desmond, and if he could do anything for me other than wait for the general election endorsement, I would appreciate it since now was the time I urgently needed backing. At that point, he offered what I hoped would prove a decisive factor: "I cannot endorse you. However, I will write a short note to the mayor saying that you are personally *very* acceptable to me and that you are the kind of person I would like to support if you receive the nomination. I'll send you a copy of the note for your files."

My elation lasted only a few hours. When I settled down in a window seat on the train back to Carbondale and, preparatory to doing some work, pulled a few papers out of my briefcase, I stared in disbelief at one of them—it was the special resume I had prepared for John Desmond and thought I had left with him. What the devil was it doing here? Then it hit me—I had, instead, given him the resume designed for the downstate people showing my membership in the Illinois Education Association. Because of the animosity between it and the Chicago Teachers Union, I felt sure that when Desmond saw my IEA affiliation he would change his mind about me. All I could hope for now was that, because Chicago's school system had relative autonomy and the superintendent position was primarily a downstate one, Desmond might stay out of it. I could not now expect his help. I could only hope my blunder would do me no harm.

Bitterly angry with myself, at first I merely bemoaned my carelessness. But then a Freudian interpretation hit me: Did I really and truly want to become superintendent? Or was it only the political challenge of a nomination and an election that appealed to me—was winning an end in itself? Did I even *want* to win? Well, I thought I could do some good as superintendent, but more than once I had questioned whether I was competent or interested enough to function in an administrative capacity. Perhaps, by leaving the wrong resume with Desmond, I was trying to tell myself something; maybe I really did not want the job.

After a while, I decided to stop whipping myself and made my way carefully through the speeding, rocking train to the club car, where I ordered a Budweiser and tried to relax. Ordinarily, I stuck to Tab (modern campaigners have to keep trim), but tonight I craved something a little stronger. Resuming my self-questioning (if not my self-flagellation), I reflected that I could always hire a capable aide, perhaps Bob Adams, to run the administrative operations, while I, relishing the external, political aspects of the job, would deal with the governor, the legislature, the media, and the party organizations. The thousand patronage jobs attached to the office of superintendent could provide a solid political springboard, I mused. I began to fantasize becoming Illinois secretary of state, with an even larger patronage army and even more county chairmen beholden to me; and after that, the United States Senate; and then, well, who knew . . . ?

Though still regretting my gaffe, by the time the train pulled into Carbondale I had more or less vanquished my demons and, dreaming of my political future, had injected myself back into the race with renewed determination. I wanted very much to capture the nomination. Even if Desmond did not endorse me (and I never did receive a copy of his promised note to Mayor Daley), I felt sure that none of the other contenders had secured his backing. Moreover, I had made contact with educators who sometimes had occasion to talk with the party leaders; so perhaps my name would come up. My major accomplishment, however, was that I had developed three good campaign issues: the need for a drastic upgrading of reading skills, for coping better with the problem of drugs in the schools, and for improving the quality of school counselling. These three points gave me a platform from which to mount a hard-hitting campaign.

But my solicitation of educators had not fared as well as my courtship of labor. True, as a college professor with a Ph.D., I felt I would appeal to the "good government" types. Since the incumbent superintendent had built his reputation upon his background as a successful basketball coach (his team had won the state championship), the contrast between us would, I assumed, make me especially appealing to college-educated people concerned with upgrading public education in Illinois. But two sets of circumstances arose that were to cause me problems.

First, a group of Carbondale parents had become disturbed about the use of corporal punishment in the Carbondale schools and had fixed on Monroe Deming, the Jackson County superintendent, as their target. Deming, an organization Democrat with many friends among the other downstate superintendents, had already offered chairman Chancey and me his support. Thus, when Sue Melching asked me to join the parent group to protest Deming's policies at the upcoming school board meeting, I felt caught between two opposing factions whose support I really wanted. Fortunately, I had an appointment in Springfield the afternoon of the evening board session, and although I could have returned in time by eating a fast-food supper, I waffled by saying I would attend if my appointment did not detain me. My Springfield meeting broke up early, but I ate a leisurely supper and made a slow trip back so that I in fact did reach Carbondale too late to join the meeting. The following day, I called Sue Melching and hypocritically cited my late return to Carbondale as my excuse.

A second difficulty at this point in my campaign was the debate about whether the state superintendent post should be made appointive rather than elective. Many reform groups and newspapers advocated "taking the schools out of politics." I personally felt that making the position appointive would merely substitute one type of politics for another. Furthermore, I was well aware that Paul Powell, whose support I desperately needed, vehemently opposed attempts to depoliticize any office. The populist Powell berated the "so-called experts" and called for "rule by the people." If I were to take a "good government" stance on this matter, Powell would lump me in with the rest of the "do-gooders."

In view of the controversial nature of the appointive/elective issue, I resolved to take no public stand at all prior to the slatemaking session. The Lindsay-Schaub newspaper chain, however, queried several prospective nominees, myself among them, as to where each of us stood. I told the reporter that, because this was a complex question, I would study it further and announce my position later if I received the party's endorsement. This answer did not wash. The Lindsay-Schaub papers, which previously had given me favorable coverage, wrote a story indicating that of all the contenders interviewed, only I had not endorsed taking the superintendent position out of politics. Even if my stance in favor of political control of the superintendent office hurt me with reformers in the general election, my immediate need was to capture the nomination, and no damage had resulted in this regard. In fact, the newspapers' statements had helped me with downstate leaders, who usually opposed reform of any type.

For good or ill, I had made some important contacts with professional educators and had gained strong labor support and financial commitments. Toting up the pluses and minuses, I felt that, on the whole, the campaign was going well.

Although I ascribed great importance to backing by labor and education, one group in particular counted above all others: the Irish inner circle. These people were uppermost in my mind, and what an advantage I held! State Senator Art McGloon, my personal political tutor and committeeman of my father-in-law's Thirty-seventh Ward, had risen to prominence in the machine family and now served as the minority leader of the Illinois state senate; moreover, his leadership position brought him quite close to the mayor. McGloon conferred with Daley weekly while the legislature was in session and conferred frequently when it was not, since McGloon headed a ward that produced handsome majorities for the machine. I had maintained my contacts with McGloon through correspondence and brief conversations with him at the state capitol during my occasional trips there.

He had told me, "Mel, if I can ever do anything for you, be sure to let me know." Now he could do me a big favor—he could team up with my downstate sponsor, Clyde Choate. McGloon could become my Chicago mentor.

But before I got around to asking him, I began to hear rumors: Bakalis had McGloon's backing. Of all the fifty wards in Chicago, Bakalis had come from McGloon's Thirty-seventh; he was a native son, whereas I was related to the ward only through marriage. Furthermore, Bakalis, it developed, had sought out McGloon much earlier in the campaign. When I finally discovered that the rumors were true, I could have kicked myself for not going after McGloon's endorsement earlier. I might not have acquired it because of Bakalis's one-of-our-own status, but I should have tried.

A second effort with the Irish was made for me by Nick Fera, Sr., the father of one of my SIU students, Nick, Jr. As I was about to make my last trip to Chicago prior to the nominating session, Nick, Junior, told me that he had spoken to his father on my behalf and that the senior Fera wanted to meet me. I assured young Nick I would see his father. But after four fruitless efforts to reach Fera through his answering service, I concentrated on seeing labor leaders instead. Only after my return to Carbondale did I learn that Fera had arranged for me to meet Matt Danaher, close personal friend and confidant to Mayor Daley, and had left the message with the answering service. I had not received it. When Danaher and I did meet two years later, we talked easily together, and I felt he would have been an effective advocate had I met him in time.

I tried to enlist Michael Howlett, the popular state auditor. Encouraged by one of his political associates, I sent Howlett a resume and requested an appointment. I did not get a response, and I later discovered that he had sponsored Mike Bakalis early on.

Faced with these major disappointments, I simply had to do the best I could with the endorsements I was sure of. Paul Powell had stressed the importance of not letting verbal endorsements stand by themselves: one needed them in writing, and they should be sent directly to Daley. Moreover, Powell emphasized, the endorsers should send me copies, which would perform two functions: I would know that the person who promised a letter had, in fact, sent it; and I would have a tangible dossier to present to Mayor Daley and the other slatemakers as proof of my endorsements.

Ray Chancey agreed to solicit such endorsements from the county chairmen in the Twenty-first Congressional District. My first step in this direction was to send them copies of my resume, after which Chancey made a personal plea at the monthly chairmen's meeting at Tony's Restaurant in Marion. Almost all chairmen, however, played the game of "downstate duck." That is, even if they favored a candidate, they were reluctant to reveal it until the Chicago contingent had reached a decision in order not to end up on the "wrong" side. It was the same old game, and few letters were forthcoming.

Chancey next had me draft, for his signature, a letter indicating my endorsement campaign's accelerating momentum and my dependability on patronage. Striking a balance between appropriate modesty and effective salesmanship caused me much difficulty, but the letter evidently worked—several county chairmen decided to risk a preslatemaking endorsement, which, as a few indicated and as I well knew, they did not give casually.

I received endorsements from other sources as well. Both the Southeast Illinois Building Trades Council and the carpenters union sent letters to Mayor Daley. Chairman Charles Mileur of the Building Trades Council wrote that, among other things, his group felt I "would be a winner and bring new life into the superintendent's office as well as being a credit to the Democratic party in Illinois." With Mileur's written endorsement, my campaign had come full circle, for it was at a monthly meeting of the business agents in Carbondale that I made my first southern Illinois campaign speech three months earlier.

Because the party was acutely conscious of the alienation of many young people from the machine, Dan Mitchell, southeastern regional director of the state's Young Democrats, sent an endorsement letter to Daley. One part of Mitchell's letter summed up quite accurately my base of support:

> I know that [Dr. Kahn] is supported by labor unions, educational groups, several newspapers, Young Democrat groups, and several county chairmen who are aware of his superb qualifications. . . .
>
> The fact that Dr. Melvin Kahn has taught at all levels of education and in all areas of our state (Cook County and Downstate) makes him a strong unity candidate and a state-wide vote getter. . . .

In the meantime, a serendipitous thing happened: Andy Gianulis, a former student, dropped in to visit and mentioned that he had talked to his father, John Gianulis, about my nomination efforts. The elder Gianulis was chairman of the Rock Island County organization, the fourth largest Democratic stronghold in the state. Andy said, "My father is interested in what I told him about you. He'd like to know more about you, especially what kind of support you have, your financial backing, and the reasons you think you could win the election." This represented a real breakthrough. All my other endorsements were from southern Illinois, and now to secure the backing of a powerful county chairman in northern Illinois would be a real coup. I went quickly to work and composed a letter that turned out to be both a fair summary of my strengths, as I saw them in early November 1969, and an outline of my plans for the last few weeks of the nomination campaign. After the customary formalities, the letter read:

> First, I genuinely enjoy a good, hard campaign. As the co-chairman of Citizens for Shapiro in the Twenty-first Congressional District, I was called on to give many talks throughout the district. Unlike a lot of people in education, I have a genuine admiration and respect for precinct committeemen because of their role as bulwarks of our two-party system. Consequently, I seem to have good rapport with them—they know I appreciate the crucial role they play.
>
> At the present time, I number the following among my backers: Representative Clyde Choate; Ray Chancey, my county chairman, who also tells me that as far as he knows, all chairmen in the Twenty-first District are behind me; Governor Sam Shapiro; Alderman Kenneth Campbell of Chicago; informal backing of many Young Democrats, who are not permitted to formally endorse; the Southern Illinois Business Agents Association; and, unofficially, John Alesia of the steelworkers. I also have reason to believe that I will soon emerge with even more labor support because of my close association with labor.
>
> Regarding finances, I have been assured that if nominated I will receive substantial backing. In a few days, I will call you by phone and be more specific.
>
> Because of coming from a union family and having extensive experience in working with unions, I should have strong access to the labor vote. I will not only speak in union halls but will go after

those who need prodding by working the factory gates throughout the state.

As a downstate teacher, I can demonstrate that I understand the problems of downstate. Also, by virtue of the contacts I made while campaigning for Shapiro in downstate Illinois, I will have ready access to many of the downstate areas.

Harry Truman proved that people like a campaigner and relish the idea that a candidate is willing to seek their vote and discuss the issues. I can assure you that if endorsed I will immediately start campaigning and actively covering the state.

Finally, I fully realize that there are professionals who know a lot more about politics than myself. I am not afraid to listen and will profit immensely by following the counsel of those in our party who are knowledgeable in the art of politics.

I was grateful to John Gianulis for initiating the sorts of questions that forced me to make the above assessment as to where I had been and where I was going in the campaign. Whenever I was plagued by doubts (which was almost constantly now), I repeated like a catechism my letter's checklist of political support. But Gianulis had asked additionally about my financial support. Not wishing to give the details in a letter, I called him and spelled out my financial sources. My phone call had another purpose—I felt I could sell myself better in conversation than within the confines of a letter. The investment paid off handsomely. Gianulis not only promised to help me but also secured backing from the cochairman of neighboring Henry County, Fred J. Brown. Gianulis sent a letter to Mayor Daley in which, although he did not give me a formal endorsement (to have done so might have put him at cross-purposes with the slatemakers if they chose another candidate), he expressed appreciation for "any consideration you may give to the candidacy of Dr. Kahn." Fred Brown sent a telegram of endorsement not to Daley but to Clyde Choate. Perhaps Brown did not understand that my endorsement should go to Daley himself; or maybe he wanted to use Choate as a sort of "half-way house," thus not irrevocably committing himself to me with Daley. Brown was a cochairman, and I did not receive the endorsement of his fellow chairman of Henry County. Nevertheless, I appreciated the help Brown and Gianulis were offering me, and I understood fully the political risk they ran by even a qualified endorsement. They had let Daley know that, as far as they were concerned, I would be a good man. I was in their debt.

With these two concrete gestures of support, I had struck gold, and, at the time, I thought that no other prospective candidate had received this type of backing outside his home county. I later would discover that Bakalis had, but now I had elicited two such communiqués from the northern part of the state, one of them from a Democratic stronghold. Most importantly, I had scored right in Mike Bakalis's own backyard. If Paul Powell were correct, this would give me powerful momentum down the backstretch and toward the finish line, where Mayor Daley and the slatemakers waited.

8
The Politics of Decision Making

The weeks of sending signals to the top were now over, and the time had come for my competitors and me to present ourselves before the slatemaking committee, the members of which would judge among us and then bestow the laurel wreath.

A word must be said regarding the uniqueness of the Illinois Democratic party's slatemaking system. First, the state central committee—composed of the committeemen from each congressional district (twenty-four in all), the president of the County Chairmen's Association, and all state officeholders—meet in Springfield. Additionally, formal invitations go to all "available" contenders, instructing them to contact the committee and schedule an appearance. Upon receiving my invitation, I decided that the best strategy would be to speak last in order to make the final impact on the committee. Because I was the first to respond, I received my preferred time slot. Adlai Stevenson III proved wiser. He requested the first slot, thereby addressing the political leaders while they were fresh and alert.

A second element in the format of the state central committee intrigued me: their requirement that aspirants appear before them twice, first in Springfield and again in Chicago. The only difference between the two, but a major difference, was that the Daley organization participated in the latter but not in the former.

Curious, I asked an experienced politician, "Why *two* meetings?"

"Daley would feel affronted if he had to travel to Springfield—it would detract from his position as the head of his party."

Dissatisfied, I asked, "Why doesn't everyone just go directly to Chicago instead of meeting in Springfield first?"

"If they did that," he answered, 'the newspapers would say that Daley is nothing but a boss. So they run it both ways, and the first time is a dress rehearsal."

Aware of this, former Governor Sam Shapiro had warned me, "Some people try to play the downstate game in Springfield and talk like a Chicagoan in Chicago. Don't do that. If you do, the people who hear you both times will react negatively."

Two days before the slatemaking session in Springfield, a devastating news story broke concerning Southern Illinois University president Delyte Morris's new home. The mansion, located in a beautiful wooded expanse, contained imported marble, elegant chandeliers, and eight bedrooms, each bedroom with an adjoining bath. The driveway lit up when cars approached, and the windows were equipped with automatic outside defrosters for the occasional southern Illinois snowfall. The cause célèbre was the revelation that the president's home would cost more than $900,000 for building material alone, its construction being financed by money siphoned from grants normally used for graduate student support and faculty research. Moreover, labor also costing more than $900,000 had been hidden in the payroll of the university physical plant. Political leaders of both parties were incensed. Paul Powell and Clyde Choate, the university's two patron saints, felt especially perturbed, for they had vetoed a proposed $70,000 house several years earlier, fearing that it would portray SIU as extravagant. Now the apparent skimming off of grant money for a $1,800,000 house was embarrassing in the extreme to both Choate and Powell.

Alerted to the danger this scandal posed, on the day of the slatemaking session I arrived early in Springfield and contacted two people whose political acumen I valued highly. Both happened to be Republicans. Ron Michelson, a graduate student writing his Ph.D. dissertation under my direction, served as a top administrative aide to Governor Richard Ogilvie. During our meeting, he told me the media had reported Mel Kahn and Gene Graves of SIU ruled out of their respective races for superintendent and state treasurer because of their identification with the university. I was in real trouble, Michelson warned, and should anticipate the problems of my SIU affiliation. I next met with Jack Van Der Slik, my colleague on leave, who expressed opinions similar to Michelson's and cautioned that I could expect some very hostile questions from the slatemaking committee.

Heeding the admonitions of Michelson and Van Der Slik, I carefully revised my fourteen-minute talk. (Because the state chairman stops the speaker after precisely fifteen minutes, I wanted to make certain I ended on time.) It then occurred to me that, regardless of the outcome and in spite of the fact that I personally did not care for what I considered the nondemocratic ways of SIU's president, simple decency forbade further attack on a man already under the gun. Therefore, I resolved to face the question squarely and defend both my institution and President Morris.

I expressed this intention to Clyde Choate, whom I encountered in the men's room prior to my appearance before the committee. Choate concurred. He also offered some sage advice on another point: "Mel, as you know, the money problem is very, very important since we're broke in the state organization. We don't have the governorship, and there are no big contributions from highway builders and supply people. The party doesn't have anything to give you. So why don't you tell them you're in good shape financially, that you won't ask for any money? It won't cost you anything because there's nothing there anyway. And you just watch—it will go over real big."

While awaiting the call to speak before the slatemakers, all the contenders remained in a special suite in the St. Nicholas Hotel. Before each one went in to speak, others offered words of encouragement. I was impressed with their quality and felt that, with one exception, I easily could support any of the fourteen men present that day.

One man, Al Penman, worked for Paul Powell and hoped eventually to win his support. He did tell me, however, that Powell had not offered him encouragement and had insisted that he not miss any work while campaigning for the nomination. Penman, who had begun his race in 1967, remarked, "Mel, if only I had your Ph.D. or you had started campaigning two years sooner, one of us would probably end up with the nomination." He well knew that with seven contenders holding the doctorate the party most likely would select one of them. When my name was called, Penman lent me his watch, put his arm on my shoulder, and said, "Best of luck, Mel." I recognized the gesture of a generous man.

The room I walked into was smoky, and I had trouble seeing

through the haze. I felt momentarily buoyed when I spotted Paul Powell in the front row, the man who had allowed me to visit with him for nearly an hour and who, while not officially endorsing me, had been very cooperative. Rumor had it that he was impressed with me and might support me at the appropriate time. Overall, however, I felt tense as I stood at the front of the long, narrow room on the hotel's second floor. My heart thumped, and my throat felt dry.

Because the issue of the SIU president's house loomed as a potentially impassable obstacle, I tackled it first: "I am proud to be from Southern Illinois University," I began, "and we can determine if improprieties occurred there only after a thorough investigation. And even if there were mistakes, Southern Illinois remains a good institution." I cited specific programs. In the field of human rehabilitation, I argued, SIU had demonstrated compassion by providing opportunities for those who otherwise would have become "tax-eaters" rather than taxpayers. Further, the talent-search project had enabled numerous students from underprivileged families to attend the university, and SIU enrolled more students through this program than did all other Illinois universities combined. As a result of its specially designed facilities for handicapped students, I pointed out, SIU had not only served them well but also had attracted faculty of worldwide renown in the area of special education.

Next, I made a calculated statement that might, I thought, become a political asset: I praised the university for its acquisition of the Vietnam Center: "Although the Center has been highly contro-versial on campus, I feel that the charges leveled against it and its leadership have been exaggerated. Of all the universities in this country wanting a Vietnam Center—including the University of California at Berkeley, the University of Chicago, and Harvard—the U.S. government has selected SIU." I had hopes that my advocacy of the Vietnam Center would be reported to the media, in which case I anticipated denouncement by some of my militant colleagues and members of the Students for a Democratic Society, an attack I reasoned could serve as a prime political asset. Overall, I attempted to turn a political deficit into profit by aligning myself staunchly with my university. Moreover, I challenged the incumbent Republican school superintendent, Ray Page, to make a political issue of the contro-versial president's house, since, as an ex officio member of the university board, it was Page who had offered the motion to build the house after the Illinois Board of Higher Education had rejected the proposal.

I next moved to the heart of my strategy on this issue, which was to play upon the antagonism many slatemakers felt toward the newspapers. Displaying a copy of the *Illinois State Register*, with its headline on the SIU "mansion scandal," I reminded the committee that the newspapers, not content to oppose our Democratic party, also insisted upon telling us how to conduct our internal affairs. "They told us in 1948 that we should not nominate Harry Truman because their polls showed that he did not have a chance. We did not bow to them then, and we're not going to allow them to dictate to us now; for the Democratic party is the party of the people, not the Republican, one-party press."

I climaxed my presentation with the statement suggested by Clyde Choate: "Organized labor and my ethnic community have assured me of substantial financing backing. In fact, I am so confident of my finances that I give you my solemn pledge that under no circumstances will I ask the party for so much as one nickel." Loud and sustained applause greeted this declaration. Winking, Clyde Choate shot me an "okay" sign, and I realized that his strategy had been correct, that this was the most important message I could have given the slatemakers.

As I spoke, I was badly disconcerted by Powell's rudeness. During most of my speech, he was not only reading a newspaper but was holding it in front of his face. I wished I could treat him as I would a boorish student—stop speaking until he realized everyone was looking at him and thus embarrass him into attention. I thought the better of it, however, because I needed Powell's support. It was not until I drew to a close and alluded to the late Vice-President Alben Barkley, Powell's good friend from Puducah, Kentucky, that he put down the newspaper and listened.

Despite Powell's apparent indifference, the speech seemed to have gone over quite well. Although slatemakers are instructed not to reveal to reporters or to "available" contenders their reactions to the presentations, some violate this norm. Irma Agoe, the state central committeewomen from downstate, slipped over and squeezed my hand. "Good job, Mel. Slow down your speech for Chicago, and you've got an excellent chance of getting the nod."

The Reverend Corneal "Deacon" Davis approached and congratulated me warmly: "Mel, I like the way you pour it on. And it's good to see people like you at SIU. Did you ever hear the story of how I integrated the college dance?"

"No, Deacon, I didn't."

"Well, some black students told me that blacks were being barred from the big dance, and so I called the SIU president and said, 'If you don't let black kids in there, I'll personally escort them in. What do you think about that?' 'I don't want any trouble,' he said. 'I agree,' I told him, 'and if there isn't any trouble, I'll see to it that the appropriations committee won't have to cut your budget.' Well, he got the message real quick, and that dance was integrated." Placing his arm on my shoulder, Davis continued, "Mel, you're my kind of speaker. I'm for you."

This direct offer of support from a Chicago politician was an unexpected boon and pleased me greatly. I was still an underdog, but I felt I had at least a reasonably good chance for the endorsement. Now, however, the Springfield appearance behind me, I began to get anxious about whether I really could raise the $200,000 to $250,000 required for conducting a successful campaign. One night, I dreamed I had come up with $1,000, called Daley to ask for the remaining $199,000, but woke up in a cold sweat before he could answer me. The absurdity of this dream sobered me into a resolve to put the money question out of my mind and concentrate instead on my next step and last hurdle, the Chicago slatemaking session.

For this event, I spent hours preparing a presentation that was politically calculated and directed solely toward achieving the endorsement. The problem boiled down to defining and then developing my case. As a preliminary measure, my wife, Adrienne, and I examined the resumes of the other "available" candidates and agreed that at least six competitors possessed administrative qualifications for the superintendent post that were better than mine. I opted for the argument that my superior political experience would allow me to wage the most effective campaign against the incumbent. Chancey and Choate approved. I would convince the slatemakers that I was a steadfast Democrat who could conduct a strenuous campaign that would put the Republicans on the defensive. The thrust of my strategy would be to tie Richard Ogilvie, the unpopular Republican governor, to the incumbent, Ray Page. Mine would be a speech as single-mindedly political as I could make it, rather than one emphasizing primarily my educational qualifications or the substantive work I would try to accomplish as superintendent.

But one issue that concerned me greatly was aid to parochial schools. Although the Chicago slatemakers perhaps were oriented toward my Jewish background, I did not take the standard Jewish position on the issue. Traditionally, Jews have opposed all public support to parochial schools. I, however, questioned the feasibility of that sentiment, given the precarious financial situation of many of the Illinois parochial schools, a particularly serious problem in Chicago, where nearly fifty percent of all students attended them. Should they close, the great influx of students to the public schools would create a critical burden.

To deal with this perplexing issue, I had researched it and had consulted with a constitutional law expert, Professor Randall Nelson, the new political science chair at SIU. I had concluded that the families of students attending parochial schools should receive limited aid in the form of an extra tax deduction on the Illinois state income tax. Parents sending their children to a parochial school inevitably paid more than their counterparts who sent their children to one of the public schools, and did so on two counts: total taxes for educational purposes plus parochial school tuition. I proposed that these parents receive some tax relief to offset the double burden they bore because of their educational choice. I planned, in addition, to advocate parochial students' enrolling in academic classes in the public schools.

After I had prepared for this problem, it was on to Chicago. I have noted earlier that the party considered the Springfield appearance of would-be candidates as just so much "window dressing," or, as one prominent county chairman called it, "eyewash." Chicago constituted the ultimate test, a test governed by rules set forth by the dominant Cook County organization. Whereas in Springfield contenders could request their own speaking time, in Chicago the machine arranged the speaking order alphabetically according to the office each prospective nominee sought.

Among the contenders for superintendent, Mike Bakalis spoke first. The following represents Bakalis's recollection of his speech.[1]

"In the introduction, I attempted to appeal to the strong ethnic component of the Cook County central committee through a reference to my grandfather, who came here as an immigrant at the end of the nineteenth century and cast his first vote for Woodrow Wilson in the election of 1912. I attempted also to suggest that my very presence before them was in many ways an embodiment of the American dream and of the principles of the Democratic party, for clearly it showed that within two generations the grandson of an uneducated immigrant could aspire to the chief educational office of a major state.

"In the second section, I tried to outline the reasons I sought the office. Essentially, these were that I wanted to present a positive program to the people of Illinois as to what quality education could be and that I was dissatisfied that our state was not the best in every category. I then tried to humanize the quest through some rhetoric about the impact of an inadequate education on youngsters in ghettos and in the rural parts of the state and also made reference to the fact that thousands of young people, while being given access to higher education, were increasingly becoming alienated from the system. I told them that I would run on a platform of asking for new standards of excellence that I believed would be a contrast to the sterile, unimaginative mediocrity that I believed symbolized the administration of Ray Page. I also told them that I sought the nomination because I was a father who was concerned about the quality of his children's education, knowing full well, of course, that it would not hurt for them to know that I did have a family.

"In the third section of my presentation, I tried to outline the reasons I believed I could win the election. Essentially, these were my experience at all levels of education, the fact that my job at Northern [Illinois University] had taken me on travels throughout the state, and also that I had generated hundreds of letters of support from educators throughout the state, which had been mailed to members of the state central committee. I also told them that I could win because I was not politically inexperienced, that I had been active since I was sixteen years old in precinct work; and I made sure that I stressed that it was in the precincts of Chicago. I indicated to them that I also served as a precinct committeeman while I lived in Evanston and that when I moved to DeKalb I organized the Democratic Club of DeKalb as well as being a member of the regular Democratic organization of that county. I tried to point out to them that I could win because I would be an aggressive candidate and that I had gone around the state seeking the support of state central committeemen in every geographic area. I tried to suggest to them that I believed I could appeal to young people, to students, to teachers, and to mothers. It is important to keep in mind that this was the first slating session after the serious negative images that Mayor Daley and the Democratic party had received as an aftermath of the national convention which was held in Chicago in 1968. Thus, part of my pitch was that we needed to appeal to a whole generation that had been alienated from the party and that I could do that. I finally indicated to them that I believed I could raise an adequate amount of money, although I was clearly involved in guesswork when I talked about this.

"I ended the presentation with some negative comments about the performance of Ray Page and said that I would present a positive program which would be such a striking contrast to him and to his administration that the election could be won."

It was later confirmed to me that the Bakalis speech had gone over splendidly, something I had deduced when, as I was awaiting my turn, Adlai Stevenson III paused in the anteroom and remarked, "Excellent job, Mike." I will not say that my heart sank; on the other hand, the shore seemed to have receded a little.

Mayor Daley had given his word, though, that the nomination would not be locked up in advance, that he had seen people come before the slatemakers, give the best talk, and walk away with it. Contrary to what Daley had told me, the conventional wisdom held that the speeches carried no weight. But chairman Jim Ronan later confirmed Daley's assertion. Over the years, Ronan said, he had seen highly touted aspirants kill their chances with mediocre or even offensive speeches. "In fact," he told me, "one guy in your group, Mel, got up there and started talking about 'reds' and 'pinkos' on college campuses. Well, he took himself out right then and there—we weren't having any of that junk." Ronan also had seen unknowns win the endorsement, he said, by the combination of an effective presentation and other positive attributes: "There was a lawyer named Parsons who contacted his committeeman at the last minute. Nobody had ever heard of him up till then. Well, he walked in and gave one helluva presentation. We were looking for a good black judge, and he sure filled the bill. We were really happy to have found a top-flight man like that to be on our ticket." If the speech to the slatemakers could make a difference, maybe Bakalis was not a foregone conclusion after all. Still, I had to generate some smoke.

In preparing for this moment, I had determined the following factors to be the core of what I had to offer the slatemaking committee: First, I would make the most dynamic campaigner, specifically, the most effective campaigner against incumbent Ray Page. Second, I was unambiguously a downstater, unlike Bakalis, whose claim to downstate status was marginal. Third, I possessed successful downstate political experience as co-campaign manager for ex-Governor Sam Shapiro. Fourth, I had done campaign work in Cook County as well. Fifth, I could function as a bridge between the generations and among various occupational groups. Lastly, I was tuned in to the ethnic make-up of the machine—if they needed a Jewish candidate to harvest votes in Cook County, I was their man.

The Jewish factor was important. The machine had been faring poorly in the North Shore wards and in the suburbs, areas occupied by a high percentage of the Jewish population. Phil Goldstick, a politically astute lawyer, confirmed this when he told me, "Daley needs a Jewish candidate in Cook County. I don't know if he's found one yet, and for this reason you might well be the man. Let the slatemakers know you're Jewish, but don't overstress it." Considering that he himself was Jewish and aspired to the county ticket, his encouragement was unselfish, for my endorsement undoubtedly would insure his omission from the slate. He gave me one other piece of advice: "The slatemakers will sit there for over nine hours hearing one candidate after another drone on as to why he is highly qualified. Loosen them up. Give them plenty of humor. They'll appreciate it, and it will help your presentation. And another thing, when you start off, tell them you're a politician, not an educator. They'll love it."

On the bitterly cold morning of the Big Day, I emerged from the Royal Style Shop shaven and neatly trimmed and began walking the two blocks to the Sherman House Hotel. But as I approached it, I got a bad scare: Picketers were parading in front of the hotel entrance. Never before had I violated a picket line, and as the one contender with labor support I could not cross this one even if I wanted to. Nearing them, however, I discovered to my relief that the picketers were just individual workers protesting against county board president George Dunne. Had they turned out to be bona fide union members, I would have faced a real dilemma.

I checked in with the receptionist and joined the other aspirants waiting outside the caucus room. And when, a few minutes later, the door opened and the speaker who had just finished emerged, I gave the doorman my dossiers for distribution to the slatemakers. Only after it was too late did I realize that my neatly typed notes were missing—I had forgotten to remove them from the special folder I had prepared for Mayor Daley. Well, so much the better; without notes I could achieve excellent eye contact. And I did know the speech well, having practiced it more than twenty times before various audiences. My listeners had included colleagues at SIU; a former student who became my captive on the train to Chicago; my wife; and my mother-in-law, Mildred Iseberg, who had had the patience to endure three separate practice sessions. Now five months of arduous campaigning had finally brought me to Judgment Day.

Entering the large meeting room, I glanced around quickly and estimated more than eighty-five political leaders present. They consisted of approximately forty-five committeemen from Cook County, the twenty-four members of the state central committee, and about sixteen to eighteen state party officials and officeholders. The room, unlike the one in Springfield, was large, well-lighted, and adequately ventilated.

As I stood behind the podium at front left and scanned the three sections of seating, I felt reassured, because I already had met most of the eighty-five slatemakers. Clyde Choate, my downstate sponsor, sat next to my potential advocate, Paul Powell. And Powell was not reading a newspaper this time. I sought out my principal ethnic backers. There was Vito Marzullo in the front row. Colonel Kenneth Campbell, the black leader, occupied a seat in the middle section. Art McGloon, in the back, would provide Irish support if Bakalis got ruled out. Also in the back sat "Deacon" Davis, who had broken the norm in Springfield by letting me know he supported me. Marshall Korshak, the Jewish leader, sat next to him rolling an elegant cigar from one side of his mouth to the other. All my ethnic advocates were on hand except for Congressman Roman Pucinski. Where was "Pooch"? He had promised a labor friend that he would support me but had also sent word that he would ask me a question pertaining to education legislation. Not having known what to expect, I felt relieved, in a way, that Pucinski was not there to catch me unawares.

Congressman Dan Rostenkowski, the chairman of the meeting, introduced me, and now I felt a quiet confidence as I addressed the three leaders at the main table and the audience facing the four of us:

"Chairman Rostenkowski, Mr. Mayor, State Chairman Ronan, and Fellow Democrats:

"Today I come before you not as Dr. Melvin Kahn, educator, but as Mel Kahn, organization Democrat. I am proud to be a Democrat, for as a student of history I know what our Democratic party has accomplished for all the people and that we have done more good than all the Republicans, do-gooders, independents, and reformers lumped together.

"It was our Democratic party, and our Democratic party alone, that spearheaded the Americanization process of free public education for everybody; that has always supported the idea that every child is entitled to become his best possible self; and that has always cured Republican depressions. Believe me, no political party in any nation, at any time, at any place, has ever accomplished for its people what our Democratic party has performed. And, most importantly, our Democratic party of Illinois, under your leadership, has marched in the forefront of our great national party.

"Because of these accomplishments, I am proud to be a member of our great party. But there is also a personal reason. Some years ago I was dating a young Chicago woman, and her father didn't think that I or any other young man was good enough for his daughter. One Friday evening, when I came to take her to a movie, she told me we would have to collect signatures on nominating petitions because her father, a precinct captain, had the flu, and ward committeeman Paul Corcoran did not accept flu as an excuse."

[Corcoran, one of the sainted Democratic leaders, had died the previous year. At the mention of his name, Mayor Daley and many of the Chicagoans became quite attentive.]

"As we collected the signatures, something very interesting happened. An elderly Jewish lady signed one petition after another until she came to one that she held on to, exclaiming, 'McGloon! He's not Jewish, is he?'

"My young lady friend said, 'No, he's not Jewish, but my father says he's the very best friend the Jewish people have in all of Austin.' "

[At this, every slatemaker turned to look and smile at state Senator McGloon. He beamed back.]

"Well, the lady signed the petition, my girlfriend and I gathered the necessary number of signatures, and, after that, the father of this young lady eased his objections and came to the conclusion that his daughter might do worse than marry a good Democrat. Fellow Democrats, proving myself as a Democratic leader in the vineyards by securing nominating petitions was the crucial factor in my life.

Today, I'm happy to say that I'm married to this young lady, and we have three very fine children. And so, to you, the Democratic leaders who will *not* accept flu as an excuse for failing to get the job done, my deepest gratitude for helping me win the hand of a tremendous young woman."

[Though I was actually engaging in hypocrisy—our marriage was somewhat rocky at this point—I figured that retouching my Democratic love story might help politically.]

"Unfortunately, when we get away from the Democratic party, we have problems, and today we have a blank page in Illinois education. What has happened is that the GOP—the Not-So-Grand Ogilvie party—working hand in glove with the Blank-Page administration, has short-changed the school kids of Illinois. Now, why do I say we have a blank page? First, we have a blank page in drug prevention. Less than five percent of Illinois schools provide adequate education programs on drugs. I say to you, our children are too valuable a resource to be shortchanged by a blank page in drug education.

"We also have a blank page in reading. One-third of the school children in Illinois cannot adequately read their textbooks. And nonreaders become high-school drop–outs, the same drop–outs who commit eighty percent of crimes.

"There's also a blank page in guidance counselling. The superintendent of public instruction sets the certification standards for guidance counselors, and yet Illinois is the only major state in the nation that doesn't require any supervised training before a person becomes a guidance counselor. If I become state superintendent, I will see to it that we no longer use school children, our most treasured resource, for on-the-job training.

"Now, I question seriously whether the present Republican administration can deal competently with our educational problems. In fact, there is a story going around about one of Page's Republican incompetents: He belonged to a club where somebody stood up and recommended ordering a new chandelier. The Republican said, 'I object! First of all, if we went to order it, nobody would know how to spell it. Second, nobody here knows how to play one. Third, if we're going to spend money on anything, what this club really needs is a new light fixture.' "

[Laughter from the audience.]

"I say to you in all due respect, I will provide leadership in meeting our critical educational needs. I have been behind the classroom doors at all three levels—elementary school, high school, and the university. I have taught in the city of Chicago, the suburbs, and now the downstate area. In addition to my background, I believe I can function as a bridge between the generations. I am the only available person for this position who has spoken before this state's Young Democrats; and at Southern Illinois University I served as a liaison between the Young Democrats and the party organization in our county.

"I've worked successfully in the downstate area, as cochairman for Governor Shapiro. When he was losing in the rest of the state, we carried Jackson County for him. Now, I don't take credit for this; mine was but a small role. But I proved that I could work in harmony with Democratic party leaders so that we functioned effectively. And, while attending the University of Chicago, I stood with the great Congressman Barratt O'Hara when he was attacked by the evil forces of racism and hatred in the South Side of Chicago. I'm proud to say that in that campaign I worked together with party leaders, blacks, labor unions, and young people in turning back the slander of that vicious campaign. Yes, fellow Democrats, I not only believe in the Democratic party, but I've demonstrated time and time again a willingness to stand, work, and win with our party whether it be in Cook County or downstate.

"Let me tell you something—we in downstate Illinois know how to treat those Ogilvie Republicans. We like to tell the story of a suburban Ogilvie Republican who was traveling in downstate Illinois. He noticed a farmer, pulled up alongside the road, and stopped.

"He said, 'Hey, Mr. Farmer! Are you one of those downstate Democrats?'

"The farmer replied, 'Sure am! And mighty proud of it!'

"With that, the Ogilvie Republican reached into his glove compartment, pulled out a gun, and sneered, 'Okay, Mr. Democrat, you're going to dance.' Then he zinged three quick shots at the farmer.

"The farmer did a little shuffle back and forth, and the Republican fired another three shots. Again, the farmer shuffled. The Ogilvie Republican chuckled loudly and obviously felt very good.

"The Democratic farmer then asked, 'Mr. Republican, you had six shots in that gun?'

" 'Yes.'

" 'And you used them all up?'

" 'Yes.'

"The farmer reached into his hay wagon, pulled out a rifle, and pointed it at the Republican, saying, 'Okay, Mr. Ogilvie Republican, have you ever kissed a mule's fanny?'

" 'No, but I'm sure looking forward to it!' "

[The audience roared. A glance at Mayor Daley assured me that he was laughing as heartily as the others, and for the first time I felt I had cracked his tough armor.]

"We downstate Democrats know how to treat those Ogilvie Republicans, and if you put one of us on the state ticket, we'll show you how it's done.

"I'd like to point out something else—there are some misguided do-gooders who look with scorn at precinct captains and committeemen. I disagree. I teach my students that the precinct worker, who prowls the precincts and knocks on doors, is the cogwheel of democracy, the direct link between the voters and the party organization. Because of my genuine respect and admiration for these vital people, I will work effectively with the precinct captains and committeemen, the real backbone of our party.

"Now let's talk realistically. Without sufficient finances, the best candidate in the world cannot become adequately known. Fellow Democrats, I have the financial resources to wage a successful campaign. John Alesia of the steelworkers has authorized me to tell you that the steelworkers will make a substantial financial contribution to my candidacy. Governor Shapiro has also assured me that I will receive a sizable contribution from my own religious group, comparable to that which any statewide candidate of my faith would receive. Fellow Democrats, I am so confident of these pledges that I make you a solemn promise—I will not, under any circumstances, ask the Democratic state central committee for one single nickel in this campaign."

[Sustained applause.]

"Most importantly, though, I am a loyal Democrat. If you choose another person, I will work as hard for him as I have always worked for the Democratic party. I will do everything asked of me plus more, for obviously there are some tremendous men available. But if you select me as our standard-bearer, I will campaign this state as it has never been campaigned before—because, quite frankly, I am a bad loser. I agree with our great leader Franklin D. Roosevelt that

'Victory is our habit.' As a good Democrat, *I believe in following that habit again and again and again!"*

[Applause.]

"I would like to close with the phrase used by our beloved Vice-President Alben Barkley, a great leader of all Democrats but particularly close to us in southern Illinois because he lived just across the river in Puducah. At the Democratic convention in 1948, he quoted Revelations: 'Behold, I stand at the door and knock. If anyone opens the door, I will enter and serve.' Fellow Democrats, I would like to serve all the people as superintendent of schools, where I could *answer* the knock of *those who need to be served.* Today, the school children of the state knock at the door. Children afflicted with the scourge of drug addiction—they knock at the door. Our most precious resource, the children who need guidance and counselling from competent people—they knock at the door. The handicapped children of our state—they knock at the door. As Democrats, the party of compassion, we cannot ignore those who knock.

"Ladies and gentlemen of the Democratic party, with your help I stand ready to lead our party to victory. But, more importantly, when we win it will mean more than a party victory—or a personal victory: It will mean victory for our school children, because they are the ones with the greatest stake in this election. Fellow Democrats, I hear the knock at the door. If you so decide, I will answer that knock and carry our Democratic banner high and proud!"

As I finished, I noticed Marshall Korshak and "Deacon" Davis grinning and nodding at each other. Colonel Campbell slapped his knee, and Choate, beaming, shot me an "okay" sign. Powell was smiling, and the usually impassive Daley was looking at me with what I interpreted to be a new interest.

Congressman Rostenkowski spoke: "Excellent presentation, Mel." [I thought this remark significant, because he had introduced me as *Dr.* Melvin Kahn. To me, this new, personal note indicated progress.] "I want to ask you a question: If you do not receive an endorsement, will you support in the primary the person we endorse?"

As with the knights of old, he was asking that I formally pledge my fealty in advance of the decision, despite my having given such assurance during my speech. I replied, "As in every primary in the past, I will enthusiastically support every single person endorsed at this meeting." That was what Rostenkowski and the others wanted to hear from all the contenders, vows of obedience that would preclude a primary fight.

When Eddie Barrett asked, "How about jobs?" I was ready:

"Loyalty and competence are necessary requirements for any worker. My aim is to hire people with the same outlook and philosophy as I have; and, since I am a strong Democrat, I will do my utmost to hire strong Democrats. Under no circumstance will I even consider hiring a Republican or independent unless there are absolutely no competent Democrats available. In addition, loyalty dictates that I will not consider anyone who does not have approval from his ward committeeman or county chairman.

"Now, this does not mean that I will automatically hire everyone recommended—as a professional educator, I cannot delegate my responsibility to determine educational competence for the policy-making positions. But, rest assured, each applicant must not only meet my standards of competency but your standards of party loyalty."

This answer apparently pleased the audience, for I noticed several heads nodding affirmatively. I later found out that Michael Bakalis had given a less detailed, more subtle, and more politically effective answer when asked his position on patronage. He had answered: "I have a young daughter whom I love very much. And I want you to know that, as a father, it makes me feel a lot better knowing that her school bus is inspected by a Democrat instead of a Republican."

As Rostenkowski was getting ready to terminate my segment, a totally unexpected question came forth; it was surprising because ward committeeman Ralph Metcalfe intended it to show me in a favorable light, though up to that moment he had seemed neutral and matter-of-fact. "Who *is* your father-in-law who is so serious about collecting petition signatures?" he asked. The Chicagoans in the audience immediately sat to attention, especially Daley, who leaned in my direction. Feeling solidly in control, and a little heady, I decided to toy with them a bit. "Well, he did such a good job that when he came before those of you from Cook County you decided to make him a judge."

Besides Metcalfe, Marshall Korshak and Izzie Horwitz knew the identity of the mysterious figure who now occupied center stage, but I could see the speculation mounting among many of the others. I continued, "I don't know if I should tell you, since the newspapers don't like judges to have political backgrounds unless they happen to be Republicans." [Smiles and laughter.] "I'll tell you on one condition—that all the newspaper reporters leave the room." This evoked some raucous laughter, because an outsider's chances of penetrating this closed meeting's security measures were too minuscule to calculate. I savored their suspense. Then I leaned forward and said quietly, "My father-in-law is Judge Harry Iseberg."

Daley, Ronan, and Rostenkowski looked at each other with apparent approval. Harry Iseberg had been a star precinct captain, one of the very best, in the legendary 1960 Kennedy victory, as well as an effective and loyal assistant corporation counsel for twenty-six years. He was a member of the machine family. As I glanced about me now, I noticed a lot of buzzing and smiling, their recognition that as Harry's son-in-law I, too, was a member of the political family. Like Harry, I could be relied on and trusted.

Chairman Dan Rostenkowski stepped in: "Mel, I want to thank you very much for appearing before us. It's been a real pleasure visiting with you."

"Thank you, Mr. Chairman." And with that, I bounded into the waiting area, confident that the speech had gone well and that I had made my mark with those who would do the deciding.

One of my fellow hopefuls came up to me and asked, "What was all the applause about?"

"I told some jokes on Republicans," I replied.

When the last speaker had finished and the slatemakers came pouring out from their long session, several paused to give complimentary greetings to other aspirants and to me. McGloon offered a pleasant comment, but I could sense that his political heart belonged to Mike Bakalis. Then Choate beckoned me inside to the now almost deserted room and put his arm on my shoulder: "Mel, in Springfield last week you were good. Today, you were terrific! But the Greek boy also did a real good job. When you started out, I told you it would be a long shot. A lot depends on what they do with the rest of the ticket. But southern Illinois is behind you, and you made some real Chicago friends. Furthermore, I'm going to be on the subcommittee, and McGloon isn't. The odds are tough, but I'm going to do everything I can inside that subcommittee."

Instead of reconvening after supper, the subcommittee decided to delay its deliberations and recommendations until the following day. Thus began the longest night of my life.

Clyde Choate had seemed surprised when, at the end of our conversation, I had told him, "Clyde, I'm going back to Carbondale tonight. If something positive breaks tomorrow, give me a call, and I'll fly right in."

"Mel, you really ought to stick around."

"I can't. If there were anything I could do to help things, I could see being here. But I'm just too uptight. I want to see my family and teach my eight-thirty class tomorrow morning. I can't just sit around."

On the way out of the Morrison Hotel, a beaming father-in-law, Judge Harry Iseberg, came striding toward me. "Mel, Bernie Neistein told me you had everybody, including Daley, in the palm of your hand!"

"Yeah, if Neistein and Korshak were Irishmen, we'd be okay," I replied.

"Are you coming home with me?"

"No, Dad, I'm going back to Carbondale."

"You ought to stay in town, Mel."

"I know, but I can't hack the waiting. Besides, I think it looks like Bakalis. I'm taking the seven o'clock train."

"Okay, Mel. Good luck. Give Adie and the kids our love."

Evidently, I was not the only one who wanted to get out of town. I later found out that Mike Bakalis had returned to DeKalb.

The antiquated Illinois Central ran even slower than usual that night. In the solitude of my thoughts, I reached back through the entire campaign: my late start, my failure to snare McGloon, the frequent difficulty of finding Choate, my mediocre performance in September when I had addressed the party organization in Vandalia. But I also thought of the high points, particularly the enthusiastic support of Chancey and the Jackson County organization and my final appearance before the slatemakers, one of the best speeches I had ever delivered. I wondered if I had a good chance.

Adrienne was waiting when the taxi delivered me to the house at three in the morning. We talked for half an hour, and then I tried to sleep. But I was too tense to do more than toss and turn for the first hour. Finally, I dozed off and began to dream. The focal point of my dream was the black telephone on Karen Zink's desk in the SIU political science office. It had taken on gargantuan proportions and now covered the whole desk. Minute after minute went by, but Clyde

Choate never called. When I awoke a few hours later, I half-believed that the dream foretold the day's otucome—that Clyde would have no reason to call me for the quick flight to Chicago.

I went to my eight-thirty political parties class without formally preparing my lecture. I did not need to, for the subject was slate-making, and I had been living this lecture during four months of participation-observation with the strongest party organization in the country.

Meanwhile, in Chicago, the subcommittee of the Democratic state committee was preparing to begin its deliberations. This body possessed the real decision-making power. Although, technically, it only "recommended" to the central committee that made the formal decisions, the latter invariably adopted these recommendations. The central committee's temporary chairman, in consultation with the mayor and the state chairman, appointed a subcommittee that contained a microcosm of the party's most influential segments; thus, it comprised the actual decision-making arena.

Every member of the state central committee possessed a formal vote equivalent to the number of votes he had received in his congressional district when elected committeeman in the party's primary. Though twelve of the twenty-four congressional districts were located downstate, downstaters invariably cast less than 38 percent of the state's total primary votes. Conversely, because the twelve Cook County districts comprised the locus of Democratic voting strength, these districts had more formal voting power and proportionately greater representation within the subcommittee. The Cook County forces could prevail on any issue on the basis of sheer numbers. But both Cook County and downstate recognized downstate votes as crucial for Democratic victories in statewide elections and for key votes on Chicago issues in the state legislature. This mutual consideration manifested itself each time the subcommittee met to discuss and deliberate.

The Cook County majority of the 1969 state subcommittee consisted of the ethnic leaders who then dominated the Chicago machine. First and foremost were members of the Irish inner circle—Richard Daley, Tom Keane, George Dunne, Parky Cullerton, and John Touhy. Irishman Jim Ronan attended in his role as state chairman, and other ethnic leaders included Polish Dan Rostenkowski, Italian Vito Marzullo, and black leader Ralph Metcalfe.

Downstate was present also: Paul Powell, Mayor Al Fields of

populous East St. Louis, Clyde Choate, Leo Fitzgerald (the downstate chairman), and southern Illinoisan Benny Cherry, president of the County Chairmen's Association. My friend Irma Agoe of Mt. Vernon served as the token woman. As Jim Ronan once told me, "We always include one woman, the same as we include at least one representative from each major ethnic group."

Although previous sessions of the subcommittee had demonstrated that Mayor Daley wielded more "clout" than any other single individual, several instances illustrate that whether the decision involved the state or the county he could not always have his way with the slatemakers. I have made earlier mention of the mayor's failure to receive approval for a nonpartisan, blue-ribbon judicial ticket in 1968 and his eventual withdrawal, under pressure from Vito Marzullo, of his proposal to slate Stanley Kusper for city treasurer. If Daley could not always carry the day even with his closest machine colleagues and even with respect to those offices acknowledged to be within the territorial imperative of the "Chicago boys," so much less easily, then, could he "boss" the slatemakers when the territory was the whole state and the offices those to which downstate Democrats could stake a legitimate claim. The methodology of slatemaking paralleled the *modus operandi* of the Cook County machine proper— bargaining, trading-off, and compromising. Downstate and Cook County needed each other, and to best achieve their mutually rewarding goals, Chairman Daley and the subcommittee followed certain unwritten norms when selecting the party's nominees:

First, each candidate must possess "winnability." There was no point in putting up a candidate who did not have a realistic chance of winning, because winning candidates provided the basis for the "better living" of both the Cook County and downstate organizations. As state chairman Jim Ronan had declared, the machine would rather win with an outsider on the ticket than lose with one of its own.

Second, each candidate must be competent. The party could not ignore the slurs perennially cast upon the caliber of Democratic party personnel in Illinois; and, while sometimes willing to slate hacks in the lower echelons, it conscientiously attempted to present well-qualified people for state and national office. The slating of men like Paul Douglas and Adlai Stevenson II, both machine outsiders, attests to how high that caliber could be.

Third, each candidate must have strong financial backing. It took hundreds of thousands of dollars to run a statewide campaign, with such major offices as U.S. senator and governor costing more than a million dollars each. The slatemakers, for this reason, focused on a prospective candidate's potential for funding a large percentage of his own campaign costs. Their attentiveness to an office seeker's financial resources heightened perceptibly when the Democratic party did not hold the governorship, an office that usually yielded great amounts of money from sources such as construction and road building.

Senator Douglas, a model of ethics in politics, well understood the drawing power of up-front money. Reportedly, Douglas once told an affluent aide, "If you ever go before the slatemaking committee, take out your checkbook, show it to them, and say that you have in your checking account all the funds necessary to run your campaign. That will let them know you mean business regarding financial acceptability."

Fourth, the candidate should provide ethnic balance. Party leaders wanted to make a broad-based appeal to the many ethnic groups residing in Cook County as well as to downstate WASPs. For this reason, the slatemakers could not afford an asymmetrical or skewed ticket, one that underrepresented any significant ethnic group.

Fifth, the candidate should provide geographical balance. In addition to adequate representation for Cook County, the party slate had to reflect various segments of downstate in order to exert the geographical pulling power necessary to deliver victory for all the party's candidates. The three major positions on the slate (U.S. senator, state treasurer, and superintendent of public instruction) were interrelated inasmuch as the party had to field a geographically balanced ticket. From where I stood, both the first two posts had to go to persons from the Cook County area if Bakalis were to be eliminated; but if either of them went to a downstater, that would eliminate me. I had a high regard for both Alan Dixon and the late entrant, Paul Simon; but my political future depended upon Lake Countian Adlai Stevenson receiving the senatorial nod.

Stevenson's place on the ticket was by no means assured. Paul Powell vehemently opposed Stevenson for reasons dating back to his dislike for the patrician and "above-party ways" of young Adlai's father. He tagged the son as a cut from the same cloth, as not having earned his own way but as having merely cloaked himself in his father's name. Neither as legislator nor state treasurer had Adlai proved himself the type of person with whom Powell could work out profitable deals. Powell could also recall the audacity of the man, when, in 1967, Adlai III had presented himself to the slatemakers as the best qualified of all the gubernatorial aspirants. Since sitting-Governor Sam Shapiro sought the party's endorsement, Powell thought him entitled to it by virtue of both his position and his long years of service in the legislature. Powell resented young Adlai's ambitions.

Powell did not stand alone in this opinion. The forty-five downstate county chairmen on his payroll naturally embraced his sentiments. Moreover, strong opposition had developed within Cook County. Powerful committeemen such as Vito Marzullo shared many of Powell's concerns and had reason to believe that Adlai the son would be like the father—undependable on patronage jobs and special deals.

Almost to a man, the members of the machine had bristled at Stevenson's epithetic outcry during Chicago's 1968 Democratic National Convention against police ("stormtroopers in blue") and mayor ("feudal lord"). Moreover, Stevenson had threatened to challenge the machine by running a Polish friend for sheriff and by moving to the city and seeking the mayor's post himself. This kind of talk made him anathema with Democratic pros, and it therefore surprised no one when, during his senatorial-bid presentation to the slatemakers, their normally bland questioning became an exercise in the third degree. One of the slatemakers later told me what had transpired:

Powell asked Stevenson, "Adlai, will you support the entire ticket regardless of who is on it?"

"I will support all qualified persons on the ticket," Stevenson replied.

Powell said, "That's not what I asked you. Will you support the *entire* ticket?"

Stevenson repeated his response.

Again: "*Will you support the entire ticket?*"

The assemblage tensed forward, anxious but thrilled at this battle of wills between the party's rural elder and its youngest favorite.

At that point, Daley stepped in: "Paul, the Stevenson family has always supported the entire Democratic ticket one hundred percent."

This, then, was the controversial background against which, in November 1969, Mayor Daley and other slatemakers began their secret subcommittee meeting. After state chairman Jim Ronan convened the session, the mayor moved to the podium and announced that he wanted to present some important figures. Reminding the assemblage that the Cook County organization long had conducted its own poll at the same time and in the same places to permit comparability through the years, Daley declared that the poll had proved reliably accurate. But this year he had ordered an independent poll to check the figures. He would present those figures now, he stated, because the purpose of the meeting was to come up with the strongest nominees for office. The first office to be considered was the U.S. Senate. Without emotion, Daley presented the poll results.

Chicago:	Stevenson, 33%	Dixon, 19%	Simon, 8%
Cook County:	Stevenson, 41%	Dixon, 18%	Simon, 10%
Downstate:	Stevenson, 42%	Dixon, 31%	Simon, 9.5%

When the nonrespondents were subtracted, Daley explained, and the race projected against newly appointed Senator Ralph Smith, Stevenson emerged by far the strongest potential candidate of the three main contenders.

Following Daley's presentation, some cursory discussion about Stevenson took place; but there was no denying that the mayor had made his case. Powell surrendered: "Well, if the mayor can eat crow, so can I." Obviously, he was referring to the fact that Stevenson not only had severely criticized Daley but actually had conducted a rally at his Libertyville farm for the purpose of liberalizing the party and diluting the power of the Daley machine. Now, however, the flexible Daley had what he wanted, the strongest possible candidate at the head of the ticket. Stevenson's candidacy would accomplish two things: First, it would potentially help the Cook County ethnics achieve a ticket-wide victory, and second, a Stevenson victory would take him out of the state to Washington, where he could no longer pose a serious threat to the machine. A defeat in the general election likewise would accomplish the same end—Stevenson would lose his political clout.

With respect to my nomination chances, Act 1 had gone fine. No downstater had received the senate nomination, and I was still in the running. But one apparent loose end puzzled me: Although the thrust of Daley's statistics, the ostensible consensus, and Powell's surrender all indicated Stevenson, the subcommittee had not as yet formally announced its choice.

According to the script I had created, in Act 2 the slatemakers would have to nominate for state treasurer someone from the Daley machine's home turf. Alan Dixon, from a town near East St. Louis, already had announced that under no circumstances would he take anything but the senatorial nomination. His firm stance on this point gave me hope, since Dixon came from my general geographical area. Even better, John Gleason, a vice-president of the First National Bank of Chicago, frequently had been mentioned for treasurer. Having served as secretary of veterans affairs in the Kennedy administration and national commander of the American Legion, he possessed excellent political credentials. More importantly yet, from where I stood, Gleason's nomination would insure that Michael Bakalis, who had strong Chicago ties and who lived in DeKalb (only sixty miles from Chicago), would be knocked out of the contest on geographical grounds. Were Gleason chosen, my prospects looked good. My script demanded that aspirants from Cook County and a "collar" county be endorsed for the two top posts; and if that script were followed, I soon would be taking center stage in Illinois politics.

In Carbondale, many miles away from the theater in which the drama was unfolding on that crucial morning, I went over and over this script in my mind, praying the actors would follow it to the letter. After finishing my class at nine-thirty, I returned to my office and asked Karen Zink whether Clyde Choate had called. "No," she replied, "if he had, I would've run over to your classroom and shouted at the top of my lungs for the whole world to hear." Karen understood fully the implications of the call. She had been with me from the start, had even typed my political correspondence during her lunch hour and after work. And she had spoken on my behalf to her influential father, vice-chairman Earl Kumpel of Sangamon County, whose powerful political organization had launched my statewide campaign.

I called my county chairman: "Ray, this is Mel. Have you heard anything this morning?"

"No, Mel, not a thing. But Irma Agoe called me last night. She said you, Bakalis, and a guy from Charleston all gave very impressive talks. She thinks it's going to be either you or Bakalis. She doesn't know which. I haven't heard anything from Clyde Choate."

"I haven't either, Ray. I'll let you know if I do."

I made extra trips to the water cooler, hoping that as I passed Karen's desk the phone would ring and it would be Choate. On my third trip, it rang; my heart skipped a beat. Maybe the dream had been a false portent, I thought to myself. But the call was not for me.

I glanced at the clock, 11:18 A.M. What was taking place in Chicago?

My friend on the subcommittee who later recounted the events of the meeting did not describe the setting. But I could imaging the room in the Sherman House Hotel, the cold November sunlight slanting through the windows. I could visualize the people gathered there, some with faces arranged and composed so as to betray nothing of a great, or even a small, anxiety; others relaxed, intermittently boisterous as they exchanged bluff jokes; all of them alert for the rustle at the head of the room that would signal a move to the business at hand.

Chairman Jim Ronan opened the meeting. There was some desultory talk, my informant said, "and then Mayor Daley, Paul Powell, and Mayor Fields [of East St. Louis] left the meeting room. They were gone quite a while. Paul came back in, sat down next to Clyde Choate and talked to him. Bill Jenkins, Benny Cherry, and I sat nearby. Clyde said to us, 'I'll explain our position later.'

"Mayor Fields and Paul Powell again left and met with Alan Dixon in the hall. There was some discussion among them, but I can't tell you exactly what was said because I could catch very little of it. I did hear Powell say, 'Alan, you've always wanted to be on the state ticket. Here's your chance.' It apparently was a deal Powell and Fields had agreed upon, but they couldn't clinch it by themselves— they had to convince Alan, get his okay.

"And there were certain things that went against their plan. For example, in the state treasurer's job you can't succeed yourself. It's often a dead end, because the four-year term always ends in the middle of a presidential term, when the only other position available is state superintendent of public instruction or, possibly, a senate seat. I'm convinced they had to promise Alan that he'd be considered in the future for a more important place on the state ticket if only he would take the treasurer post now.

"But after all this, Alan still wanted to talk it over with his wife and with Paul Simon. Finally, though, he said, 'Yes.'"

So this was the reason the subcommittee had delayed its statement that Stevenson had been slated for the Senate. Now, however, chairman Ronan could announce a consensus—Stevenson for senator and Dixon for state treasurer. Daley had succeeded in mollifying Powell and other anti-Stevenson forces; and Daley, Powell, and Fields had molded a unified team for the two top positions. It looked as though Dixon of Belleville had taken me out geographically.

My informant told me what had happened next.

The subcommittee began its discussion of the state superintendent position. John Touhy, the powerful Chicago legislative leader, spoke for Bakalis, emphasizing his educational qualifications, his effectiveness as a campaigner, and his strong financial backing. But Clyde Choate, as if unaware of my now-crippling geographical handicap, went all out for me:

"Mel Kahn's a worker in the vineyards who gives the sweat of his brow to the party and has never asked anything in return. Mel has worked directly with me in running winning campaigns throughout downstate."

And then the bellringer:

"Mel isn't some run-of-the-mill professor. He's one of us. He talks, thinks, and practices politics the same way we do. He's the kind of man we can deal with, a man who will arouse the precinct workers to go all out. Most important, Mel Kahn will give real strength to our local tickets."

But in spite of Choate's impassioned plea, the subcommittee recommended Mike Bakalis; and except for "Deacon" Davis, who gave a stirring presentation for me, the full committee readily accepted the subcommittee's recommendations. Ironically, what I had hoped for had come to pass: The choice of the state treasurer had delivered a knockout blow. But I, not Bakalis, had gone down for the count.

As my office clock dragged toward twelve, my expectations plummeted from "maybe" to "faintly," until the noon buzzer brought home the stark realization that my political quest was at an end. Foreman Daley and his jury obviously had brought in a verdict against me.

So I joined some colleagues for lunch. They attempted to cheer me up and to hold out some hope, but I could only pick at my food. I thought of calling Clyde Choate but backed off; he had told me he would phone if the decision were favorable, and he had not called. Even if I could track him down, I intuitively knew the truth and did not want to face it.

At about three-thirty, I picked up a copy of the *Southern Illinoisan*. A front-page headline leaped out at me: "Kahn Fails in Nomination Try." That morning, as my hopes had faded with the passing of each hour, I had given an interview to a reporter (one of my former students) in which I had allowed myself to express my pessimism. Here now, in the text of that interview, I was the source of my own notification of the defeat. The inside of the paper provided official confirmation, a wire-service story reporting the expected— Mike Bakalis had won the party's endorsement.

When I went home at five o'clock, Adrienne told me that we were going out to dinner and a movie and that she had already arranged for a sitter. As I was getting ready, the finality of it all hit me. My political dreams were shattered. The opportunity represented by winning the superintendent's post, a first step to higher offices, had eluded me. I knew that I should call Mike Bakalis and congratulate him, but I could not bring myself to dial the number. So acute was my disappointment that I was afraid I would crack over the phone.

We had a good steak dinner at the LBJ Restaurant and then went to the movie theater. I felt better and started to call Mike from the lobby but again could not go through with it. Finally, half-way through the film, I went out and phoned. The background sounds indicated that the Bakalises were celebrating. Mike was a gracious winner and verbalized some nice things to me. When he said he wanted to consult with me throughout his campaign, I readily agreed.

In the days that followed, I often wondered about the details of the subcommittee's choice of Bakalis instead of me. State chairman Ronan subsequently provided some insight: "You were strongly in the running until we went down to your region and selected Al Dixon. Now, you weren't as strong as Mike Bakalis. But once we took Dixon, that eliminated you right on the spot, because there's no way we were going to give two places to the downstate area when there were only three places on the entire ticket. You guys are already overrepresented."

Another member of the subcommittee later described his reactions to the slate: "We were not pressured at all. It was merely a case of presenting the facts, and the facts seemed to speak for themselves: It had to be Stevenson because he was the logical contender. It had to be Alan Dixon because, after all his years of service in the legislature, he was entitled to something. He had been the main competitor against Stevenson, and he represented southern Illinois. It had to be Bakalis because not only had he made an excellent presentation to the slatemakers, he was also from the right geographical area. And he had done the best job of campaigning before the slatemakers met. I am honestly convinced that these three men constituted the best possible ticket that could have been fielded, and, as a Democrat, I felt quite proud of it."

Unopposed in the primary, Mike Bakalis went on to win election as state superintendent of public instruction and later became state comptroller, serving with distinction in both positions. Bakalis received his party's highest honor in 1978 when he became the Democratic nominee for governor against incumbent Jim Thompson. Although he lost this race, as the Democratic party's standard-bearer he nonetheless had won the best the party had to offer him, the nomination itself.

I returned to teaching politics. And then one day, it occurred to met that it might be interesting to write a book about the slatemaking process in the state that was once home to the most efficient and most consistently victorious political organization in the nation.

I say "once" because, over the next decade, the vast changes taking place in Chicago politics saw the machine floundering in its efforts to adapt and survive. A brief examination of the flurries and alarums that characterized politics in the Chicago of the 1970s may allow us to make some guesses about the machine's future.

Epilogue I
From Ethnic Accommodation
to Racial Politics

In the wake of the social upheavals of the 1960s and the raised political consciousness they stimulated, two forces in Cook County that had been gathering restlessly throughout the preceding decade came together in 1972 and launched a frontal attack on the Daley machine in the primaries as well as in the general election. The first of these was a growing black population, with a concomitantly stronger power base, that demanded a louder voice in local government and the economic and social gains this would bring about. The second was an increasingly better organized and more active white liberal bloc that espoused local and state government reform. The impressive power exhibited by the blacks and white reformers in 1972 seemed the harbinger of things to come—a new coalition, a new counter-machine.

But a coalition failed to materialize in the next several years. While there were some joint efforts in specific legislative and city council races and marked success in Ralph Metcalfe's 1976 congressional campaign, blacks and reformers failed to forge a consistent Chicago-wide united front. The machine demonstrated its resiliency as it succeeded in coopting some reform candidates after they had been elected. The best example occurred later in the decade when blacks and liberals allowed themselves to be taken in by the glib promises of an "anti-machine" mayoral candidate, who, after her election, coopted herself into a machine regular.

As for the machine, it also had its peaks and valleys. After its devastating losses in 1972, it handily won the 1975 and 1977 city primaries. At the state level, it managed to slate a moderately successful ticket in 1975, which, however, was only partially successful in the 1976 general election. After Mayor Daley's death in December 1976, the lack of leadership produced less effective procedures in slating state tickets. On the local level, power was divided as George Dunne became party chairman and an Irish-led coalition strongly influenced the political decisions of Mayor Michael Bilandic. Provincial interest prevailed over the idea of a balanced ticket, and the fragmentation of power in the Cook County Democratic central committee, in which first one and then another politician socialized intraparty conflict into the public arena, left the gate open in 1983 for the election of Chicago's first black mayor.

In the first election of the decade, the blue-ribbon 1970 state ticket of Adlai Stevenson III, Alan Dixon, and Michael Bakalis was skillfully designed to recapture the Democrats and independents who had become disenchanted over the 1968 Democratic convention debacle of Mayor Daley and the Chicago machine. Stevenson bore a distinguished name, Dixon was a gifted orator, and Bakalis was an impressive young college dean who particularly appealed to well-educated people. This ticket would certainly reunify the party and would undoubtedly attract independents and, possibly, moderate Republicans.

Even with this eminently winnable ticket, however, the machine still faced serious challenges from that year on, challenges that, however various and distinct they might appear, boiled down to two major problems. First, the delicate balance between the white ethnics and the growing numbers of blacks became increasingly precarious. The 1969 Black Panther raids by state's attorney Edward Hanrahan's police had created strained feelings in the black community, and in late 1971 a decision would be made on whether to reslate him. Complicating the accelerating destabilization of the ethnic coalition was the dilemma of how to reapportion congressional districts without alienating any ethnic group. The second major difficulty the machine faced was the mobilization of the reformers, who, having made inroads during the sixties, were now organized at the precinct level in several wards. They already had defeated several machine candidates for Illinois constitutional convention delegate positions and would cause further damage and embarrassment. To meet these challenges, the machine had to restore its public image and keep its varied segments unified.

Continuing the traditional machine policy of responding to political demands in proportion to the intensity and voting strength of those who made them, Daley and other machine leaders began to raise the payoff level to black politicians in the early 1970s by slating more of them for office. Not enough were slated to satisfy black middle-class voters, but the threat of white-ethnic alienation from the party prevented the organization from supporting more black candidates.

The need to broker between blacks and white ethnics with regard to prestigious congressional nominations was emphasized by the reapportionment controversy prior to the 1972 elections. A top party leader stated the problem:

"Nixon was paranoid about Wallace throwing the [presidential] election into the U.S. House of Representatives and was particularly upset about Illinois, where we had a split delegation. So he was determined that we would reapportion Illinois; and with the Republican legislature, he counted on picking up a Republican seat, which would mean a vote for him in the House. The result was that [Congressmen] Frank Annunzio and George Collins [a black] were thrown into the same congressional district.

"Daley first suggested to Annunzio that if he would step down, he would be taken care of. Annunzio raised all kinds of hell and let it be known that he wouldn't do it. Daley then suggested the same thing to Collins, and his response was 'hell, no.' Daley was paid a visit by one hundred and fifty black ministers who said that they would bolt the ticket if Collins weren't reslated. Daley's face turned white.

"I told him that he had enough trouble with [State's Attorney] Hanrahan and that this would really confound things. So Daley prevailed upon Pucinski to have Annunzio run for his seat [for the U.S. House of Representatives], since Pucinski was now running for the Senate. Pucinski thought that Annunzio could win it, but since Pucinski was a long shot for the Senate, he wanted a House seat to go back to, he told Daley. Daley answered that the organization just *had* to resolve this nomination problem and that Pucinski would be taken care of. Pucinski finally agreed, and thereby solved a sure-loss dilemma of choosing between a black and a white ethnic."

The tension between the white ethnics and the blacks expressed itself also when Mike Bakalis, now Illinois superintendent of public instruction, issued desegregation guidelines for the state school system. He received a phone call from the mayor expressing Daley's deep disappointment that Mike had not consulted with him prior to this action. The guidelines, Daley told him, were creating strongly negative reactions among the white ethnics on the northwest and southwest sides. This communication from the mayor was highly unusual, because Daley had not, up to then, requested policy favors from Bakalis nor suggested to him how he should run his office. But the reaction of Chicago's white ethnics to school desegregation proposals was so serious, however, that he had broken the norm and had alerted Bakalis to the political harm his decision had posed to the machine.

The question of whether to reslate controversial state's attorney Edward Hanrahan for the 1972 general election was the issue upon which the lines were clearly drawn, with the white ethnics on one side and the blacks and white liberals on the other. Hanrahan had been indicted for obstruction of justice in preventing the prosecution of policemen involved in the 1969 killing of two Black Panther leaders (one of them in his bed) during the Hanrahan-led raid on their apartment. His cover-up role had generated intense friction in the community at large, and his indictment caused many prestigious groups to urge his leave of absence while the criminal charges were pending. These groups included the Chicago Bar Association, the Better Government Association, the Chicago Crime Commission, the Chicago Association of Lawyers, the city's four major newspapers, as well as many white and black civil rights leaders.

The machine, in December 1971, endorsed Hanrahan for reelection despite his indictment, the objections from professional organizations, opposition from prestigious liberals (including Senator Adlai Stevenson III), and the antagonism of the black community. One slatemaker told me what occurred at the slatemaking session: "Claude Holman [a black ward committeeman] led off for Hanrahan, twenty-eight people in a row spoke on his behalf, and Hanrahan ended up with the endorsement. Daley sat there like a stoic. He didn't scratch his nose, move his eyes, raise an eyebrow, or do anything to indicate that he'd had any part in it. Obviously, he had." Hanrahan was known to be Daley's fair-haired boy and a likely choice to succeed him.

The news of Hanrahan's slating caused a whirlwind of adverse reaction. A petition signed by 500,000 people, biting newspaper editorials, and Stevenson's flat refusal to support Hanrahan sparked widespread dissension. Those party members nominated to state and national office by the state central committee had been put in jeopardy by the county's bungling of its slating responsibilities, one of which certainly was to field a slate of candidates who would not antagonize a major voting segment in Cook County and thus provoke morally outraged voters to defect from the entire ticket in the general election. Gubernatorial candidate Paul Simon (a downstater), senatorial candidate Roman Pucinski, and county board president George Dunne went to Daley with the same message: Hanrahan will drag everybody on the ticket down to defeat. It was this argument that finally got through to Daley. Laying aside his preference for Hanrahan, he acquiesced to the pressure and in an unprecedented move called a "postslating" meeting for Sunday, December 21.

One participant gave me the following account of the events of the meeting and its aftermath: "Hanrahan threatened to take us all to court if we stripped him of the endorsement. But we went ahead and replaced him with Judge Ray Berg. The judge was on a snowmobile trip somewhere in Wisconsin with his family, and nobody knew how to get hold of him—the problem was that the next day was the deadline for filing. Well, they finally tracked Berg down, and he gave his okay. The next day, they got the petitions and, though they had only a couple of hours to go out and get the signatures, they did get them."

To no avail, as it turned out. Excluded from the party's official slate of candidates, Ed Hanrahan proceeded to "endorse" himself. He campaigned vigorously among law and order constituents and won the three-cornered primary race against Berg and reformer Donald Page Moore, splitting the anti-Hanrahan vote and amassing 43 percent of the total. Daley, having regained a now legitimated favorite, threw the full force of the machine into Hanrahan's campaign. He did so for two reasons: First, the state's attorney's office possessed a number of choice patronage plums, and second, a friendly Democratic state's attorney could avoid or minimize, the prosecution of Democrats for graft and vote fraud. Conversely, an unfriendly Republican could build a career for himself by exposing election fraud and sending Democratic politicians to jail.

The more affluent south-side blacks voted overwhelmingly in the general election for Republican Bernie Carey, while the "controlled" west side blacks (who usually provided Democratic margins of 80 to 90 percent) barely delivered the Democratic ticket in their wards. The bolters, white reformers, and suburban Republicans combined to hand

Hanrahan and the machine a stinging defeat. According to one of my informants, Hanrahan's past record made it ironic that he would become the heavy in the Black Panthers case. A ward committeeman explained: "The FBI was going to do the raid originally, but they couldn't make it. On top of that, a lot of blacks initially liked Hanrahan because of the way he cracked down on the street gangs in their neighborhoods. Then, too, Hanrahan was personal friends with blacks. He even brought some of his black friends to Mass, and it created quite a stir among the whites. It was certainly an odd twist of fate that Hanrahan of all people would end up being Mister Bad Guy among the blacks." Ed Hanrahan has been characterized by others, however, as a man of uncertain temper and enormous ego.

During the entire process, the machine proved itself inept. To begin with, it endorsed a man who was awaiting trial on criminal charges, thereby antagonizing blacks and liberals. Its subsequent withdrawal of the endorsement angered white ethnics who admired Hanrahan's get-tough stance with blacks. It then lost the primary to Hanrahan and gave blacks their first excuse to bolt the machine since Daley had assumed the party chairmanship in 1953. Finally, Daley and the white machine brass made Hanrahan's campaign their most important contest, providing substance to charges by Ralph Metcalfe (the machine's most prominent black leader) and others that the organization was racist. The overt, and seemingly substantiated, charge of racism encouraged blacks to defect again in the general election and cast their votes for Republican Carey. Through these blunders, the machine had let slip its mask, had revealed itself as unwilling to serve its black components at the expense of the white-ethnic vote. The blacks, thoroughly antagonized by the Hanrahan affair, proved they could, and would, desert the party when race was the issue, just as in the past the Poles had rebelled against the machine's neglect of Polish candidates.

In early 1971, speculation about the party's 1972 gubernatorial choice focused on three men: Lieutenant Governor Paul Simon, U.S. District Attorney Tom Foran, and Secretary of State Mike Howlett. A key slatemaker told me that the "smart money" was on Foran, since he had compiled a superior law and order record as U.S. attorney. But this slatemaker underestimated Simon. Now that Paul Powell had died (in 1970) Simon, a liberal, was able to garner strong downstate backing and, on the basis of his prolabor record, to secure substantial labor support, particularly from the large industrial unions.

Without attacking the machine, Simon nevertheless hinted that he would run in the Democratic primary in 1972. Some party leaders did not cotton to the independent Simon, but rather than risk his defeating Foran or Howlett, and beset by both blacks and white reformists, the machine endorsed him. A man of sterling credentials, he was appealing to labor, rank-and-file voters, independent reformers, and the media, which admired his performance as a public servant. Daley and the machine had slated wisely.

The media and the political pros had snickered at maverick Dan Walker's announcement, in November 1970, that he would seek the Democratic nomination for governor of Illinois in 1972. Everyone knew that mavericks without a political base did not defeat endorsed candidates in statewide Democratic primaries. True, this had occurred in 1936, when Governor Henry Horner defeated the machine's Dr. Herman Bundenson, but Horner had been the incumbent, whereas Walker had never held elective office.

Walker, who had graduated second in his law class at Northwestern University, had served as a middle-level aide to Governor Adlai Stevenson II and later as legal counsel and an $118,000-a-year vice-president for Marcor, Montgomery Ward's parent company.[1] Walker had failed in his bid for the party's endorsement for attorney general in 1968 but achieved national prominence when the National Commission on the Causes and Prevention of Violence asked him to investigate the disruption of the 1968 Democratic National Convention. He personally wrote the controversial summary characterizing it as a "police riot." This work, soon known as the "Walker Report," had attracted nationwide publicity and the animosity of Mayor Daley, who had placed the blame squarely on radical leaders such as Abbie Hoffman.

In the early, name-recognition stage of his campaign, Walker cleverly made use of his surname for a strategy that captured the attention of the media and the public fancy—he hiked around the entire state shaking hands with the people on the farms and in the small towns and the cities. Apart from this piece of showmanship, he carried credentials as a reformer and centered his attack on Simon, the epitome of honesty in politics, on Simon's ties with the venal machine. Walker chided Simon for "going behind closed doors" to court the very elements that plundered the public treasury. "Paul Simon doesn't talk about paring payrolls and cutting waste" sneered Walker. "He'd be stepping on the hands that feed him."[2]

The pivotal point in the campaign was reached when Simon advocated reducing taxes on food, real estate, and personal property by increasing the income tax. Senatorial candidate Roman Pucinski told Simon, "You'd better clear it up, or it will blow the election." Simon replied, "That's what I believe, and I'm going to stick with it." When Art McGloon heard Simon's statement on television, he called him: "Don't you realize that Touhy and I put Ogilvie in the casket on the tax issue and nailed the lid shut? Why don't you leave it alone? You're supposed to be candid about your *opponent* before the election; after you get elected is the time to be candid about *your* program, not before!" Mayor Daley exclaimed to one party leader, "What the hell is the guy doing? He's blowing the election!" In previous general election campaigns, Daley had worked with the slated candidates; but, evidently, this did not occur in 1972, or Simon would have been led through some rather thorough campaigning paces.

Walker homed in on the tax issue. He had a better alternative, he claimed—the elimination of waste and graft. He also made points by opposing Daley's pet project of a crosstown expressway. While the project would have created several thousand jobs and linked O'Hare and Midway airports and the major Chicago expressways, it would have forced the relocation of several thousand people. These persons rallied to Walker's banner, while Simon remained silent. Even though many drivers undoubtedly favored the proposal, the expressway issue created far less intensity for them than for its opponents, who stood to lose their homes.

A week before the election, all of the Twenty-first Congressional District's county chairmen gathered at the Ramada Inn in Carbondale. There, Clyde Choate, Alan Dixon, and Simon's trusted aide, Gene Callahan stressed the importance of rolling out the voters for Simon, because worrisome reports were beginning to trickle in from around the state.

Choate went around the room asking how things looked in each county. Jim Knott of Randolph County struck the initial tone: "If Walker gets one vote in Randolph County, I don't know where it's coming from." One chairman after another reflected Knott's optimism, until it was Chancey's turn: "Paul is in real trouble in Jackson County. We will lose by fifteen hundred votes." The three visitors were shocked. Choate finally said, "Well, you'll turn that around, won't you?" Chancey responded, "We'll do our very best, because you know what we think of Paul. But we won't be able to win it.

Walker has run too smart a campaign." Incredulity reigned. Chancey was the outstanding chairman of the downstate county that usually carried the banner in producing Democratic majorities. Simon, moreover, had run very strongly in Jackson County in his 1968 election for lieutenant governor.

But Chancey had spoken truly. This year Simon lost Jackson County by 500 votes as Walker carried the state in a stunning upset. Walker, the antimachine primary candidate, now dropped his criticism of the machine and turned his guns against incumbent Governor Richard Ogilvie. Expediently, the machine offered Walker both its blessing and a $55,000 contribution, and Walker accepted both. On election night, Richard Daley, the broker-mediator, stated only, "We all know—everyone knows—Dan Walker will make a great governor."

In addition to the loss to Walker, the machine faced other problems with the reform Democrats. Alderman Dick Simpson had founded the Independent Precinct Organization (IPO) for the purpose of nominating reform candidates in both parties. And, as the occasion arose, they would work against unacceptable Democrats in general elections, supporting Republican Bernie Carey, for example, over Edward Hanrahan for state's attorney. The IPO caused embarrassment to the machine by helping defeat Hanrahan, winning aldermanic seats in the city council, and capturing several legislative seats. While the IPO consisted primarily of white, middle-class professionals, it often provided money, organization, and workers to black reformers who challenged machine candidates.

Members of the IPO, under the leadership of Bill Singer, combined forces with Jesse Jackson to challenge machine-elected delegates to the 1972 Democratic National Convention. When Roman Pucinski suggested to Mayor Daley that since the reformers could control the convention the Chicago delegates might be rejected, the mayor laughed off the idea. But the national committee appointed a special hearing officer, Cecil F. Poole, who ruled that the machine had violated the delegate selection rules. In the caucuses held for selecting the challengers' slate of delegates, an ugly atmosphere prevailed. Joe Mathewson describes the havoc at one of the eight caucuses: "The regulars surged forward out of the pews toward [Wayne] Whalen [the presiding officer]. They surrounded him, pushed him, and knocked him down."[3] The Chicago newspapers gave this mayhem the full treatment: "'Daley Men Raid Caucuses,' the

Tribune emblazoned across page one. 'Daley Raiders Rout Delegation Rivals!' shrieked the *Sun-Times*. Pictures showed the shouting
and yelling, even Alderman Vrdolyak seizing Wayne Whalen's
papers from the lectern, and Whalen on the floor trying to gather them
up. 'Muscle politics,' the *Sun-Times* declared in an angry editorial.
Chicago Today's editorial termed the regulars 'Chicago's own storm
troopers.'"[4] Members of the machine emerged from this confrontation
with the party's reform faction as schoolyard bullies. The machine
was out of control.

The reformers caused difficulty on yet another front. They
supported Adlai Stevenson for the chairmanship of Illinois's delegation to the national convention. Although Stevenson had opposed
Hanrahan, he and Daley had "made up" and had established a
satisfactory working relationship. Now his prospective chairmanship
constituted a significant challenge to the mayor's leadership of the
state party. Stevenson had extracted a pledge from a majority of the
delegates, but the Daley forces went to work exerting the pressure of
threatened job loss and so recaptured some of Stevenson's delegates.
The *coup de grâce* was delivered at the convention itself when the
bloc of alternate delegates was seated and the machine delegation
refused admission. Daley, who had maintained contact with his
delegates from his Michigan hideaway, returned to Chicago a bitter
man. He had been castigated by the national media in 1968, and now
his own political party had denied him and his cohorts their traditional
and time honored participation in their party's most publicized
nomination event. Daley was crushed.
for the good of the local ticket, the organization had to support
McGovern. According to a mutual friend of the two men, Daley
furiously asserted that under no circumstances would he do so.
McGovern had visited Daley during the campaign to assure him that
he wanted to unify the party; and, since McGovern's people
controlled the convention, he could have made possible the honorable
seating of the machine delegation. As a result of their exclusion, the
local reform opposition, led by Bill Singer and Jesse Jackson, were
nationally lionized as Chicago's representatives. When Touhy left
Daley, he well knew that Daley was not receptive to his argument
that expediency demanded active machine support for McGovern in
the election campaign. But the next morning, at six o'clock, Daley
phoned Touhy: "You're right," he said, "McGovern is a Democrat,
and to elect Hanrahan and the rest of the ticket we've got to get behind

McGovern." Once more, the influence of a subordinate had changed Daley's mind. Vito Marzullo, however, made up his own mind and endorsed Republican Nixon, without retribution from the machine.

The evidence suggests that 1972 marked a sharp decline in the strength of the machine. At the crucial nomination stage, the machine suffered serious setbacks at the hands of the blacks and the white reformers. But it would be a mistake to give these two segments full credit—the flawed political judgment of Richard J. Daley also played a significant role in this new state of affairs. The aging Daley had turned seventy and would suffer a major stroke in 1974. The intransigence that led to the initial slating of Ed Hanrahan as state's attorney in 1972 despite the vehement protests of blacks and white liberals reveals a Daley turned rigid, unyielding—the flex had gone. The result was, for the first time in fifty years, massive black defections from the party. Never again would the machine be able to count on an automatic straight-party vote by blacks for the entire slate regardless of who was on it. Blacks would no longer settle for a few political crumbs and general exclusion from the city and state tickets.

Loss of the Democratic gubernatorial primary to Dan Walker damaged the machine's image further. But, certainly, the organization had slated what, at the time, seemed a strong choice—the able and effective campaigner Paul Simon, who provided a strong bridge to the reform Democrats. Walker's primary victory resulted both from his highly effective campaign and from Simon's unfortunate espousal of higher taxes. The image of "good government" that Simon presented was offset by the machine's general election support of Hanrahan, whose negative image it was that stuck to the party. With this loss of a state primary for the first time in thirty-six years, the "blue smoke" was beginning to dissipate.

Finally, the combination of blacks and white liberals that succeeded in representing Chicago at the 1972 national convention represented a crippling blow. Mayor Daley and the machine had built a reputation as national Democratic party power-brokers during the sixties, and after their 1968 convention debacle they were most anxious to reprise the public image (and self-image) of earlier years. But the ignominy of their rejection from their own national convention in 1972 must have brought home to the mayor the sober realities of the present. The machine had lost the key nomination struggles at each level: Hanrahan had won his county race; Walker had won at the state level; and the Jesse Jackson-led blacks and Bill Singer-led reformers had won at the national convention. If the appearance of power is power, the reverse must also hold: the appearance of impotence is impotence. For the Daley machine, the glory days were over.

Mayor Daley long had espoused the slogan, "Good government is good politics." But during the first half of the 1970s, the good-government image vanished behind a cloud of scandals involving senior members of the machine family. Federal Judge and former Governor Otto Kerner, the "Mr. Clean" of Illinois politics, was sentenced to federal prison because of illegal race track stock dealings. Machine luminaries such as the powerful Tom Keane (Thirty-first Ward committeeman and floor leader of the city council), Alderman Paul Wigoda, Earl Bush (Daley's press secretary), Fred Hubbard (a coopted liberal black alderman and director of the Chicago Plan), and Eddie Barrett (county clerk) were all sentenced to federal prison. The clean image of Mayor Daley himself was stained when, during his three-month convalescence from a major stroke in 1974, the *Sun-Times* broke the news that the mayor had, for seventeen years, owned a real estate and holding company with current assets of more than $200,000. Questions surfaced also about lucrative deals involving city business in which sons Michael and John had engaged.

Because Republican State's Attorney Bernard Carey would not protect violators of state laws as would a Democrat, prosecution soon ceased to be a novelty. Forty-seven policemen were convicted of shaking down tavern operators; a state insurance examiner was found guilty of changing the allegedly wrong answers on the insurance-broker's exam of Daley's son William; and more than forty election workers were indicted for vote fraud. Other transgressions included illegal wire taps on the home and office phones of State's Attorney Carey himself and infiltration by police department undercover agents of organizations that included Jesse Jackson's People United to Save Humanity (PUSH). The media gave full play to these activities, and although the mayor denied having authorized them and averred that they had been halted, public outrage reigned.

As Lieutenant Governor Neil Hartigan had predicted on election night, the Cook County organization suffered through a difficult four years with Governor Walker. An early controversy involved the Chicago Transit Aid Bill. The legislature had authorized $18.9

million dollars in emergency funds, of which the state would provide $12.6 million and Chicago and Cook County the remaining $6.3 million. The governor, however, using his amendatory veto, reduced the state's share and raised the local contribution so that each would put up $9.45 million.[5] After he had left the governorship, Walker justified his actions with respect to this bill:

> People said, "Why didn't you ever work with Daley?" Of course my response to that was, "Why don't people ask the question, 'Why doesn't Daley work with the governor?' . . .
> . . . If we had just said, "Yes, Mayor," then that would have been the end of the ball game in terms of my having any real power with respect to what was going to happen on the Democratic side of the aisle in the legislature. Daley would have had the ball game.
> We had to fight, from a political, practical standpoint, we had to fight. Even if we lost we had to fight. It was a good issue to fight on, I thought, because substantively we were right, and what he was proposing, a very dangerous precedent for state government, because once you go to a two to one match on one program you're going to get stuck with a two to one match on another program and so on down the line.[6]

Walker worked hard to create the image of a tight-fisted fiscal conservative and continued to use his veto power in a dramatic and well-publicized manner, a tactic that frequently brought him into conflict with Daley. Walker's veto of nearly $80 million in state aid for public education led to a bitter showdown. Daley came to the capitol with hundreds of parents and politicians, inundating legislative halls with lobbyists. Daley the humanitarian was very much evident when he told the legislators, "As long as I'm around, I will raise my voice for the school children, especially for the school kids of the inner cities. . . . You can talk all you want about law and order and crime, but if the kids haven't gotten the opportunity for a good education, they are out of luck. We spend millions for prisons. Let's spend something for the school kids of Illinois."[7] Walker had opposed the increase in order to honor his pledge that under no circumstances would he raise taxes. Daley indicated what he thought of that stance by praising former Republican Richard Ogilvie, who had spearheaded the drive for a state income and corporation tax package in 1968:

"[N]o one in politics who doesn't have guts and courage should be in public office."[8]

The constant scuffling between Governor Dan Walker and Mayor Richard Daley damaged the party. One state officeholder characterized the situation: "The internal friction between Daley and Walker zapped the energies of the organization to a tremendous extent. Walker was attempting to become head of the state party and use this as a springboard to the presidency. What we had was four years of bickering and debilitation within the party." The machine's failure to secure the gubernatorial nomination for their slated choice, Paul Simon, created problems far more serious and longer-lasting than the temporary embarrassment of losing in its own party's primary.

The fading away, in 1972, of the machine's image of invulnerability offered encouragement to reformers—black and white—to challenge machine incumbents for both the legislature and the city council. Ralph Metcalfe provides an especially meaningful focus for analyzing the changing role of blacks vis-à-vis the machine during the latter part of the Daley era.

Metcalfe had achieved popularity as a gold-medal winner and teammate of the legendary Jesse Owens during the 1936 Olympics. In the fifties, he was employed by a property management firm in Chicago, and much of his work involved handling slum housing, a job unlikely to make him popular with the inhabitants of the tenement districts. But black leader William Dawson recruited him into politics, and Metcalfe became a member of the Chicago human relations committee, an appointment that gave him status in the black community. Metcalfe carried good educational credentials; he held a master's degree from the University of Southern California and had been a political science instructor and track coach at Xavier University in New Orleans.[9]

During the sixties, Daley took a fancy to him, struck by Metcalfe's brightness, his loyalty to the machine, and his Catholicism. During these years, Metcalfe's formal positions of state representative and Third Ward committeeman made him the most prominent black in Cook County politics and thus the machine's informal troubleshooter. When negotiations had to take place with building contractors reluctant to hire blacks, Metcalfe was assigned the delicate task of working out the agreements. When the 1968 Democratic

National Convention delegates were delaying the proceedings with their time-consuming tributes to the martyred Robert Kennedy, it was Metcalfe who strode to the podium and requested a moment of silence for Dr. Martin Luther King, Jr. And, when serving in the city council, Metcalfe was assigned to counteract charges of discrimination leveled against that body by civil rights advocate Alderman Leon Despres, and others.

In the 1970 congressional primary campaign, reformer A. A. "Sammy" Rayner attacked Metcalfe's role as a machine captive, a role, however, Metcalfe vigorously defended: "People want service, not a bunch of hollering. . . . We get out twelve-hundred Christmas baskets every Christmas. These things still cost."[10] Later in the campaign, he continued this theme: "We get street lights when we need them. To get street lights, you must be part of the team. My ward was the first to get things. Rayner's was the last."[11]

For five years, Metcalfe's son, Ralph, Jr., had attempted to convince his father that blacks were being severely mistreated, but his arguments did not then shake the senior Metcalfe's faith in the machine. In 1972, however, two dramatic incidents that touched him personally transformed Metcalfe from machine apologist to ardent civil rights leader. One of his close friends had been arrested and treated as a drunk, although he in fact had suffered a stroke. Detained for fifteen hours, when he was finally transferred to a hospital, he died. Another friend, who served Metcalfe as chairman of the First Congressional Citizens Committee, was arrested, ordered to spread-eagle over his car, and allegedly roughed up by police.

Metcalfe quietly went to police chief James Conlisk, from whom he received a sympathetic hearing but nothing else. Blacks continued to complain about police brutality. Metcalfe went public: "The police abuse black people verbally and physically . . . , arresting and molesting motorists on the flimsiest excuse. The police call blacks 'nigger.' They have no respect for our women. They say they're all whores, and they even abuse them in front of their children. . . . Mayor Daley is not God. I only worship God. I will not sell out my people."[12] After continuing skirmishes with the machine by Metcalfe, Daley finally cut off his patronage. Metcalfe responded, "Daley may try to take my patronage away, but I'm not concerned. . . . I'm concerned with looking in the mirror and asking, 'am I representing the group who elected me?'"[13]

Ralph Metcalfe, Sr., had tried to serve his people's interests and work for their betterment through the established power structure because it had been, for so very many years, the only game in town. Now his dramatic turnaround represented the rude awakening of a man of conscience to the machine's heel-dragging in the matter of civil rights. But more than that, it symbolized the emerging political consciousness of a large segment of Chicago's black community in the 1970s. Previously, the black wards had comprised one of the machine's crucial electoral bases, had been, of all voting blocs, the most deliverable. A machine-endorsed white candidate would win overwhelmingly against a black candidate in these wards, whether the contest occurred in a primary or in a general election. From the time of Metcalfe's new civil rights stance, however, which found its most productive expression in the anti-Hanrahan role Metcalfe played in 1972, the black vote would never again be deliverable at the sole behest of the white-dominated machine.

After their successes in 1972, some blacks and reformers had reason to believe that they could continue to turn away machine-endorsed Democratic candidates. As the 1975 slatemaking session for the city election drew near, the Daley organization seemed vulnerable. But having suffered through the valley of 1972, the machine, demonstrating the determination, toughness, and resiliency that had been the hallmarks of its prime years, doggedly sought higher ground. It slated its first black for a city-wide office—city treasurer candidate Joe Bertrand. The response of the blacks and the white reformers was naïve in the extreme: Bill Singer, a white liberal, and Richard Newhouse, a black, both announced for the mayor's race. Since it was obvious that they would split the anti-Daley vote, neither carried any credibility as a prospective winner. Had one of them stayed out of the race, the other's chances would have improved, for he would have been able to mobilize more volunteers and attract more campaign money. Few people will work for or contribute money to the campaign of a likely loser. With both Singer and Newhouse in the running, the white liberal/black united front that had worked so successfully against Hanrahan and against the Daley-led national convention delegation in 1972 had evaporated. Mayor Daley won with 57 percent of the vote overall, and 48.4 percent in the old "Dawson" black wards, in contrast to the 82.8 percent he had averaged in these wards in his two previously contested primaries.[14]

But despite this dramatic drop in the black vote, the machine had managed to patch up the cracks in its image and live to fight another day.[15]

The Daley organization had two top priorities at the 1975 slatemaking session: to nominate candidates who would win the 1976 primaries against Ralph Metcalfe for both his congressional seat and his Third Ward committeeman post, and to defeat incumbent Governor Dan Walker.

Toward the first of these goals, the machine slated Tyrone Kenner, the ward's alderman, for Metcalfe's committeemanship. To defeat Metcalfe at the ward level would be to remove him from the Cook County central committee. Slated for Metcalfe's congressional seat was Erwin France, a real estate developer who worked for the department of planning and who was in charge of the poverty program. One ward committeeman characterized France as "a real favorite of the mayor, a man who spoke very well and who did everything that the mayor and the machine wanted." Throughout the campaign, Metcalfe struck the theme, "If we're not successful, blacks will be moved further and further back."[16] France, on the other hand, defined the issue as "who can deliver the best services,"[17] the campaign message Metcalfe himself had delivered four years earlier when challenged by antimachine candidate Rayner. Former alderman Leon Despres said of France, "He had an advanced degree when he went with the Department of Planning. I went after him for conflict of interest because he remained on the advisory panel of the group of developers he'd been associated with, and I felt he was making money out of Planning at the same time he was working with the city."

Vivid evidence of the machine's internal fragmentation came when Senator Adlai Stevenson, the machine-endorsed, favorite "son" candidate for president in 1976 and its realistic contender for the vice-presidential nomination, intervened against the machine by endorsing Metcalfe. Even so, Metcalfe started his congressional primary campaign at a distinct disadvantage. As the incumbent, he had good name recognition; but he had been stripped of his patronage and thus had no jobs to offer. Despres described Metcalfe's campaign: "Since his patronage had been cut off, he couldn't get anyone appointed to anything. And his captains began turning against him because their jobs were insecure. More than that, Metcalfe didn't know how to organize his campaign. He had never done that before and had no idea how to go about it. He'd always been given a lot of workers and had always been accustomed to others' taking care of things; now here he was, stripped of everything he was used to. Well, people rallied to him. I was active in the campaign then, and I was part of the larger campaign committee, though not the innermost committee."

On election day, Metcalfe, considered a slight underdog as he faced France and the machine foot soldiers, nevertheless scored a smashing victory with 71 percent of the vote. No longer willing to settle for second- and third-line patronage, blacks now showed themselves ready to go after the biggest prizes available. One white committeeman expressed his view of the situation: "The blacks are out of control."

With respect to the governorship, the slatemakers in 1975 wanted a candidate from Cook County in order to maximize its chance of defeating Governor Walker in the 1976 primary. For secretary of state, it endorsed Neil Hartigan, who, as lieutenant governor under Walker, had been extremely frustrated by the way in which Walker had completely shut him out. To round out the top of the ticket, the machine wanted downstater Alan Dixon for lieutenant governor. But Dixon, well aware that this office was a political dead end, refused the endorsement. He would consider only the governorship, he said, or the patronage-rich office of secretary of state.

Illinois Secretary of State Mike Howlett was enormously popular in Cook County, and the machine preferred him for the governor's slot on the ticket. Howlett, however, made it clear that he would not accept the party's endorsement if Dixon continued in the gubernatorial race. Howlett had no desire to face Dixon in a primary. Dixon understood perfectly the double bind in which he had placed the machine: If he insisted on the secretary of state position (since Howlett was the committee's gubernatorial choice), Hartigan would have to go for the lieutenant governorship. But because both Hartigan and Howlett were Roman Catholic, Irish machine politicians from Chicago, the end result would be an unbalanced ticket. State Senator Kenneth Buzbee of Carbondale, himself aspiring to the lieutenant governorship and cognizant of the slatemakers' dilemma when he appeared before them, urged them to devise a ticket balanced with respect to geography, age, political philosophy, and religion. The last category raised Mayor Daley's dander: "Religion is *not* a factor— President Kennedy put a stop to that!" he retorted testily. Buzbee said: "I worked hard for John F. Kennedy, and I'm of course not advocating a religious test. What I want is for the ticket to be

balanced—it's important to represent all major religious faiths."
Mollified, Mayor Daley began to cool down, and the slatemakers
proceeded with their candidate interviews.

State chairman John Touhy asked Alan Dixon, "Will you
support the state ticket if you don't get the position you want?" Dixon
replied: "I've always supported the Democratic ticket, but this time I
will have to see the slate before I pledge to support it."[18] The machine
endorsed Dixon for secretary of state and Hartigan for lieutenant
governor.

The slating of senate president Cecil Partee, a black, for attorney
general was designed as a sop to the black community to counteract
blacks' wrath at machine efforts to defeat Ralph Metcalfe for ward
committeeman and congressman. The endorsement of former Superintendent of Public Instruction Michael Bakalis for state comptroller
gave the slate what the Chicago *Tribune* called "a touch of
independence and intellectuality."[19] Bakalis had requested endorsement for lieutenant governor, but after his appearance before the
slatemakers he received a call from the mayor. Speaking courteously,
Daley had said, "Mike, something's come up where we have to do
some shifting around. We sure need you on the ticket. Would you be
willing to run for comptroller?" Here was Daley the master ticket
builder in operation. But it should be noted that, contrary to the
charges of critics, Daley almost always attempted to find candidates
of intelligence and ability who were capable of carrying out the duties
of the offices for which they were slated. Bakalis accepted Daley's
offer and, no exception to the rule, performed the comptroller's job
with his usual competency and efficiency.

Except for the two Irish-Catholic Chicagoans at the top of the
ticket, the slatemakers produced a balanced slate in 1976. Howlett,
Hartigan, Dixon, and Bakalis had all demonstrated their success as
statewide campaigners. And it was hoped that Partee's name on the
state ticket would prevent a recurrence of the firestorm that had
gutted the machine's outpost in the black wards during the Metcalfe
battle.

The 1976 elections were the last before Mayor Daley died, and
the organization recouped some of the prestige lost in its 1972
election contests. Now, while it had failed to unseat Metcalfe and had
lost the governorship to Republican James Thompson, the machine
leadership could rejoice at having defeated Dan Walker in the
primary. After all, the Cook County organization had done very well

for itself in its past working relationships with Republican governors. Mayor Daley now also had the personal satisfaction, in a private meeting requested by Ralph Metcalfe, of hearing the latter ask for restoration of his patronage privileges.[20] Daley refused.

When Richard J. Daley died on December 20, 1976, the only certainty about a successor was that the city council had to schedule an election for the unexpired term within six months of his death and that it would have to install an acting mayor for the interim. When George Dunne decided to seek Daley's county chairmanship, he faced determined opposition from committeeman Edmond Kelley, but Dunne managed to carry the day. Dunne was willing enough to accept the acting mayoralty, too, if a ground swell developed. It did not. What did develop, though, was a claim on the acting mayor position that was not easily disposed of. Wilson Frost, a black alderman, announced that as president pro tem of the city council he was the legitimate heir to the job and that, furthermore, the mayor had let him know that had the stroke Daley suffered in 1974 been fatal Frost would have replaced him. On the basis of these considerations, Frost attempted to hold a press conference in Mayor Daley's office. But upon discovering that the office already had been sealed off, he transferred the conference to the council chambers, where, however, city workers materialized out of nowhere and began to make "considerable clanking noise" with their buckets and ladders. Corporation counsel William Quinlan gave an opinion that, at the moment, there was no acting mayor and that Frost could not discharge any mayoral functions. Ed Vrdolyak tried to line up support for himself but could muster only nine votes. Although Vrdolyak and Frost between them could count on twenty-seven of the fifty votes, Tom Donovan, Daley's patronage chief, had been working diligently for Michael Bilandic, Daley's Eleventh Ward alderman, who served also as chairman of the powerful finance committee. As political analyst Charles Cleveland has described the situation, Donovan enjoyed a distinct advantage because, as patronage chief, he "knew what almost nobody else did: how many jobs there were and who had them. In politics, that's like having the combination to the secret safe."[21]

The original "deal" was for Bilandic to become acting mayor, Vrdolyak to chair the finance committee, and Eddie Burke to chair the lucrative building and zoning committee. This arrangement, however, produced an outcry from both the media and the black community.

Blacks wanted Frost to go all out for the acting mayor's job, and several white committeemen and aldermen insisted that the Bilandic-Vrdolyak-Burke deal be nullified—blacks must be given a leadership position. Other aldermen concurred, and new negotiations took place in a meeting on December 26. If he would not seek the acting mayoralty, Frost was told, he could have both the chairmanship of the finance committee and the position of floor leader. The black machine politicians urged him to take the offer, since the chairmanship of the finance committee was the most powerful position in the city council and, further, Bilandic had already clinched the votes for the acting-mayor's job. But black civil rights leaders, led by Jesse Jackson and publisher Gus Savage, thought Frost's position as president pro tem entitled him to become acting mayor. He should not compromise, they said. These sentiments were echoed by the black community at large, and Frost assured them he would not give in. But when questioned by the media, he temporized—he would run, he said, if he could get the necessary votes.

To many blacks, the city council meeting on December 26 offered the promise of an historical decision—the selection of Chicago's first black mayor. To the city hall politicos, the word was "Bilandic." But whatever the outcome, the excitement of witnessing the selection of Chicago's first new mayor in twenty-two years filled the meeting room. The council session was heavily attended by blacks, Jesse Jackson among them, who had come to support fellow black Wilson Frost's bid for the late Mayor Daley's job. Once more, however, city workers had been called in, this time to occupy the seats on the main floor; and when Frost's supporters began to arrive, they were shunted off to the glass-plated balcony. Roger Simon, of the *Sun-Times*, infuses the essence of the meeting with his own special flavor, which, in the following excerpts, remains full-bodied:

THE COUNCIL MEETING . . . was like a movie whose ending you already knew. You knew they were going to drive a stake through Dracula's heart, but you had to watch anyway. . . .

. . . The boys immediately started to caucus. There was a black caucus and a Polish caucus, and even a Jewish caucus—the last, a group that had trouble even in agreeing on a meeting place or who was going to bring the sweet rolls. . . .

. . . Frost . . . already was claiming the acting-mayor post. But when it got right down to it the boys decided that Wilson Frost had about as much chance to be named mayor as Ray Charles.

So the boys scratched their heads and searched their souls and asked themselves: If the Old Man were here, what would he do? The answer came to them in a roll of thunder: Boys, cut a deal.

So they did. If Frost would give up his delusions of becoming the first mayor, he would be made Finance Committee chairman and floor leader. . . .

. . . And so the deal was cut. . . . Michael Bilandic would be elected acting mayor. . . .

. . . And so, in the closing minutes before noon, Frost made his concession speech. It sounded very brave until you realized what he was doing. It all added up to, "Why should I be the one to take the suicide jump?"

Which translates to: "I wasn't going to do it unless the fix was in." . . . But it took a man of God, the minister who gave the opening prayer for the Council meeting to sum things up best. The minister commented that it was sad not to see Mayor Daley in the room.

"But we know his beloved spirit remains with us," the minister said.

And the boys said amen to that.[23]

Michael Bilandic, the Croatian "honorary Irishman" from Daley's Eleventh Ward, became acting mayor with the help of the Eleventh Ward power-brokers, to whom he had proved himself, as alderman, cooperative and knowledgeable in the intricacies of finance. He was also, of course, committed to the continued success of the Eleventh Ward Democratic organization. "Bilandic is as Irish as we are," one Eleventh Warder declared. "He really spells his name D-A-L-E-Y." Other leaders had acquiesced in his selection because he was competent and would keep things stable until such time as they chose a new mayor. The ward committeemen were pleased with Bilandic's performance and with the continuation of benefits through his patronage chief, Tom Donovan.

When, in 1977, Bilandic decided to seek election to fill Daley's unexpired term, he drew spirited opposition from candidates willing to remind him that he was breaking his pledge not to run. Roman Pucinski already had announced his candidacy, and when asked how he would respond to the slatemakers' ritual question, "Will you support the party's choice regardless of who is selected?" he smiled and said, "I wouldn't pledge my support. It's a whole new ball game now." Pucinski, the savvy machine veteran, knowing that Bilandic likely would acquire the endorsement, knew also that machine strength had waned. As a prominent Pole, he could run a strong primary race independent of the organization. He even considered a proposition put to him by the Republican party leadership: "In 1977," he told me recently, "the Republicans approached me. In fact, Governor Thompson specifically sent [Ray] Terrell to ask me about running on a fusion ticket, since it didn't look like the Republicans had anybody. We met at the Plaza Motel in Rosemont. I was told that the Republican slatemakers would be very receptive; in fact, I had appeared before them, and things had gone well. The Democrats obviously had got word about what was going on in regard to the possible fusion ticket, because Lar "America First" Daly [a perennial candidate] submitted [Republican] candidate petitions that were impeccable. He must have had help from certain people in the Democratic party to get them signed so quickly and so perfectly."

Pucinski's statement that things had changed was correct. Here was a machine stalwart, one of the most prominent of Chicago's ward committeemen, who had not only declared his candidacy without party endorsement but had made a serious move toward running a Republican campaign against his machine cohorts. That the man who have given up his seniority in the U.S. House of Representatives to run a suicidal campaign for the U.S. Senate for the sake of the local ticket would contemplate such actions indicated that party discipline had lost its hold.

Pucinski could not run as a Republican, but he ran in the Democratic primary and received a respectable 32.7 percent of the vote against the machine-backed Bilandic's 51 percent. The black candidate, Harold Washington, received 10.7 percent of the total vote. In the former Dawson wards, machine candidate Bilandic received 49.7 in comparison with Mayor Daley's 48.4 percent in 1975. Even with black candidate Washington in the contest, the turnout in these wards was only 25.6 percent, in contrast to a 32.9 turnout in 1975, when a black ran against Daley.[23] Kathleen Kemp and Robert Lineberry have commented on this low-voter phenomenon: "Either black voters feel pressures from several sources and choose to stay at home, or the appeal of a black candidate is not enough for them to reverse the trend of not voting in elections. The result is an irregular, but clear decline in the deliverability of black wards in Chicago."[24]

The white machine leadership had little reason to be upset, however; their power base lay in the northwest and southwest race-conscious, white-ethnic wards. The white liberals and the blacks had given no indication that they could recreate the city-wide partnership that had paid off so handsomely against Hanrahan in 1972, although they had accomplished this in a limited geographical area in the Metcalfe race. The coalition would be reforged, however, in 1979; and although the candidate on whose behalf it would be activated would fail to satisfy, 1983's elections would offer more promise.

The absence of Mayor Daley was felt at the 1977 state slatemaking session. While George Dunne had become county chairman of the Democratic central committee, he lacked the vast patronage power that Mayor Daley had held as both county chairman and mayor. Patronage control was divided between Tom Donovan, Mayor Bilandic's patronage chief, and various ward committeemen who ruled over fiefdoms such as the Chicago sanitary district, the Chicago park district, and the board of election commissioners. This fragmentation manifested itself in many ways: Since Republican Governor James Thompson had served less than one year of his special two-year term, he was considered unbeatable; and the strongest Democrat, Secretary of State Alan Dixon, who had sought the governorship two years earlier, refused to seek it again. Comptroller Mike Bakalis realized that it would be a difficult race but figured that, since he was not a machine "insider," it would be his only opportunity to run for governor, and he acquired the Democratic endorsement backing of all other Democrats almost by default. No officeholder was willing to take on Senator Charles Percy. In the absence of an effective leader like Mayor Daley, there was no one who could employ both the carrot and the stick to entice and goad established Democrats such as Dixon, Lieutenant Governor Neil Hartigan, and state Senator Phil Rock to run for the top positions, in the manner that Daley had recruited the reluctant Roman Pucinski and Mike Howlett to run.

County chairman Dunne and state chairman John Touhy did select a balanced slate that was approved by Bakalis, Dixon, and a few ward committeemen. The proposed ticket contained, in addition to Bakalis and Dixon, a woman and a black. But when, two weeks later, the Democrats held their new "open" slatemaking session, they replaced the woman and the black endorsees with two men who had the backing of influential ward committeemen. Sanitary district commissioner Richard Troy replaced Chicago attorney Patrick Murphy for attorney general. Troy's father-in-law was ward committeeman Matthew Bieszcsat, who allegedly convinced many of his fellow ward committeemen to put pressure on members of the state central committee on behalf of his son-in-law. And Jerry Cosentino (like Troy, a sanitary district commissioner) replaced Grace Mary Stern of Lake County for the state treasurer position. Consentino enjoyed strong labor support as well as the backing of ward committeeman Vito Marzullo. These actions produced an unbalanced ticket that was weighted heavily in favor of Cook County. The weakness of this slate was revealed in the machine's inability to find a viable nominee for lieutenant governor. The slatemakers attempted to deal with this problem by commissioning Bakalis to recruit his own running mate subject to their later approval. It took him two weeks to find one.

When Richard Daley was party chairman, there was a commitment to meeting the needs of geography and ethnicity, with primary emphasis placed upon constructing a ticket with widespread appeal. Political atomization now characterized the machine leadership, and individual ward committeemen used their muscle to secure endorsements for their favorites irrespective of whether these represented essential constituencies. The Chicago *Tribune* editorialized the point: "The state slate was an attempt at compromise between attracting voters and appeasing a few powerful committeemen from Chicago's machine wards. The result was a ticket so heavily weighted against downstate—and for politicians against voters—that it's likely to sink without a trace outside the Chicago area."[25]

Alan Dixon's and Adlai Stevenson's reactions were indicative of how things stood: Dixon refused to endorse either Troy or Cosentino in the primary; after all, the Chicago ward leaders had vetoed the ticket that Dixon had helped put together. Stevenson attempted, unsuccessfully, to convince Cosentino and Troy to withdraw; then he announced that he would endorse no state candidate for the 1978 primary.

Although the machine had lost much of its effectiveness, the ward committeemen and the labor unions generally felt that Bilandic was doing a reasonably good job as mayor. As for the business and financial community, they were smugly satisfied at having one of their own in the mayor's chair. Disenchantment continued among Chicago's blacks and those who abhorred "politics as usual"—for them, nothing had changed. And that was all right with the white ethnics. There had, however, been one public relations problem—Jane Bryne, the commissioner of consumer affairs, had attacked him in the media for "greasing" an 11 percent hike in taxi fares. Bilandic fired her and continued to serve through 1978 without any real difficulties. Two political scientists analyzed the situation concerning Bilandic's candidacy for the 1979 election. "His only opponent of note is former city consumer commissioner Jane Bryne, who lacks any base of support within the party or among the voters. The fact is that Bilandic is unbeatable in 1979."[26]

The machine, sharing this view, unanimously slated Bilandic for the four-year term, but one of his confidants suggested the precaution of running another candidate to split the antimachine vote. Bilandic dismissed the idea as unnecessary. Jane Bryne, however, ran a hard-hitting campaign in which she sharply attacked Bilandic for not providing adequate services. The political frustrations of blacks and liberals had been intensified by a bitter winter and a record seven and one-half feet of snow. The city's snow-clearance activity had been sluggish, bus and train service irregular (often bypassing stops in the black wards to make up lost time), and the mayor had responded to complaints with peevish defensiveness.

Byrne capitalized on the situation and bested Bilandic and the machine in the primary by more than 16,000 votes, receiving two-thirds of the black vote and a similar vote ratio of people in the eighteen to thirty-four age group. Professional pollster Steve Teichner's exit survey on the 1979 primary indicated the impact of citizen frustration: "What the snow did was to raise the alienation that people felt about the city government—the contracts, the corruption, the blandness of Bilandic, the fact that the city that's supposed to work wasn't working."[27] Teichner also found that fewer people, particularly blacks, were identifying with the Democratic party; he concluded that Byrne had drawn especially from the disaffected and the previously disenfranchised.[28] The turnout of 59 percent of the registered voters in the Democratic party was significantly higher than the 49 percent average of the previous six primaries. Obviously, many of the nonvoters felt sufficiently aroused to turn out and vote against the status quo.

Although Byrne's campaign centered on Bilandic and the machine (that "evil cabal of men," as she referred to them), she wasted no time in reaching a rapprochement with those whom she had attacked, reminding them of her firm commitment to political patronage and making her peace particularly with Ed Vrdolyak and Eddie Burke. She soon established herself as a tough political leader. Martin Oberman, an independent alderman who initially had supported her, later characterized her running of the city council as "even more repressive" than Mayor Daley's and further labeled her more abusive than either Daley or Bilandic on patronage matters.[29]

Jane Byrne, having assumed the mantle of leadership, could not, however, vanquish the Eleventh Ward. The late Mayor Daley had been her mentor, but nothing of that mutual accord carried over into her relationship with his son Richie. As the Eleventh Ward's committeeman and as state senator, young Daley began to make his power potential felt. In October 1979, for example, he cautioned fellow committee members against following Byrne's lead in endorsing Senator Ted Kennedy over President Carter. Byrne retaliated by firing from their city jobs thirty persons whom Daley and his political ally, Nineteenth Ward committeeman Tom Hynes, had sponsored. About this time, the media revealed the heretofore secret information that the Cook County Democratic central committee had paid Mayor Daley an annual salary of $25,000 and in late December publicized the fact that two of the Daley brothers had been profiting from selling insurance to contractors doing business with the city. After this last news story broke, Richie Daley's office claimed that the data had been leaked by the city, and Daley personally accused Byrne of attempting to defame the Daley name.

The handwriting on the wall, which had been growing ever more legible, delivered up its full message on November 19, when Daley requested that the Cook County central committee endorse him for state's attorney in the 1980 primary: Daley was readying himself to challenge Byrne for the mayoralty in 1983. In an effort to keep him from the state's attorney office, which would have given him additional political credentials and served as the launching pad for his attempt at the mayoralty, Byrne recruited her own candidate, Alderman Eddie Burke, for the state's attorney post two weeks after Daley made his formal request of the committee. It was evident to Daley that Byrne had the votes, however, and so he withdrew his bid and announced that he would run independently of the machine in the Democratic primary.

The 1980 primary forged another link in the lengthening chain of evidence that the machine could no longer defeat its challengers, and this time around, Jane Byrne's view was that of defender of the machine fortress. Richie Daley defeated the machine's choice, Eddie Burke, for state's attorney by a spread of 63 percent to 37 percent of the vote. When Daley's victory was announced, the well-wishers at his mayoralty election changed, "Daley in '83." The machine-endorsed candidate for president, Ted Kennedy, won only fourteen of the thirty-nine Cook County delegate positions to the Democratic National Convention. Two congressional seats formerly held by machine-sponsored blacks were lost to independent Democrats Harold Washington and Gus Savage. And Judge Frank Lorenz, the machine-endorsed candidate for the Illinois Supreme Court, lost decisively to a former party maverick, Judge Seymour Simon. Alan Dixon, who easily won his primary for the U.S. Senate, came from downstate Belleville, and the machine could not claim credit for his victory. Byrne commented, "The organization did its best, but it's not what the people wanted."[30]

The battle between Byrne and Daley intensified after the 1980 primary, when Byrne at first pledged her support for Daley for the general election but then withdrew it. She accused Daley and Tom Hynes of influencing the rejection of building permits to people who would rent to blacks and Latinos. Daley sharply denied the charges, claiming that Byrne was trying to sabotage his race by calling it a "campaign of hate."[31] Byrne's husband and press secretary, Jay McMullen, also had sharp words for Daley whom, he said, was "sick and paranoid and neurotic."[32]

At a rally before Democratic precinct captains, Daley lashed back. Columnist Paul Michael Green characterized the attack as issuing "out of necessity and anger":

> The speech ... was without precedent in Chicago's political history. ... [Daley] charged her with being in collusion with [Republican Bernard] Carey to defeat his candidacy and of engaging "in a hit-and-run campaign full of innuendos, smears and false charges." He compared her to the late Wisconsin Sen. Joseph McCarthy and claimed like McCarthy, she was using the technique of the big lie in her racial discrimination charges against him and his 11th Ward. Finally, Daley told the stunned audience: "There isn't a precinct captain, a Democratic worker, a business-man, or a professional who does business with the city who does not fear Mayor Byrne ... [and] everyone in this room knows it."

... Finley Peter Dunne's fictional bartender, Mr. Dooley, said that "Chicago politics was not bean bag." However, even Mr. Dooley would have been impressed by the ferocity of the Daley-Byrne battle—it had, in fact, turned into a bare knuckles barroom fight.[33]

Daley's rock 'em, sock 'em counterattack paid off. Despite bitter opposition by Byrne, he won the primary and then went on to defeat incumbent Republican Bernard Carey in the general election, thereby establishing himself as a viable contender against Byrne in the 1983 mayoralty election.

Jane Byrne the mayor fell short of Jane Byrne the candidate. She had campaigned on a promise to appoint more minorities to key positions and had amassed a two-to-one ratio in the black community in her 1979 victory over Bilandic, but a number of her mayoral decisions exposed her to blacks as a political chameleon. For police superintendent, she by-passed the popular black deputy superintendent, Sam Nolan, on the grounds that she wanted to hire an outsider but then selected white insider Richard Brzeczek. For interim school superintendent, she hired Angeline Caruso, a white, and by-passed Manfred Boyd, a black deputy superintendent, whose assistant Caruso had been. When she replaced two prodesegregation black school board members with two segregationist whites, Alderman Allan Streeter, a black whom Byrne had appointed to the city council, bitterly denounced her action and voted against confirmation of her two choices. The court later invalidated Streeter's appointment to the council and ordered a special election, in which Byrne actively involved herself against him. She next telephoned several journalists to inform them that the federal government was investigating Streeter for allegedly taking kickbacks from businesses that had government contracts with a program he once had directed. The U.S. attorney later announced that there was no substance to the charges, and Streeter won the election.

The 1981 slatemaking process featured two major contenders—former Governor Dan Walker and former Senator Adlai Stevenson, both vying for the party's gubernatorial endorsement. Dan Walker, who had carried on a running feud with the machine and the late Mayor Daley, now presented himself as a proper "company man," letting it be known that he wanted the slatemakers to pick the candidate for the lieutenant governorship. It would be arrogant of him to choose his own running mate, he said: "That role should belong to the slatemakers." Walker wished to curry favor with the Cook County ward committeemen who had engineered his stinging defeat in the 1976 primary against Chicagoan Mike Howlett. Adlai Stevenson, however, gave every indication that he would run in the primary, with the slatemakers' endorsement or without it. They endorsed Stevenson.

Mayor Jane Byrne, who had used her patronage power to oust county chairman George Dunne, figured prominently in the slating of Neil Hartigan for attorney general over her sharpest city council critic, Martin Oberman. In contrast to 1977, the slatemakers fielded a full ticket, which also included a woman for lieutenant governor. Evidently, the Democrats had profited from their experience of four years previously. The slatemaking session was marred, however, with the sort of internal squabbling that had, it seemed, settled in for good. Roman Pucinski criticized Stevenson for Stevenson's lack of support among labor leaders, challenging him, "What do you intend to do to repair the damage?"[34] Stevenson did not recapture any of the lukewarm labor leadership when he responded that whatever support he might lose in one area he would make up in others. Such an approach could help neither Stevenson nor his party, which historically had relied on support from the industrial unions. But then Stevenson's name permitted him to eschew excessive dependence upon the party.

Slim Coleman, a white professional neighborhood organizer, and Jesse Jackson capitalized on the discontent in the black community and generated an intensive voter registration drive that netted almost 200,000 new black registrants. (Because race is not identifiable on voter registration forms, a precise figure is not available.) This effort translated into a massive margin in the black wards for underdog Adlai Stevenson, the 1982 Democratic gubernatorial candidate. Stevenson, who had trailed by 20 percent in the polls, came within 5,000 votes of winning the governor's race.

The redistricting plan approved by the Chicago city council and Mayor Byrne created an additional source of controversy surrounding the mayor. Despite the fact that blacks and Hispanics accounted for more than 50 percent of the population, the new apportionment plan would have provided for only sixteen council seats for blacks and two for Hispanics on the fifty-seat council. Charging violation of the Voting Rights Act, a Jesse Jackson-led group of organizations filed a federal court suit, which the U.S. Justice Department later joined on behalf of the plaintiffs. The court declared the apportionment plan unconstitutional.

Heartened by their registration turnout in the 1982 general election, blacks sought an alternative to Jane Byrne and also to Richie Daley. There was a tremendous ground swell for a strong black candidate who would take the bit by the teeth and run more than a token campaign. Harold Washington concurred on the need for such a man but did not, at first, see himself as making a second effort at the mayoralty (he had run in 1977). Washington enjoyed his congressional role and would not put it on the line for another futile local race. After the highly successful registration drive, however, he agreed to run in response to what he termed "a massive draft."[35]

The 1983 endorsement process was unique. Even though the organization in the past had lost primaries to Walker, Hanrahan, and Metcalfe, the slatemakers yet had presented a united front in making their endorsements. This time, however, thirteen of the fifty ward committeemen, or 26 percent, refused to endorse their own incumbent, Jane Byrne. The majority vote gave her the party's endorsement, but the absence of the traditional unanimity told the story as to the state of the Cook County Democratic organization in 1982.

Although the black community overwhelmingly backed Washington, this was not true of several black leaders. John Stroger, committeeman of the Eighth Ward and Cook County commissioner, had asked Washington twice if he would run for mayor and, after the second negative response, had joined with Daley. In a conversation I had with Stroger, he indicated that he had received a lot of pressure, as well as threats of personal harm, from blacks who thought he was disloyal. In an interview with *Chicago* magazine, he justified his decision:

> As far as the current mayoral race, I've supported Daley from the beginning. When nobody else was going to his affairs, I was there, because I was turned off by Jane Byrne. She had not been sensitive to my organization or to our community. . . . I didn't like the manner in which she tried to block Daley's nomination for state's attorney. From there on it was personally downhill. . . . I didn't like Byrne's appointments to the school board . . . or her lack of sensitivity to the problems of the neighborhoods. . . .
> . . . My allies are President George Dunne, Tom Hynes, and other people who were against Jane Byrne. No one ever has asked

me to be a part of the drive for a black mayor. I attend PUSH meetings, so I knew that Reverend Jackson would like to see a black mayor, and I supported the voter registration drive, but no one had surfaced to be a candidate.[36]

Jane Byrne did have some black support. Thirteen black legislators from Chicago endorsed her, as did James Taylor, a $70,000-a-year aide to Bryne who was also the committeeman of the Sixteenth Ward. Washington accused Taylor of intimidating his campaign workers. In a campaign appearance in Taylor's ward, Washington lashed out, referring to Taylor and his ward organization as disgraceful.

Daley ran on his record as a progressive state senator who had championed the cause of mental health and consumer protection. He also emphasized his record as a successful prosecutor who was especially attuned to the protection of the rights of minorities and women. Daley hit hard at Byrne's lack of leadership and criticized her appointments and financial management of the city's operations. Byrne tried to present a new, positive image in the campaign, talking about her accomplishments rather than attacking her opponents, and emphasizing her record on behalf of women and fiscal responsibility (she had wiped out an alleged $1 billion debt that she claimed she had inherited from her predecessor). Throughout the campaign, Byrne led the polls.

In the closing days, both the Washington and Byrne camps stressed the question of race. Before one church group, Washington said, "I am bold enough to tell you that your black son is asking for every one of those votes."[37] County chairman Ed Vrdolyak injected overt racism into the campaign when he told precinct captains, "A vote for Daley is a vote for Washington. It's a two-person race. It would be the worst day in the history of Chicago if your candidate . . . was not elected. It's a racial thing. Don't kid yourself. I'm calling on you to save your city, to save your precinct. We're fighting to keep the city the way it is."[38] And Daley attacked Byrne with gusto, accusing her of following a "strategy of fear, emotionalism, and hysteria."[39]

Harold Washington won, receiving 84 percent of the black vote. The city-wide results were Washington 36.5 percent, Byrne 33.4 percent, and Daley 29.7 percent.

Washington's Republican opponent in the general election was Bernard Epton. Jane Byrne's staff made an effort to have the White

House pressure Epton to bow out so that she could appear on the voting machines as the Republican candidate. She also announced a short-lived write-in campaign, which, however, was characterized by its inability to attract either a campaign manager or sizable contributions.

Epton, a Jewish millionaire attorney, had formerly represented the liberal Hyde Park (University of Chicago) area in the state legislature. He compiled a strong pro-civil rights record as a legislator and initially announced that he would not run a racist campaign. Under the tutelage of media consultant John Deardourf, Epton waged a racist campaign that featured the slogan, "Vote Epton—before it's too late." He also hit hard at Washington's personal liabilities: a forty-day prison sentence for failing to file income tax returns for four years, suspension of his attorney's license, and censure by the Chicago Bar Association for taking money from clients without rendering the promised legal services.

A controversial area was Washington's pledge to dismantle the patronage system. This upset many of the ward committeemen, for patronage was the lifeblood of their ward organizations. Vito Marzullo told me, "The _____ is talking about dismantling the machine. What kind of talk is that for a guy who expects to have the support of the committeemen? What about my people, who've been supporting me for over fifty-six years? Don't I owe something to them? This guy wants to slap them in the face. To hell with him!"

Many of the ward committeemen felt cross-pressured. Mindful that Washington was favored to win, they realized that he could deprive them of traditional political plums. At the same time, many were reluctant to upset their antiblack voters and so followed the policy of endorsing Washington officially to satisfy him but instructing their precinct captains not to campaign for him.

County chairman Ed Vrdolyak announced for Washington and gave him a $2,000 contribution. But when Vrdolyak called a meeting of ward committeemen to endorse Washington, he provided for a voice vote so that those torn between the mayor's patronage and their own constituents could avoid going on record. Two prominent Polish ward leaders took opposing positions. Alderman Roman Pucinski supported Epton, while Congressman Dan Rostenkowski endorsed Washington.

An interesting aspect of the campaign was the influx into Chicago of national Democratic figures to show support for Harold Washington: Tip O'Neill, Ted Kennedy, John Glenn, Allen Cranston, and national Democratic chairman Charles Manatt. Former budget director Bert Lance led a contingent of Democratic state chairmen from the South into the white wards to campaign for him.[40]

Washington won overwhelmingly in the black wards and benefited from both the huge registration increase and the heavy voter turnout. He also made inroads into the lakefront liberal white areas. Epton scored big in the traditional white ethnic wards and ran the closest race of any Republican since "Big Bill" Thompson ran and won in 1927.

A key factor in Washington's victory was the Hispanic vote. The exit poll of the Midwest Voter Registration Education Project indicated that Washington received 75.3 percent of the Hispanic vote to Epton's 16.6 percent. (Eight percent did not answer the question.) The authors estimate that this translated into totals of 45,062 to 9,952, or a margin for Washington of roughly 35,000.[41]

Kenneth Janda, writing in *Vox Pop*, has underscored these findings through ward-level voting analysis. He found that the six wards in which Washington gained at least 25 percentage points from the primary to the general election possessed Hispanic pluralities. And in the Thirty-first Ward, which contains an Hispanic majority, Washington soared from 17 percent in February to 60.4 percent in the April election. Perhaps one reason for this abrupt turnabout in the Hispanic vote, from strong opposition to Washington to strong support, was the racist campaign waged by the Republican candidate Bernard Epton.[42]

Race constituted the paramount issue in the 1983 Chicago mayoral election. While Washington received a scant 51.5 percent of the vote, his Democratic party running mates for city clerk, white incumbent Walter B. Kozubowski, and city treasurer, black incumbent Cecil Partee, received 83.1 percent and 79.3 percent respectively. An examination of the six wards with the highest percentage of voting age whites (a composite percentage of 94 percent) reveals that Washington received 6.2 percent, Kozubowski 77.4 percent, and Partee 60.8 percent. In the absence of specific data, it is not possible to divine why black candidate Partee achieved ten times the percentage of his black running mate, Washington. Speculatively, one might consider Partee's incumbency, his status as a safe machine black, and the fact that he was running for a low-visibility office. As for Washington, his 6 percent of the vote in the wards containing 6 percent non-white voting-age citizens indicates that he received but scant support from white voters in those wards.

The six strongest black wards with the highest voting age population (a composite percentage of 98 percent) voted a straight Democratic ticket, since the white candidate Kozubowski received a high 93.8 percent. This compares quite favorably with black running mates Washington and Partee, who received 99.1 and 98.2 percent respectively. While some may be quick to cite this as evidence of the persistence of party identification in the black areas, it might be worthwhile to reflect on how Kozubowski might have fared had he faced a black opponent. Speculation based on electoral data carries severe limitations, since it fails to discern motivations. Additional survey research is necessary to discern the strength of variables such as office importance, incumbency, ideology, and voter ethnicity.[43]

An integral part of both Washington's primary and general election campaigns was the promise of political reform, and a top priority was to replace old-guard city council leaders. Washington knew he could count on the sixteen blacks and the four liberals; if he could pick up just five of the other thirty, he would match the strength of the old guard and cast the tie-breaker in organizing the city council. When word of his intentions became known, Alderman Ed Vrdolyak created a coalition of twenty-nine aldermen who agreed to stick together for purposes of organizing the city council. This entailed creating new city council committees as well as giving up his own positions as president pro tem and zoning committee chairman. A key move was the replacement of the most powerful black, Wilson Frost, as finance committee chairman. Vrdolyak felt betrayed because, he claimed, Frost had promised that Vrdolyak would not lose his zoning committee chairmanship. Then he found out that Frost was "going around offering my job as chairman of the building and zoning committee to five or six guys."[44] Washington's strong inaugural speech, reiterating a new era of reform and the abolition of old-style politics, solidified the twenty-nine man majority.

At the first meeting, Washington realized that he did not have the votes and attempted to postpone the meeting. The council requested a vote, and Washington hastily adjourned. The twenty-nine aldermen met, with Vrdolyak presiding, and accepted the committee chairmanship assignments. Washington disputed the legality of this, but the Illinois Supreme Court upheld the actions of the Twenty-Nine. Clearly, the Washington team had boasted too early and had demonstrated an inability to count. The big loser was former inner-circle member Wilson Frost, who, now looked upon as a pariah for attempting to oust his fellow insiders, lost the most powerful post in the city council, the chairmanship of the finance committee.

Harold Washington, who had campaigned as a reformer opposed to patronage, received a shock shortly after taking office. He discovered that the federal court allowed him only 254 patronage jobs. He complained that this would not permit him sufficient loyal staff to implement his programs. Michael Shakman, who had brought the antipatronage suit, accused Washington of "political treachery."[45] The Vrdolyak people, who originally had opposed the Shakman decisions banning political hiring and firing, now agreed with Shakman that Washington should be limited to a small number of patronage jobs. They relished the idea of blanketing the departments of city government with their own appointees. Washington argued that he needed at least 1,200 patronage positions. The absurdity of the situation was that in 1979 city council attorney Jerome Torshen had argued that 3,000 such appointees were not enough. Without patronage to reward and punish, a weak executive is in a disadvantageous position with respect to bargaining with a strong legislative body. Mayor Washington appeared to be hung up on his own reform petard.

At the beginning of the 1970s, the machine still operated as an ethnic coalition. It answered the complaints of its dissident liberals and blacks by slating more of them. This worked fairly well with the liberals and even gave strength to the machine's state and local tickets. But the blacks wanted more than recognition politics in the form of prestigious offices for the few. More jobs for all, better education, and fair treatment by the police comprised the main complaints that the machine did not adequately address.

The machine was aware that the race-conscious white ethnics in the southwest and northwest areas were now its bastions of strength, and in a zero-sum game any major benefits for the blacks would cost too much in white support. When blacks and liberals united, they were highly effective, as in the 1972 Hanrahan and Walker contests as well as in the 1979 and 1983 mayoralty campaigns. But as long as the machine stayed unified and the blacks and liberals divided, the machine triumphed.

After Mayor Daley died, leadership fragmented, and individual ward leaders looked after their provincial interests rather than those of the state party. The individual sub-leaders, not charged with system maintenance, did not grant reciprocal deference to the smaller units as Mayor Daley had done. In 1983, the Irish split internally, as did other white ethnic groups, and blacks united behind Harold Washington, who won only because of the white split. But more important than the party itself was the nature of the new polity. Racial conflict had replaced ethnic accommodation.

Epilogue II
How Responsive?

Most political scientists and concerned citizens would assess a government according to a traditional concept of democratic theory, with its attendant requisites of massive participation and active involvement. But as E. E. Schattschneider has argued persuasively, the central problem is not how to get the people at large to run a democracy—their numbers and their private responsibilities make that impossible—but, rather, how to make a political community sensitive to the people's needs.[1] The central challenge, then, of a multi-ethnic, multi-class, and multi-religious society is to fashion a consensus that responds to its diverse components and that permits a high degree of stability—in short, a government that most people can live with.

Because the Daley machine served as a broker of policies and of those who espoused them, it was able to govern Chicago relatively well. When Daniel Moynihan called it "the best run city in America," he was referring to governance, not to garbage collection. Critics correctly point out, however, that Chicago's political equilibrium carried a high cost: poor schools, segregation, slum housing, police abuse of citizens, and graft and corruption. These failures it shared with other U.S. cities, large and small, particularly those that had to contend with the ever escalating in-migration of the unskilled, ill-educated, minority poor. But many Chicagoans were unwilling to pay the increasing costs of providing more benefits to the deprived, and the politicians went along. Walter Lippmann has stated the problem: "In order to magnify the purposes of the state it is obviously necessary to forget the limitations of men. But in reality the limitations prevail and the behavior of the state must conform to them. Governments can do no more than they can do."[2]

If all governments are constrained by the failings of the human beings who do the governing, we must suppose that when one form of government is abandoned and another takes its place, one set, and one sort, of failings replaces the other. It may be that, despite their weaknesses, Mayor Daley and the machine chose candidates wisely and governed more responsibly than a reform mayor will find it possible to do. If, as Carl McGowan observed, much can be accomplished for the public good when an enlightened leader and a powerful political organization work in tandem, a leader who pursues idealistic ends without securing the means by which to realize them may be of little use to those citizens he seeks to serve. He may in fact waste time that might more profitably be put to work for his constituency by a leader less idealistic but more willing and able to adapt and compromise because he wants to stay in office.

Mayor Richard J. Daley was the latter sort of politician. Andrew Greeley has described the prototype:

> The ethnic politician's slogan that social progress is good politics is neither phony nor cynical but simply a statement of political reality as he sees it. He knows that if he is too "conservative" the balance he has established will not shift rapidly enough to keep up with the changing state of his city; and if he is too "liberal" he may attempt to force change on the city before there is a broad enough consensus to support it. In the thirties he supports the trade unions and in the sixties the black demand for power, but he supports both such demands in ways that will not drive other groups out of his coalition. There may be a tendency in such an approach to move too slowly, especially if the organization has poor communication links with a minority group. But the political leader is much less sanguine than his academic critic about the ability of any leadership to correct most social problems in a brief period of time.[3]

In the late sixties and in the seventies, events moved too swiftly, the machine responded and adapted too slowly (its operational style of reciprocal deference, multi-factional accommodation, and compromise did not permit rapid change) and, consequently, its strength declined. While the machine was resilient and could often pacify or coopt the party's liberals, it lost control of the blacks. During this period, in accordance with national trends, the machine witnessed a loosening of party ties by local Democrats, and in both Chicago and the suburbs there was a quantum leap in split-ticket voting as party loyalty waned. As David Everson and Joan Parker have pointed out, the resultant weak parties often have lacked the strength to work out agreements that will attract majority support within a legislative body.[4] As the party machines diminish in power, however, we find a proliferation of interests that push their single-issue causes but share little concern about the need for developing a consensus. At a time when society is rent with divisiveness, intense frustration, and anger, the movement into the shadows of the traditional mediator—the strong party organization—exacerbates the situation. In Chicago, after Mayor Daley's death, the politics of ethnic accommodation devolved into racial politics; and in 1983 the politics of reform quickly became a politics of stalemate that often led to acrimonious legal proceedings.

James Q. Wilson, writing in 1962, addressed the question of whether an exclusively reform-minded leadership can govern effectively. Presented with the contrasting aims of the reformer politician—politics based upon principle—and the professional (or ethnic) politician—politics based upon self-interest—men and women of conscience likely would choose the former. What would appear to be a clear enough choice might, however, have adverse implications and ramifications for good government:

> Institutions should be judged by the ends they serve, not by the motives of their members, and on this basis it is an open question whether the professional politician is not the person best equipped to operate a democratic government in a way that will produce desirable policies. A preoccupation with the propriety of methods, while a legitimate concern, can be carried too far. No one used the power of patronage more ruthlessly than Abraham Lincoln; no one appealed more cleverly or more successfully to "irrational" sentiments of nationalism and race pride than Fiorello H. La Guardia; no one relied more heavily on big-city machines than Franklin D. Roosevelt.[5]

Wilson then notes Adlai Stevenson II's concern with the problem of idealism versus pragmatism. Stevenson asked:

> What are the effects of an almost exclusively "ideological" political motivation? Is some degree of instability the likely price

of a lack of the restraint of economic interest and of part-time interest in politics? What are the implications of all-out election campaigning by highly vocal groups who assume little responsibility for legislative follow-up of either their nominees or their programs? What is necessary to prevent hit-and-run politics—even by one's highest minded political friends? . . . [6]

To these queries as to who should govern, Stevenson, the prototype of the idealistic candidate, offered no answers. But the questions he raised suggest a related one: What kind of candidates have strong party organizations produced? The Daley machine sometimes slated incompetents, though more often for lower than for higher office. But the bureaucracies of every city in the nation, including those with city manager and/or commission forms of government, abound with civil servants whose job security relieves them of the necessity of overmuch vigilance in the performance of their duties. Government hacks are ubiquitous. And not all candidates elected in open primaries, for low office or high, prove equal to the task of governing either wisely or well. With respect to state and national office particularly, the Daley machine consistently awarded nominations to worthy persons such as the Stevensons, father and son, Paul Douglas, Paul Simon, and Michael Bakalis. The machine, moreover, was not a closed operation. It welcomed independent challengers (reformer Bill Singer, for example) into the fold once they had won office, especially if the erstwhile reformer indicated a new understanding of the pragmatic realities involved in governing. And when Democratic organization candidates lost in the general election, the machine accepted the responsibility of working out agreements with its Republican legislative counterparts and with Republican governors.

Because the machine could discipline, it could carry out its policies. But elected officials who do not have at their disposal inducements or incentives other than the appeal to conscience or persuasive talk experience difficulty in implementing their programs. James Q. Wilson has argued, "Agreement on programs can be won without modifying the program if the party leaders have non-programmatic resources with which they can bargain. These resources are principally two: control over party nominations for office and control over the patronage resources of the government. The direct primary has weakened the former and the merit system the latter."[7] The steady decomposition of the American political machine qua machine is inevitable if it can neither discipline nor reward by means of nominations withheld or proffered. It cannot exact commitments from those who win without its help. The uncontrolled primary possesses two main defects: one, a lack of meaningful results in low turnout primaries, whose voters are not representative of general election voters; two, a great weakening of the political party as an informal mediating institution between the public and those charged with formulating public policy.

This is not a clarion call for placing unchecked nomination power in the hands of political machines. It is, however, a defense of strong political parties in the interests of effective government. The danger posed by special-interest and single-issue politics is that they can divide up the majority of mainstream voters, thus permitting an extremist to prevail. In the political taxonomy, the species known as the machine may be endangered, but the genus party survives. As William Grimshaw has stated it, "[W]hile the party is unquestionably weaker and badly troubled now, under the circumstances it, like the fabled one-eyed man in the land of the blind, remains a force with which to reckon."[8] It does, however, need the attention of political ecologists.

The atomization of party leadership in Chicago raises questions about the city's political future that are difficult to answer. For example, will the party organization become a black-dominated machine? I purposely do not focus on Mayor Washington, who may or may not win reelection, but ask, rather, if and when a majority of ward committeemen will consist of blacks, with or without their white liberal allies. And will the white liberals make common cause with the blacks as they did in 1972, 1979, and 1983, or will they opt out? The future role of the heterogeneous Hispanics, who range from conservative, affluent, well-educated Cubans to impoverished Mexican-Americans, raises another question for this rapidly growing group that in 1983 comprised an estimated 14 percent of the population of Chicago but only 6 percent of the registered voters. They must overcome many hurdles to gain significant political strength. Will one of the steps they take be the forming of a coalition with the blacks?

Another consideration is suburbia, which has witnessed an influx of both people and jobs. Lawrence Hansen has suggested that by the year 2000 the suburbanites of Cook County will outnumber Chicago residents. "One result," Hansen predicts, "will be a transformed

Democratic Party, whose outlook and appeal will be more consistently statewide in nature. Chicago's domination of the party will end, as will its ability to orchestrate events, like slatemaking, to serve its own parochial and internal political needs."[9]

However the political future of Chicago may sort itself out, demography dictates that, to survive, the Cook County Democratic organization will have to adapt itself to the changes that are taking place in its natural habitat. After having acrimoniously hammered out a budget in the summer of 1983, the bitterly polarized factions of the city council resumed hostilities as usual. And in the November slatemaking sessions, the pattern of intraparty struggle continued. On the county level, Washingtonite Wilson Frost resisted the machine's attempt to manipulate him into a seat on the county board of tax appeals. Frost sought the post of recorder of deeds, a position that would have meant a gain for blacks, who had never held an executive countywide office. Three prominent Democratic office-holders, Comptroller Roland Burris (a black), state Senator Phil Rock, and Congressman Paul Simon, contended for the state central committee's endorsement for the U.S. Senate seat. The committee slated Rock; and the Cook County contingent, fearing that Burris would siphon votes away from Rock and allow Simon to win the primary, tried to induce Burris to withdraw by offering to slate more black candidates for county offices. Burris, like Frost, refused. Senator Charles Percy was regarded as vulnerable, but the chances were minimal that the Democratic nominee would emerge from the primary with the support of a united party electorate.

In mid-1983, the Illinois Democratic party symbolized a divided government, a divided organization, and a divided Democratic electorate. The old machine had failed. The factionalized party needed to construct an ethnic coalition that would appeal to both the new plurality and the traditional European ethnics. A crucial test will be whether the machine can once again fashion slates acceptable to its ethnic components as well as to its prospective candidates.

Notes

PROLOGUE

1. The term "machine" is not used pejoratively. I prefer Edward C. Banfield's definition: "A 'machine' is a party of a particular kind: one which relies characteristically upon the attraction of material rewards rather than enthusiasm for political principles." Edward C. Banfield, *Political Influence* (New York: The Free Press of Glencoe, 1961), p. 237.

2. E. E. Schattschneider, *Party Government* (New York: Farrar and Rinehart, 1942), p. 100.

3. Hugh Heclo, "Presidential and Prime Ministerial Selection," in *Perspectives on Presidential Selection*, ed. Donald R. Matthews (Washington, D.C.: The Brookings Institution, 1973), p. 21.

4. Leon D. Epstein, *Political Parties in Western Democracies*, 3d printing (New York: Praeger, 1972), p. 77.

5. Schattschneider, *Party Government*, p. 64.

6. The Court's Shakman I and Shakman II decisions make it illegal to fire or hire on the basis of political activity. Despite these rulings, Chicago and other cities will likely maintain the patronage system for many years to come. Ironically, Mayor Harold Washington of Chicago, a reform Democrat, found his hands tied with respect to firing the political appointees of his machine opponents. Conversely, the machine regulars who bitterly opposed Shakman now take great delight in the protection given their patronage appointees.

7. Frank J. Sorauf, *Political Parties in America*, 4th ed. (Boston: Little, Brown, 1980), pp. 202–3.

8. See Angus Campbell, Phillip E. Converse, Warren E. Miller, and Donald E. Stokes, *The American Voter* (New York: John Wiley & Sons, 1960).

9. Ferdinand Tönnies, *Community and Society (Gemeinschaft und Gesellschaft)*, trans. and ed. by Charles P. Loomis (London: Routledge & Kegan Paul, 1955). I am indebted to my friend and teacher, Earl S. Johnson, for first apprising me of the *Gemeinschaft-Gesellschaft* concept. See Earl S. Johnson, "How to Live in Two Worlds without Confusing Them or Ourselves," *Journal of Community Psychology* 5 (1977):189–96.

10. Samuel J. Eldersveld, *Political Parties in American Society* (New York: Basic Books, 1982), pp. 99, 133–34.

11. Lasswell's and Kaplan's definition of stratarchy is as follows: "Intermediate between an oligarchy and a republic is a type of rule which might be called *stratarchy*. The ruling group proliferates into an extensive hierarchy, to such a degree that a high proportion of the body politic may be exercising some weight of power. The oligarchy has been stratified and considerably enlarged. Such a form of rule is closer to republicanism than autocracy in that considerable numbers of the domain of power participate in the process of decision making, although, to be sure, their participation may be limited to the administrative rather than legislative phase." Harold D.

Lasswell and Abraham Kaplan, *Power and Society: A Framework for Political Inquiry* (New Haven , Conn.: Yale University Press, 1950), pp. 219–20.

12. Eldersveld, *Political Parties*, p. 99.

13. Ibid., p. 134.

14. Milton L. Rakove, *Don't Make No Waves, Don't Back No Losers: An Insider's Analysis of the Daley Machine* (Bloomington: Indiana University Press, 1975), quoted and summarized in Eldersveld, pp.150–53.

15. Eldersveld, *Political Parties*, p. 99.

16. See Mike Royko, *Boss: Richard J. Daley of Chicago* (New York: E. P. Dutton, 1971).

CHAPTER ONE

1. Michael Bilandic had agreed to serve as mayor for a few months until the special mayoral election. He originally made it clear that he would not be a candidate; later, he changed his mind and won election to the unexpired two years of Mayor Daley's term.

2. All towns and cities mentioned in the manuscript are located in the state of Illinois.

3. The boundaries of the Twenty-first Congressional District changed after the 1970 census.

4. After Powell's death, Chancey did accept a patronage position with Secretary of State Michael Howlett.

5. Technically, endorsement means being slated by the party. Prior to 1972, it was a foregone conclusion that endorsed persons would win nomination in the primary. Although technically incorrect, many politicians equate endorsement with nomination.

CHAPTER TWO

1. Milton M. Gordon, "Assimilation in America: Theory and Reality," in *The Ethnic Factor in American Politics*, ed. Brett W. Hawkins and Robert A. Lorinskas (Columbus, Ohio: Charles E. Merrill, 1970), pp. 39–40. Reprinted from *Daedalus, Journal of the American Academy of Arts and Sciences* 90 (Spring 1961).

2. Chicago *Sun-Times*, 10 June 1971, p. 5.

3. Chicago *Defender*, 11 June 1983, p. 4.

4. Edgar Litt, *Beyond Pluralism: Ethnic Politics in America* (Glenview, Ill.: Scott, Foresman, 1970), p. 66.

5. Raymond E. Wolfinger, "Some Consequences of Ethnic Politics," in *The Electoral Process*, ed. M. Kent Jennings and L. Harmon Zeigler (Englewood Cliffs, N.J.: Prentice-Hall, 1966), p. 47.

6. Chicago *Tribune*, 10 October 1971, sec. 1A, pp. 1, 7.

7. Editorial in *Dziennik Chicagoski*, 3 November 1894, in *Chicago Foreign Language Press Survey*, Polish sec., 1-F1, no. 918.

8. *Dziennik Chicagoski*, 3 April 1896, in *Chicago Foreign Language Press Survey*, Polish sec., 1-F, quoted in Edward R. Kantowicz, *Polish-American Politics in Chicago: 1888–1940* (Chicago: University of Chicago Press, 1975), p. 52.

9. Kantowicz, *Polish-American Politics in Chicago*, p. 52.

10. Ibid., pp. 174–75.

11. Ibid., p. 147.

12. Ibid., p. 152.

13. Lois Wille, "Fear Rises in the Suburbs," a reprint from the Chicago *Daily News*, in *The Anxious Majority* (New York: Institute for Human Relations, 1970), p. 8, quoted in Michael Novak, *The Rise of the Unmeltable Ethnics: Politics and Culture in the Seventies*, paperback ed. (Macmillan, 1973), p. 71.

14. Chicago *Tribune*, 10 October 1971, sec. 1A, p. 22.

15. John M. Allswang, "The Chicago Negro Voter and the Democratic Consensus: A Case Study, 1918–1936," *Journal of the Illinois State Historical Society* 60 (Summer 1967):157.

16. James Q. Wilson, *Negro Politics: The Search for Leadership* (Glencoe, Ill.: Free Press, 1960), p. 78.

17. James Q. Wilson has suggested that analysts have overrated the impact of New Deal social welfare policies, since a greater increase in Democratic voting took place in the black middle-class wards than in the lower-class wards. Nevertheless, it is clear that New Deal programs enabled the Democratic party to appear as the helpmate of the blacks and of have-not groups in general. Ibid., pp. 78–79, footnote 1.

18. Ibid., pp. 80–81.

19. Ibid., p. 53.

20. Andrew M. Greeley, *Why Can't They Be Like Us? America's White Ethnic Groups* (New York: E. P. Dutton, 1971), p. 207.

21. Ibid., p. 208.

22. Nathan Glazer and Daniel Patrick Moynihan, *Beyond the Melting Pot: The Negroes, Puerto Ricans, Jews, Italians, and Irish of New York City*, 2d ed. (Cambridge, Mass.: The M.I.T. Press, 1963), p. 224.

23. See W. E. H. Lecky, *A History of Ireland in the Eighteenth Century*, abridged and with an introduction by L. P. Curtis, Jr. (Chicago: University of Chicago Press, 1972), p. 43.

24. George Potter, *To the Golden Door: The Story of the Irish in America* (Westport, Conn.: Greenwood Press, 1960), p. 68.

25. Thomas N. Brown, "Nationalism and the Irish Peasant," *The Review of Politics* 15 (October 1953):407, quoted in Paul Michael Green, "Irish Chicago: The Multiethnic Road to Machine Success,"in *Ethnic Chicago*, ed. Peter d'A. Jones and Melvin G. Holi (Grand Rapids, Mich.: William B. Eerdmans, 1981), p. 318.

26. Potter, *To the Golden Door*, p. 66.

27. Glazer and Moynihan, *Beyond the Melting Pot*, p. 224.

28. Ibid., pp. 225–26.

29. Lloyd Wendt and Herman Kogan, *Bosses in Lusty Chicago: The Story of Bathhouse John and Hinky Dink*, Midland Books ed. (Bloomington: Indiana University Press, 1967), p. 19.

30. Ibid., pp. 75–76.

31. Ibid., p. 91.

32. Edward M. Levine, *The Irish and Irish Politicians: A Study of Cultural and Social Alienation* (South Bend, Ind.: Notre Dame Press, 1966), p. 129.

33. Ibid., p. 134.

34. For an excellent documentation of Irish dominance in Chicago, see Milton L. Rakove, *Don't Make No Waves, Don't Back No Losers: An Insider's Analysis of the Daley Machine* (Bloomington: Indiana University Press, 1975), pp. 32–42.

35. Levine, *The Irish and Irish Politicians*, p. 190.

36. Ibid., p. 190.

37. Ibid., p. 172.

38. For a discussion of ethnic politics covering the Daley years and extending through 1980, see the ethnically relevant articles in Samuel K. Gove and Louis H. Masotti, *After Daley: Chicago Politics in Transition* (Urbana: University of Illinois Press, 1982), pp. 1–158.

CHAPTER THREE

1. Raymond E. Wolfinger's 1972 study, "Why Political Machines Have Not Withered Away and Other Revisionist Thoughts," indicates that in other cities also the civil service label was applied to what, in reality, were patronage jobs. "Cities in New York . . . can keep jobs from being covered by civil service by classifying them as 'provisional,' i.e., temporary, or 'noncompetitive,' which means that satisfactory tests cannot be devised" (p. 371). And: "During the first three years of Mayor Lindsay's regime the number of 'provisional' employees increased from 1,500 to 12,800. Under Mayor Wagner the City of New York also had 50,000 'noncompetitive' jobs; 24,000 more 'noncompetitive' positions were added after Lindsay took office. In the last year of the Wagner administration the city let $8 million in consulting contracts without competitive bidding. By 1969, the city's annual expenditure for outside consultants had risen to $75 million, with many indications that Lindsay was using these contracts as a form of patronage. In addition to the jobs and contracts at his disposal, the Mayor of New York also can wield tremendous patronage power through his control of the municipal agencies that grant zoning variances. Lindsay has made good use of this power for political purposes" (p. 372). And in a footnote to this passage, Wolfinger observes: "Lindsay's expansion of patronage is in dramatic contrast to his image as a reformer, and to the widespread interpretation that his election was yet another sign of the decline of machine politics" (p. 372). Raymond E. Wolfinger, "Why Political Machines Have Not Withered Away and Other Revisionist Thoughts," *The Journal of Politics* 34 (May 1972):365–98.

2. In Illinois, as in several other states, voters can pull a party lever that automatically casts ballots for each person on the party ticket.

3. After Mayor Daley's death, Pucinski did buck the organization in a primary and ran very strongly in the Polish wards (see Epilogue I, this book).

4. See David Kenney, Jack Van Der Slik, and Samuel J. Pernacciaro, *Roll Call! Patterns of Voting in the Sixth Illinois Constitutional Convention* (Urbana:

University of Illinois Press for the Institute of Government and Public Affairs, 1975), pp. 9–12.

5. Senator Paul H. Douglas, Introduction to Lloyd Wendt and Herman Kogan, *Bosses in Lusty Chicago: The Story of Bathhouse John and Hinky Dink*, Midland Book ed. (Bloomington: Indiana University Press, 1967), p. xii.

6. Ibid.

7. Most law schools did not require a college degree during this time period.

8. Wolfinger, "Why Political Machines Have Not Withered Away," p. 389.

9. Ibid.

CHAPTER FOUR

1. Earl S. Johnson, "How to Live in Two Worlds without Confusing Them or Ourselves," *Journal of Community Psychology* 5 (1977):190.

2. John Bartlow Martin, *Adlai Stevenson of Illinois: The Life of Adlai E. Stevenson* (Garden City, N.Y.: Doubleday, 1976), p. 359.

3. Eugene Kennedy, *Himself! The Life and Times of Mayor Richard J. Daley* (New York: The Viking Press, 1978), p. 83.

4. Ibid., p. 83.

5. Ibid., p. 56.

6. Walter Johnson, ed., *The Papers of Adlai E. Stevenson: Governor of Illinois, 1949–1952*, 3 vols. (Boston: Little, Brown, 1973), v. 3, p. 333, footnote.

7. Milton L. Rakove, *Don't Make No Waves, Don't Back No Losers: An Insider's Analysis of the Daley Machine* (Bloomington: Indiana University Press, 1975), p. 146.

8. Kennedy, *Himself!*, p. 84.

9. Len O'Connor, *Clout: Mayor Daley and His City* (Chicago: Henry Regnery, 1975), pp. 99–100.

10. Ibid., pp. 145–46.

11. Chicago *Sun-Times*, 13 February 1971, p. 4.

12. Ibid., p. 10.

13. David Halberstam, "Daley of Chicago," *Harper's Magazine* 239 (August 1968):29.

14. George Potter, *To the Golden Door: The Story of the Irish in Ireland and America* (Westport, Conn.: Greenwood Press, 1960), p. 66.

15. For an effective analysis of this technique, especially in dealing with civic groups, see Edward C. Banfield, *Political Influence* (New York: The Free Press of Glencoe, 1961).

16. Former Illinois Governor Richard Ogilvie, quoted in Mike Lawrence, "Ogilvie Revisited," *Illinois Issues* 8 (December 1982):26.

17. Paul E. Peterson, *School Politics Chicago Style* (Chicago: University of Chicago Press, 1976), p. 235.

18. A local ordinance requiring the registration of handguns was enacted in Chicago in the mid-sixties and was reported in a *Look* magazine article in September 1968. See Gereon Zimmermann, "Chicago's Mayor: Durable Dick Daley," *Look* 32 (September 3, 1968):23.

268 / The Winning Ticket

19. Halberstam, "Daley of Chicago," p. 32.

20. Kennedy, *Himself!*, p. 206.

21. Andrew Patner, "A Time to Listen: Black and Hispanic Voices Speak Out," *Chicago* 9 (February 1983):110.

22. Halberstam, "Daley of Chicago," p. 30.

23. Ibid.

24. Conversation with Professor Kenneth Janda at Northwestern University, March 24, 1983.

25. Sidney Verba, "Leadership and the Norms of the Group," in Sidney Verba, *Small Groups and Political Behavior: A Study of Leadership* (Princeton, N.J.: Princeton University Press, 1961), p. 185.

26. Banfield, *Political Influence*, p. 5.

27. Ibid., p. 243.

28. Sanford J. Ungar, "Chicago: A.D. (After Daley)," *Atlantic* 239 (March 1977):6.

29. Zimmermann, "Chicago's Mayor: Durable Dick Daley," p. 20.

CHAPTER FIVE

1. Milton L. Rakove, *Don't Make No Waves, Don't Back No Losers: An Insider's Analysis of the Daley Machine* (Bloomington: Indiana University Press, 1975), p. 142.

2. Ibid., p. 154.

3. Austin Ranney adds a qualified fourth possible distribution of the three votes: "[T]here is reason to believe that [the voter] may also mark a 2 in one candidate's box and a 1 in another's, in which case the equivalent number of votes will be tallied for each candidate." Austin Ranney, *Illinois Politics* (New York: New York University Press, 1960), p. 21. Cumulative voting was abolished in 1970.

4. Walter Johnson, ed., *The Papers of Adlai E. Stevenson: Governor of Illinois, 1949–1953*, 3 vols. (Boston: Little, Brown, 1973), v. 3, p. 156.

5. John Bartlow Martin, *Adlai Stevenson of Illinois: The Life of Adlai E. Stevenson* (Garden City, N.Y.: Doubleday, 1976), p. 369.

6. State Senator Paul Simon, as told to Alfred Balk, "The Illinois Legislature: A Study in Corruption," *Harper's* (September 1964):75–76.

7. Walter Johnson quotes Governor Stevenson's friend and associate, Carl McGowan, as saying, "Stevenson never had a venomous feeling toward Powell. It was one of regret." Walter Johnson, *The Papers of Adlai E. Stevenson*, p. 363, footnote.

8. For background material in the following section, I have relied extensively on lengthy interviews with three former legislative leaders as well as on Thomas B. Littlewood's perceptive study, *Cases in Practical Politics: Bipartisan Coalition in Illinois* (New York: McGraw-Hill, 1960).

9. Littlewood, *Cases in Practical Politics*, p. 20.

10. Ibid.

11. Ibid., p. 21.

12. Ibid., p. 3.

CHAPTER SIX

1. Copies of speeches were provided by Michael Bakalis's office. Dates were not given.
2. Jerry Owens, *Illinois State Register*, 13 July 1969, p. 4.

CHAPTER SEVEN

1. Jimmy Breslin, *How the Good Guys Finally Won: Notes from an Impeachment Summer* (New York: Ballantine Books, 1975), p. 31.
2. Metcalfe ultimately broke with the machine over the issue of police brutality. The machine attempted to defeat him as both ward committeeman and congressman, but he survived their most concerted efforts.
3. While I enjoyed good rapport with students, I abhorred those who engaged in violence. I had had firsthand experience with student troublemakers when cherry bombs had been exploded outside my classroom as well as the classrooms of some colleagues.
4. Jerry Owens, *Illinois State Register*, 23 October 1969, p. 7.
5. The business agent is elected by the membership. This full-time position requires that he negotiate contracts for the union and serve as the union representative to other unions as well as its spokesman and representative to the outside world.

CHAPTER EIGHT

1. Letter from Michael Bakalis to Melvin Kahn, 24 February 1977.

EPILOGUE I

1. Joe Mathewson, *Up Against Daley* (LaSalle, Ill.: Open Court, 1974), p. 224.
2. Ibid., p. 229.
3. Ibid., p. 210.
4. Ibid., p. 211.
5. *Wall Street Journal*, 20 March 1973, p. 22.
6. Oral History Office, Sangamon State University, "Stories of the Governorship," *Illinois Issues* (December 1982), p. 23.
7. *New York Times*, 26 October 1975, p. 43.
8. Ibid.
9. Mathewson, *Up Against Daley*, p. 186.
10. *New York Times*, 21 February 1970, p. 15.
11. *New York Times*, 19 March 1970, p. 27.
12. Mathewson, *Up Against Daley*, p. 189.

13. Ibid., p. 190.

14. Kathleen A. Kemp and Robert L. Lineberry, "The Last of the Great Urban Machines and the Last of the Great Urban Mayors? Chicago Politics, 1955–77," in *After Daley: Chicago Politics in Transition*, ed. Samuel K. Gove and Louis H. Masotti (Urbana: University of Illinois Press, 1982), p. 16.

15. Ibid., p. 16.

16. *New York Times*, 8 February 1976, p. 41.

17. Ibid.

18. Chicago *Tribune*, 24 November 1975, p. 13.

19. Chicago *Tribune*, 3 December 1975, p. 2.

20. Telephone interview with Ralph Metcalfe, Jr., 13 July 1984.

21. Charles B. Cleveland, "Bilandic: How Did He Get the Mayor's Job?" in *Illinois Issues Annual 1977–78*, ed. Caroline A. Gherardini and Leon S. Cohen (Springfield, Ill.: *Illinois Issues*, Sangamon State University, 1978), p. 79. Reprinted from *Illinois Issues*, July 1977.

22. Roger Simon, Chicago *Sun-Times*, 27 December 1976, p. 6.

23. Kemp and Lineberry, "The Last of the Great Urban Machines," p. 16.

24. Ibid., p. 17.

25. Chicago *Tribune*, 19 November 1977, p. 12.

26. Peter W. Colby and Paul Michael Green, "The Consolidation of Clout: The Vote Power of Chicago Democrats from Cermak to Bilandic," in *Illinois Elections*, 2d ed., ed. Caroline A. Gherardini, J. Michael Lennon, Richard J. Shereikis, and Larry R. Smith (Springfield, Ill.: *Illinois Issues*, Sangamon State University, 1982), p. 31. Reprinted from *Illinois Issues*, February 1979.

27. *New York Times*, 2 March 1979, p. 28.

28. Ibid.

29. *New York Times*, 24 December 1979, p. 10.

30. *New York Times*, 20 March 1980, p. 10.

31. *New York Times*, 27 October 1980, p. 16.

32. *New York Times*, 11 November 1982, p. 24.

33. Paul Michael Green, "Daley's Victory—a Prelude to the Big Brawl," in *Illinois Elections*, ed. Gherardini *et al.*, p. 51. Reprinted from *Illinois Issues*, January 1981.

34. Chicago *Sun-Times*, 19 November 1981, p. 6.

35. *New York Times*, 11 November 1982, p. 24.

36. Andrew Patner, "A Time to Listen: Black and Hispanic Voices Speak Out," *Chicago* (February 1983), pp. 109–10.

37. Chicago *Sun-Times*, 14 February 1983, p. 11.

38. *Wichita Eagle-Beacon*, 22 February 1983, p. 3B.

39. Ibid.

40. Much of the description of the ward committeeman's roles in the 1983 campaign originally appeared in Melvin A. Kahn, "Racial Politics in Chicago: The Decline of the Irish," *Wichita Eagle-Beacon*, 3 April 1983, p. 3B.

41. *Final Exit Poll Report: Chicago Mayoral Election, April 12, 1983*, prepared by Juan Andrade, Jr., and Wilfredo Nieves (Columbus, Ohio: Midwest Voter Registration Education Project, April 1983), p. 8.

42. Kenneth Janda, "More on the 1983 Chicago Mayoral Election," *Vox Pop: The Newsletter of Political Organizations & Parties* 2 (Spring 1983):7.

43. The above data were drawn from two sources: The election results came from the Chicago Election Commission, Official Canvas of Ward Totals, April 12, 1983. The identification of and data on the white wards and black wards came from Janda, "More on the 1983 Chicago Mayoral Election."

44. Chicago *Sun-Times*, 8 May 1983, p. 22.

45. Chicago *Sun-Times*, 14 May 1983, p. 10.

EPILOGUE II

1. E. E. Schattschneider, *The Semisovereign People: A Realist's View of Democracy in America* (New York: Holt, Rinehart and Winston, 1960), p. 130.

2. Walter Lippmann, *The Good Society* (New York: Grosset and Dunlap, 1936), p. 26.

3. Andrew M. Greeley, "Take Heart From the Heartland," *The New Republic*, December 12, 1970, p. 18.

4. See David H. Everson and Joan A. Parker, "Ticket Splitting: An Ominous Sign of Party Weakness," in *Illinois Elections,* 2d. ed. Caroline A. Gherardini, J. Michael Lennon, Richard J. Shereikis, and Larry R. Smith (Springfield, Ill.: *Illinois Issues*, Sangamon State University, 1982), pp. 79–82.

5. James Q. Wilson, *The Amateur Democrat: Club Politics in Three Cities* (Chicago: The University of Chicago Press, 1962), p. 22.

6. Adlai Stevenson II, "So You Want To Be in Politics?" Review of *Elm Street Politics*, by Stephen A. Mitchell, in *New York Times Book Review*, April 12, 1959, p. 1, quoted in Wilson, *The Amateur Democrat*, p. 22.

7. Wilson, *The Amateur Democrat*, p. 350.

8. William J. Grimshaw, "The Daley Legacy: A Declining Politics of Party, Race, and Public Unions," in *After Daley: Chicago Politics in Transition*, ed. Samuel K. Gove and Louis H. Masotti (Urbana: University of Illinois Press, 1982), p. 85.

9. Lawrence N. Hansen, "Suburban Politics and the Decline of the One-City Party," in *After Daley: Chicago Politics in Transition*, ed. Samuel K. Gove and Louis H. Masotti (Urbana: University of Illinois Press, 1982), p. 180.

Index

About the Authors

MELVIN A. KAHN is Professor of Political Science at Wichita State University. He received his Ph.D. in Political Science from Indiana University and his M.A. in Social Science from the University of Chicago. He has served as a gubernatorial campaign manager and as a professional campaign consultant; he sought the Daley machine's endorsement for state office in 1970.

Kahn has published a book, *The Politics of American Labor* and written the following monographs: *Legislative Politics in Indiana* (with Kenneth Janda et al); *A Lobbying Triumph* (with Robert Allegrucci); *Older Citizens and the Policy Process* (with Robert Allegrucci) and *The Making of a Political Scientist* (with Norman Luttbeg). He has published articles in *Trans-Action* and *The Midwest Journal of Political Science*.

FRANCES J. MAJORS is a former instructor of college English at Wichita State University and at Wilbur Wright Junior College in Chicago. She received her B.A. in English from the University of Wichita in 1955 and her M.A. in English at the University of Arkansas in 1957. She has co-authored a textbook in English composition, *The Source Book: An Inductive Approach to Composition* (Longman, Inc., 1981). In recent years, Majors has worked as a free-lance editor and writer and presently works in manuscript preparation for the College of Liberal Arts and Sciences, Wichita State University.